describes the nonnegotia[...]
for which they advocated[...]
success in reaching their goals; and insights
into the limitations they faced. Through the
plurality of voices and insider perspectives,
Human Rights and Disability Advocacy
presents fresh perspectives on the shift
toward a new diplomacy and explores the
implication of this model for human rights
advocacy more generally.

Maya Sabatello teaches international law
at the Center for Global Affairs of New York
University.

Marianne Schulze is a human rights
consultant based in Vienna.

Pennsylvania Studies in Human Rights
Bert B. Lockwood, Jr., Series Editor

Jacket design by Kiss Me I'm Polish LLC, New York.

Human Rights and
Disability Advocacy

PENNSYLVANIA STUDIES IN HUMAN RIGHTS

Bert B. Lockwood, Jr., Series Editor

A complete list of books in the series
is available from the publisher.

Human Rights and Disability Advocacy

Edited by

Maya Sabatello

and

Marianne Schulze

PENN

UNIVERSITY OF PENNSYLVANIA PRESS

PHILADELPHIA

Published by
University of Pennsylvania Press
Philadelphia, Pennsylvania 19104-4112
www.upenn.edu/pennpress

Printed in the United States of America
on acid-free paper
10 9 8 7 6 5 4 3 2 1

Library of Congress Cataloging-in-Publication Data

Human rights and disability advocacy / edited by Maya Sabatello and Marianne
Schulze — 1st ed.
    p. cm. — (Pennsylvania studies in human rights)
    Includes bibliographical references and index.
    ISBN 978-0-8122-4547-9 (hardcover : alk. paper)
    1. People with disabilities—Civil rights—History. 2. People with disabilities—Legal
status, laws, etc.—History. 3. Human rights advocacy—History. 4. Convention on the
Rights of Persons with Disabilities and Optional Protocol (2007 March 30) 5. Non-
governmental organizations—Political activity. 6. Civil society. I. Sabatello, Maya.
II. Schulze, Marianne, 1975–. III. Series: Pennsylvania studies in human rights.
HV1568.H855   2013
323.3—dc23
                                                          2013020966

Worse than not seeing and not hearing is not to be seen and not to be heard.

—Helen Keller

CONTENTS

ABBREVIATIONS

AHC/Ad Hoc Committee	Ad Hoc Committee on a Comprehensive and Integral International Convention on the Protection and Promotion of the Rights and Dignity of Persons with Disabilities
APF	Asia Pacific Forum of National Human Rights Institutions
Bangkok Draft	Bangkok Draft: Proposed Elements for a Comprehensive and Integral International Convention to Promote and Protect the Rights and Dignity of Persons with Disabilities
CAT	Convention Against Torture and Other Cruel, Inhuman or Degrading Treatment or Punishment
CEDAW	Convention on the Elimination of All Forms of Discrimination against Women
CICC	Coalition for the International Criminal Court
CESCR	UN Committee on Economic, Social and Cultural Rights
CRC	Convention on the Rights of the Child
CRESOR	Corporation of Real Citizenry of the Deaf in Chile
CRPD / the Convention	Convention on the Rights of Persons with Disabilities
CSIE	Centre for Studies on Inclusive Education
CSO(s)	civil society organization(s)
DPO(s)	disabled people's organizations
DRI	Disability Rights International
ECOSOC	United Nations Economic and Social Council
GA	United Nations General Assembly
GRULAC	Group of Latin American and Caribbean Countries
ICBL	International Campaign to Ban Landmines

ICCPR	International Covenant on Civil and Political Rights
ICC-NHRI	International Coordinating Committee of National Human Rights Institutions
ICESCR	International Covenant on Economic, Social and Cultural Rights
IDA	International Disability Alliance
IDC	International Disability Caucus
ILO	International Labour Organization
LSN	Landmine Survivors Network
MDRI	Mental Disability Rights International
NDAC	National Disability Advisory Council of Australia
NGO(s)	nongovernmental organization(s)
NHRI(s)	national human rights institution(s)
OHCHR	United Nations Office of the High Commissioner for Human Rights
Paris Principles	Principles relating to the status of national institutions for the promotion and protection of human rights
PWD-Australia	People with Disability Australia
Standard Rules	Standard Rules on the Equalization of Opportunities for Persons with Disabilities
UNDRIP	United Nations Declaration on the Rights of Indigenous People
UNESCAP	United Nations Economic and Social Council for Asia and the Pacific
UNESCO	United Nations Educational, Scientific and Cultural Organization
UNFPA	United Nations Population Fund
UNICEF	United Nations Children's Fund
Vienna Declaration	Vienna Declaration and Programme of Action
WFD	World Federation of the Deaf
WFDB	World Federation of the Deafblind
WG	Working Group on the Convention on the Rights of Persons with Disabilities
WGIP	Working Group on Indigenous Populations
WHO	World Health Organization
WNUSP	World Network of Users and Survivors of Psychiatry

FOREWORD

Don MacKay, Chair, Ad Hoc Committee (2005-6)

The adoption of the Convention on the Rights of Persons with Disabilities by the United Nations General Assembly on 13 December 2006 marked the end of a long journey by civil society.

For many years the international disability community had tried to persuade states that a new convention was required to ensure the full enjoyment of human rights by persons with disabilities. It was an uphill battle, but once states had finally accepted that proposition, we saw the development of a remarkable negotiating partnership between civil society and the member states of the United Nations.

As a result of that negotiating partnership, the text of the Convention itself also bears the firm imprint of civil society.

As the secretary-general of the United Nations said on the adoption of the Convention, "It was the community of the disabled themselves that worked tirelessly and insistently to promote this Convention, and the United Nations responded. In three short years, the Convention became a landmark several times over: it is the first human rights treaty to be adopted in the twenty-first century; the most rapidly negotiated human rights treaty in the history of international law; and the first to emerge from lobbying conducted extensively through the Internet."

It is therefore appropriate and timely to have this book that focuses on civil society's involvement in the drafting of the Convention. The two editors of this volume are intimately familiar with the negotiating process and have brought together a group of contributors who were also closely involved and are well placed to write about their respective subject areas.

The Convention on the Rights of Persons with Disabilities is a comprehensive and detailed document, and civil society bears much of the responsibility for that. In contributing to its negotiation, disabilities organizations had in the forefront of their minds the practical problems faced by their constituencies. They wanted to ensure that real world problems were carefully dealt with in the Convention, and that it rose above the mere theoretical.

The need for that was clear. The existing generic human rights instruments had fallen far short in their protection of the human rights and fundamental freedoms of persons with disabilities. For the most part this was not due to a deliberate avoidance by states of their obligations. The problem had been in the application of those existing generic rights and obligations with regard to a specific group of people: persons with disabilities. The enjoyment of rights and freedoms by persons with disabilities may require adaptation by states to accommodate the disability in question, but often this has not happened. Often, too, the generic human rights treaties have left gray areas and gaps for their practical implementation with respect to particular groups. The Convention clarifies those gray areas and fills the gaps with regard to persons with disabilities.

It is unfortunately true that persons with disabilities have also been subject to marginalization and discrimination, sometimes through the policies of governments, but often by our societies at large. To quote the secretary-general again on the Convention's adoption, "While it focuses on the rights and development of people with disabilities, it also speaks about our societies as a whole—and about the need to enable every person to contribute to the best of their abilities and potential."

During the negotiations, civil society emphasized the need for a "paradigm shift" in the way that governments and societies deal with matters relating to disabilities. Central to the Convention is this "paradigm shift" in the treatment of persons with disabilities, from being objects of the law to being subjects of the law with the same rights as everybody else.

Just as the paradigm shift guided us in our negotiations, it will need to guide states in their implementation of the new Convention.

Implementation will also require a continuation of the remarkable partnership that developed between governments and civil society. The Convention is quite specific in requiring governments to actively involve disability organizations in the development of policies and action to implement the Convention. Good practice suggests that governments would do this anyway. But governments need to move beyond just the black letter of the law and ensure that this happens in a meaningful way. Policy development will benefit from that, as will our societies overall.

Attitudes need to change in society and in governments. Our world needs to better accommodate diversity, and our societies need to be much more inclusive and accessible. Persons with disabilities need to be more empowered. This is what the Convention seeks to achieve, but ultimately its effective implementation will be the key. It is therefore essential, when we consider the history of the disability rights movement and the Convention, that we do so (in the words of the editors) "with a look to the future." This book is an invaluable contribution to that process.

Ron C. McCallum AO, Chair, UN Committee
on the Rights of Persons with Disabilities

The UN Convention on the Rights of Persons with Disabilities came into force on Saturday 3 May 2008, thirty days after the twentieth nation had deposited its documents of ratification with the United Nations (Article 45(1)). It had taken relatively little time for twenty countries to ratify the CRPD since it was opened for signing in March 2007, and remarkably, when France deposited its document of ratification in February 2010, it became the eightieth nation to do so.

The CRPD takes a rather modern and pragmatic approach to the rights of us persons with disabilities. First, Article 3 sets forth eight key principles, including nondiscrimination and equality, with my favorite principle being inherent dignity. Second, as well as including civil and political rights, it also encompasses economic, social, and cultural rights. Thus, the rights to adequate health information and care and education come squarely within the scope of the CRPD. Third, the special plight of women and children with disabilities are recognized in Articles 6 and 7 of the CRPD. In other words, as well as having the burden of disability, women and children are also discriminated on the grounds of sex or age. Finally, although Article 35 requires states parties to periodically report in much the same way as do the other UN treaty bodies, the CRPD goes farther by requiring them to establish a domestic body to both monitor and implement the CRPD. Under Article 33, as well as erecting one or more focal points in government, states parties are required to establish a framework to monitor and implement the CRPD. This framework may contain human rights agencies, but two other groups must be represented. They are disabled people's organizations and persons with disabilities acting in their individual capacities. In a book of this nature, it is not for its preface to chart the history of the CRPD. However, it is essential to appreciate that the "movers and shakers" for the CRPD were civil society, that is, DPOs and persons with disabilities. Without the expertise and pressure from civil society that changed the minds of many governments, I venture to conclude that we would not have this convention at the present time.

This splendid volume, edited by Maya Sabatello and Marianne Schulze, tells the story of how the CRPD was negotiated. They both were participants in these negotiations. The narratives set forth in this book's pages are viewed from the varying perspectives of the authors of its chapters, and these contributions piece together the article-by-article negotiations. These essays, which are both analytical and explanatory, give the background of the articles of the CRPD.

As one of the twelve inaugural members of the Committee on the Rights of Persons with Disabilities, whose primary function is to monitor the CRPD, I find this volume a splendid tool for those of us seeking to operate the CRPD. The editors and the contributors are to be applauded for their fine work, which illuminates this most special of conventions.

Introduction

The Convention on the Rights of Persons with Disabilities entered into force on 3 May 2008. It is the first human rights treaty to be adopted after the end of the Cold War; the first one to be adopted since the highly successful 1993 World Conference on Human Rights and the Vienna Declaration and Programme of Action that conference yielded; the first one to be drafted and adopted at the beginning of this century; and the first human rights convention to be open for signature to regional integration organizations. The establishments of the UN High Commissioner for Human Rights and of national human rights institutions since the World Conference have also been instrumental developments in the disability context. The rise of transnational civil society, which includes not only nongovernmental organizations, but also, inter alia, peoples' movements, formal and informal associations, grassroots coalitions and indigenous peoples' organizations,[1] as well as media and communication technologies, have significantly strengthened the national and international discourse on the issue. These developments in combination have enabled the dialogue on disability rights to take place. They enabled the transnational disability rights movement to plant roots and later on, to mushroom to unprecedented levels in an otherwise unwelcoming world. They enabled the global community to think and to rethink about what disability is and how we treat—or how we shall treat—our members of society who are prone to be more vulnerable. Moreover, they enabled the global community to reflect on what universal notions of human rights, subjectivity, and dignity mean at the beginning of the twenty-first century.

The eighth UN "core" human rights treaty marks a shift that elevates persons with disabilities from being remarkably invisible within human rights discourse to being protected by a multilateral treaty that frames all human rights as accessible and inclusive. Very much in line with the seminal report by Gerard Quinn and Theresia Degener, two internationally known disability rights experts and leaders for the first working session of the convention process,[2] the Convention replaces the hitherto prevalent medical approach to disability with the social model as the basis for the rights of persons with disabilities. Rather than focusing on impairment as a personal trait that needs to be "corrected," and possibly "eliminated," it emphasizes the need to remove the social and environmental barriers that exclude persons with disabilities from full and effective participation in society and enjoyment of all human rights. The Convention comprehensively examines the rights of persons with disabilities, so as to ensure a human-rights-based approach to inclusion; as a historic first, it also enshrines general principles, among them the need to "respect difference" (Article 3(d)).

In light of this achievement, it is timely and important to step back and reflect on the path that has brought about this paradigm shift. What were the successes? What are the shortcomings? And what caused either?

As the Convention has entered into force, with 130 countries and the European Community having already ratified it and signatures from more than 25 other states,[3] there is perhaps no better time to evaluate the drafting process of the first human rights treaty of the twenty-first century.

Why a New Convention?

For the international disability rights movement, the primary questions were why a new international convention was needed, and what form it would have. Indeed, previous efforts to draft such a convention on the international level have failed,[4] and the issue of disability rights seemed to have gained only mild interest beyond the realm of disability rights activists. The lack of interest was further perpetuated by the principle response that persons with disabilities fall within the scope of existing international human rights treaties and thus are inherently entitled to similar respect, protection, and treatment. An additional treaty, it was held, would be redundant; moreover, the overtheorization of rights would reduce the value of already stipulated rights.[5] The strategy to rectify any arguable discrimination against persons with disabilities was therefore to improve the enforcement of existing treaties through the authorized bodies (committees under the treaties, general comments, special rapporteurs, and so on).[6]

Indeed, efforts have been made to further disability rights on the international level. In addition to the application of the general human rights provisions within the framework of international law, specific reference to persons with disabilities can be found in Articles 2 and 23 of the Convention on the Rights of the Child, and in a few conventions of the International Labour Organization that concern the occupation(s) of persons with disabilities. Additionally, in the past two decades, a number of so-called "soft law" instruments covering different aspects of human rights of persons with disabilities were adopted. These include the Declaration of the Rights of Mentally Retarded Persons (1971) and the Declaration on the Rights of Disabled Persons (1975), as well as with specific references in World Programmes of Action, such as the International Decade of Disabled People.

A turning point in disability rights—and in fact in the general understanding of human rights—occurred following the 1993 World Conference on Human Rights. This conference was sealed with the subsequent adoption, by consensus, of the Vienna Declaration and Programme of Action. Among other things, the latter called for the creation of instruments to further protect the rights of vulnerable groups, including women, children, indigenous people, and persons with disabilities.[7] Paragraph 63 of part B(6) of the Vienna Declaration and Programme of Action, titled "The Rights of the Disabled Person," unequivocally reaffirms that

> all human rights and fundamental freedoms are universal and thus unreservedly include persons with disabilities. Every person is born equal and has the same rights to life and welfare, education and work, living independently and active participation in all aspects of society. Any direct discrimination or other negative discriminatory treatment of a disabled person is therefore a violation of his or her rights. The World Conference on Human Rights calls on Governments, where necessary, to adopt or adjust legislation to assure access to these and other rights for disabled persons.

Significantly, Paragraph 64 further states that

> The place of disabled persons is everywhere. Persons with disabilities should be guaranteed equal opportunity through the elimination of all socially determined barriers, be they physical, financial, social or psychological, which exclude or restrict full participation in society.

Two other major developments have taken place following the recommendations stipulated in the Vienna Declaration. First is that, in line with paragraph 65, the 1993 Standard Rules on the Equalization of Opportunities for Persons with Disabilities were also adopted. The impact of these rules should not be understated. Although not officially legally binding, some argue that the Standard Rules attained a binding character as they hold a moral obligation and a strong political commitment.[8] The Preamble to the Standard Rules put up front the goal to ensure full equalization, participation, and enjoyment of all human rights of and by persons with disabilities and to provide "accommodating" models for political decision making to attain this goal.

The other development was the materialization of the Vienna Declaration's call for the establishment of the UN High Commissioner for Human Rights on 20 December 1993. The OHCHR is the principal UN office mandated to promote and protect human rights. It was established with the goal to "provide a forum for identifying, highlighting, and developing responses to today's human rights challenges, and [to] act as the principal focal point of human rights research, education, public information, and advocacy activities in the UN system." Its method of work has focused on standard setting, monitoring, and implementation on the ground. Importantly, and in line with Paragraph 100 of the Vienna Declaration, the OHCHR worked in partnership not only with governments and the UN system, but also with civil society and NHRIs. The Vienna Declaration in fact explicitly recognized the invaluable role of national institutions in the promotion and protection of human rights and, moreover, encouraged their establishment and strengthening (Para. 36). The latter bodies' provision of information and input with regard to the monitoring and implementation of disability rights within the work of the OHCHR and of individual governments has therefore given further hope that disability rights, as well as all other human rights, will be properly enforced.

In practice, this strategy has consistently failed. Historically and culturally, persons with disabilities have been excluded from "rights talk" and discriminated against. National and international nondiscrimination legislation, as well as global changes in the approach to disability (see discussion below and elsewhere in this volume) had little impact. As Theresia Degener observed in her comprehensive study, the application of the legal categories under which disability can be protected (criminal, constitutional, civil, or social welfare laws) has been highly dependent on the will and power of the judiciary and hence, implicitly, on the self-advocacy of persons with disabilities—which does not always exist.[9] Furthermore, it became clear that discrimination against persons with disabilities occurs on multiple levels: from staggering rates of unemployment to institutionalization; from being treated as social and political outcasts to violence and abuse; from lack of accessibility to essential services to family rights; and others. Reports have continuously shown that women, children, indigenous people, and other minority groups suffered double, triple, and multiple levels of discrimination. There was therefore a real need in making the case for disability rights, and there was no question that it had to come "from below."

"New Diplomacy" at Work

The adoption of the Convention was preceded by at least two decades of activism. Although the most visible origin of the disability rights movement is rooted in Western NGOs and individual activism, it was not long before disability activism spanned across the globe. An intensified process of democratization,[10] a significant rise in the involvement of the so-called "third force" (that is, civil society) in international affairs,[11] globalization, and the evolvement of new, high-tech means of communication[12] have all played major roles in this trend. Information sharing within and across states, as well as between civil society organizations, states, and the UN bodies that are responsible for the promotion of human rights, have opened the door for many actors from smaller, newer, and less powerful nations to raise their own voice in a manner previously unheard of. The culminating impact was significant. While historically diverse and—like many other organizations with shared interests—often prone to disagreements, through their representative organizations (often called disabled people's organizations, or DPOs), a variety of NGOs, and individual experts, persons with disabilities played an instrumental role in the effort to mobilize the international community to take disability rights seriously, particularly during the drafting process. More than that, civil society participation in the process exceeded by far previous cases of involvement in the formulation of international human rights treaties. It has, in fact, taken the idea of "new diplomacy," referring to civil society's involvement in international processes,[13] to a new level.

Following Mexico's initiative to draft a new treaty, the UN General Assembly adopted a resolution in December 2001 that established an Ad Hoc Committee on a Comprehensive and Integral International Convention on the Protection and Promotion of the Rights and Dignity of Persons with Disabilities to consider the drafting of a disability rights convention and invited NGOs, along with states and other relevant bodies, to make contributions to the work entrusted to the AHC.[14] It quickly became apparent, however, that this vague reference to "involvement" would not be sufficient. The resolution permitted NGOs to make contributions "based on the practice of the UN," yet many DPOs did not have consultative status in the UN Economic and Social Council,[15] and the process for such accreditation is often too long to be feasible. Nor was specific mention made of NHRIs. Subsequently, the NGOs community, including NHRIs, initiated an intense lobbying campaign during the first AHC session in 2002, after which two important resolutions were adopted.

The first, dealing with access to the Committee's discussions, invited NHRIs to contribute to the proceedings and enabled a separate accreditation process for those groups who currently lacked it.[16] Thus, in comparison to the 30 individual representatives who attended the first AHC, representatives of 42 NGOs and additional disability-affiliated representatives attended the second session, for a total of about 200 individuals[17]. By the seventh session, 110 disability organizations were accredited to participate in the sessions;[18] almost 500 individuals, mostly persons with disabilities, attended the final round of negotiations.[19]

The second resolution, on the modalities for NGO participation in the AHC, allowed accredited NGOs to attend any public meeting of the Committee (this permission was later extended to informal consultations and closed meetings),[20] to intervene in the plenary, to receive copies of the official documents, and to make written or other presentations. NGOs were also permitted to make their materials available to delegations in areas designated by the Secretariat.[21]

The door opened by the resolution quickly translated into another important achievement: the decision to establish a Working Group on the Convention on the Rights of Persons with Disabilities (WG) mandated to prepare and present a text for a convention, composed of twenty-seven government representatives and, importantly, twelve accredited NGO representatives (especially DPOs) and one representative of an NHRI.[22] This too reflected a first-time achievement, as in no prior drafting process of a core human rights treaty at the UN had representatives of civil society organizations been granted formal seats in a working group. Beyond that, because the outcome of the WG was used as the basic negotiation text for the treaty in the following AHC sessions (the Chair's Draft), NGO participation was invaluable.[23]

The work of civil society organizations was also highly effective. Much of the work of the disability rights movement was organized through the International Disability Caucus, established as the "official" body to represent the disability community and characterized by a rather loose structure. Mobilized by NGO representatives who attended the first session, the International Disability Alliance (an international umbrella group established in 1999), Centre for Rehabilitation, and Landmine Survivor Network held the dominant leadership. Learning from the experience of the children's rights movement, but also from the more recent efforts of NGOs on international forums for the International Campaign to Ban Landmines and the Coalition for the International Criminal Court, the goal was to advocate for disability rights as much as possible in a coordinated manner and by consensus.

At least one Caucus meeting was held daily, and other meetings were held by the various working groups that were composed to facilitate civil society's activity. A steering committee was established, composed of representatives from the IDA, regional representation, and other NGO representatives. The IDC also included a drafting group to develop joint position statements on behalf of the disability community (after their approval by the IDC) to be delivered at the plenary meetings. Additional regional, non-alliance NGOs and communication working groups were established, and for many of the draft provisions a facilitation team was appointed (or voluntarily took on the role).

Another interesting and unique characteristic of the involvement of civil society in the process was evident in the relationships that developed with states' delegates. In addition to unusually "open doors" for discussions with DPOs/NGOs, representatives of DPOs were also included in official state delegations. Furthermore, states made a point of sending a government representative with disabilities. The rise of and respect for NHRIs, which often included—and were led by—persons with disabilities, have also been important in this context. Indeed, the negotiation of the CRPD was the first time that NHRIs participated and contributed significantly to the drafting of a core human rights treaty, giving them a prime opportunity to share their insights and utilize them for the purpose of a new human rights convention.

The impacts were obvious. For one, persons with disabilities were made visible. Second, voices "from within" were in fact taking over places of power of those "from outside," shifting the dynamics of the negotiations. Indeed, this close collaboration between civil society and states' delegates led some to believe that without the consent of the disability community, the Convention would not have been adopted. Thus, having "supporting representatives" from within the all-states institution has arguably played an important role in the ultimate result. Considered to be the shortest negotiation period for a human rights treaty, the deliberations were further expedited by a string of regional meetings, seminars, and workshops with various stakeholders in Manila, Bangkok, Madrid, Johannesburg, Quito, Beirut, and elsewhere[24] to ensure the maximum representation of those who could not bear the costs, travel, and other burdens of coming to New York. Ultimately, it took only eight AHC sessions and a WG meeting in January 2004 to conclude the negotiations on the treaty by August 2006.[25]

But was this really so? To what extent could civil society delegates wearing a "formal hat" really pull the strings when necessary? And how does that affect the overall relationship between civil society and states? The authors in this book reflect on their experience to discuss how DPOs and NGOs have been able to break through the common invisibility of persons with disabilities and to what extent this may account for the successes—and failures—of the negotiations.

Civil Society: Politics from Within

Civil society's work was very well organized and, no doubt, efficient. Generally, most of the organizations were represented through the IDC, and several committees were established to coordinate and facilitate the work of the caucus. And while each representative had the option of voting for the proposals and agenda that were discussed, the IDC's ultimate goal was to work by consensus. Accordingly, messages to the government representatives were generally delivered in one voice. This coordination impacted the way in which the IDC was viewed by state delegates. As the representative of the "disability community," the IDC was granted the right to make statements on the floor. Its daily newsletters were read carefully, and its arguments for or against a particular proposal were taken seriously, frequently being incorporated into governments' proposals.

Naturally, however, the disability community was not free of tensions. Questions about the "authentic" representation of organizations *for* persons with disabilities (in contrast to organizations *of* persons with disabilities) surfaced. Representatives of organizations who were not only representing disability rights were not always easily brought into the fold. Disagreements also occurred within the "core" disability rights community. Aside from the particular disability-related interests the DPOs tried to promote, controversies also arose with regard to the policies the Convention should adopt. South-North divides were also present. Consequently, while some representatives tried to negotiate their positions within the IDC, others chose to stay outside. Yet as all the voices contributed to the overall result, the implications of this diversity from within are critical if we are to develop a greater understanding of what it means to involve transnational members of civil society in UN-level negotiations.

This book is a first attempt to understand what happened by bringing together a collection of the many voices that were heard in the process. While the final chapter of the book proposes a more comprehensive and observational outlook on the process, including a comparison with previous negotiations on the international level, the individual chapters separately discuss how the authors' work with—and without—the coalition of NGOs facilitated their advocacy. Coming from Western and "Southern" states, from developed and developing countries, from a variety of ethnicities and social groups (demonstrating diversity of gender, age, indigenous and religious backgrounds, and so on) these authors have in common the many barriers—social, cultural, and legal—that they faced in their advocacy campaigns.

Why Care About the Drafting Process?

While the emerging concept of "new diplomacy" has played a critical role in the drafting of the CRPD and other recent international human rights instruments,[26] relatively little scholarship exists on the process itself.[27] Yet there is much value to be derived from such an account. Aside from providing a historical perspective on the most recent international human rights movement, an examination of the historical drafting process is also a powerful tool to look into both the past and the future. To what extent was the collaboration between DPOs/NGOs and governments in this process successful? Were challenges raised in previous international law processes of similar nature addressed? How did the organizations locate *themselves* in the bigger picture of the drafting process?

The book attempts to provide a unique perspective on these events by incorporating the variety of views from within. The influence of DPOs/NGOs is discussed not only in light of the final legal document, but also in relation to other actors, particularly their NGO colleagues. Indeed, the authors in this book reflect on the pluralistic nature of the negotiations: they represent NGOs of different size and purpose, with different organizational missions— organizations *of* or *for* persons with disabilities. This rich fabric of activism allows for internal discussion on the successes and failures attributed to working with the coalition or outside it. By bringing in the plurality of voices, the book offers a fresh and one-of-a-kind look into the politics of civil society organizations from *within*.

Second, the entry into force of the Convention is a new beginning. In fact, the challenge now is far greater. How will the theoretical protections of the Convention be translated into practice? How will the legal implementation of the Convention be ensured worldwide? There is no doubt that persons with disabilities and their representative organizations will remain involved in this process. Yet what challenges do the NGOs/DPOs involved in the drafting process face in making the spirit of the Convention a reality?

Structure of the Book

This book tells the story of the contemporary history of the disability rights movement with a look to the future. It comprises an array of essays written by individuals who in their respective roles as representatives of DPOs, NGOs, indigenous people's organizations, states, or national institutions have had a leading role in the drafting process of the Convention. Each describes, from the authors' viewpoint, the "un-negotiable key issues" for which they advocated; the extent of success in reaching their goals; and their insights about the limitations they faced doing so.

A point of clarification is important in this regard. This book is not an analysis of the specific provisions called for by the CRPD. Rather, it concentrates on the process of advocacy and on the actors who mobilized the amendments and therewith legal change. While a substantive discussion, including the difficulties that arose while communicating the substantive issues, is essential in order for the authors to explain their nonnegotiable points and how they did—or did not—achieve their goals, the principal goal here is to explore the strategies used throughout the negotiation process to reach those goals. The questions this book is thus concerned with are how well did the activists do in achieving their goals? When they were not successful, what went wrong? Retrospectively, would there have been viable alternatives? Given that much work still needs to be done toward the implementation of the Convention, several authors provide recommendations about how the disability rights network should work to further advance their interests.

The book is organized to accomplish two things. First, it moves from more specific issues to overarching themes: from the crucial issue of legal capacity to inclusion, to some groups who tend to be more vulnerable and whose extent of success in incorporating their interests in the Convention varies, to the advocacy efforts of regional alliances, while keeping the discussion in the last two chapters on questions of international and national monitoring. They reflect an overarching theme that was not advocated as part of the mission of one or a few NGOs and featured debates that focused more on procedural, rather than substantial, matters.

Second, the chapters are intended to demonstrate diversity in the kinds of NGOs and civil society representatives involved in the process. Advocates for similar substantive issues (e.g., legal capacity, inclusive education) advocated in different ways depending on their organization's size and geographical scope of action (global, regional, national; North, South). In the same way, the mission of the organizations—of and for persons with disabilities, and general human rights organizations—affect their familiarity with international processes and the strategies used. Finally, the authors' membership (or lack thereof) in the IDC played a role in their overall experience of the negotiation process. Certainly, the discussion of representation has inherent limits—the issue recurred in the negotiation process and proved to be fraught with challenges, including in the mere acknowledgment of their presence. Nonetheless, the issue is built into the various chapters as the authors identify and view themselves, making the book a testament to the increased involvement of a variety of grassroots human rights activists in international forums.

The concluding chapter summarizes the main observations and examines some of the theoretical aspects behind the work of the various organizations and their representatives. By doing so, it aims to provide an analysis of the emerging trends in the disability rights movement in comparison to previous similar international processes and, by extension, in the international human rights movement as a whole in light of the expanding notion of "new diplomacy."

CHAPTER 1

A Short History of the International Disability Rights Movement

Maya Sabatello

The adoption of the Convention on the Rights of Persons with Disabilities marks a significant achievement for disability rights. This success is commonly attributed to the involvement of persons with disabilities and their representative organizations in the drafting process at the United Nations. This chapter briefly recounts the history of the international disability rights movement—from individuals' activism to the formation of an organized and powerful coalition. It describes two main challenges along the way: the dominance of the medical approach to disability and its alternatives as well as the complexities associated with defining what constitutes a disability along with the implications of these issues in the drafting process. Finally, it outlines the five overarching themes enshrined in the CRPD and pinpoints some of the challenges ahead.

The Mobilization of Disability Rights

Activism by individual persons with disabilities can be traced back to the nineteenth century. It was not until the 1960s and 1970s, however, that collective mobilization around issues of disability rights began.[1] This social movement of persons with disabilities challenged the common traditional perception of the white, middle-class, male "abled" body as the "normal" body for medical observation, calling attention to the inappropriateness of scientific knowledge about "sickness and diseases" in the context of disabilities.[2]

Beyond the medical realm, disability rights activists have increasingly demanded citizenship rights and participation, contested their incarceration in institutions, and drawn attention to the exclusion and discrimination they encounter in daily life.[3] Moreover, the disability rights movement is best characterized as a movement "from below," with most of the leadership in the hands of persons with disabilities. This emergent notion of self-advocacy was reflected in the motto of the disability rights movement during the drafting process of the Convention on the Rights of Persons with Disabilities—"Nothing About Us Without Us!"

A simultaneous boost to the disability rights movement has been the global rise of a human rights movement, both in the UN and elsewhere. The 1993 World Conference on Human Rights was the largest gathering ever on that topic. Given the timing of the conference shortly after the collapse of the Soviet Union, hopes were high that the UN might finally find a way beyond its long history, stalemate, and deadlock.[4] More than 7,000 individuals attended, representing 171 nations and 800 NGOs.[5] Beyond this remarkable participation, however, the main result of the conference was the Vienna Declaration and Programme of Action.

The Vienna Declaration was adopted by consensus and marked a significant turn in the international conceptualization of human rights. Moreover, this emerging new understanding of human rights corresponded well with the demands of disability activists. Among the most important aspects of the Vienna Declaration are its recognition of the interdependence of democracy, economic development, and human rights, and the entrenchment of the notion of universality, indivisibility, interdependency, and interrelatedness of civil, political, economic, social, and cultural rights.[6] The Vienna Declaration also highlighted the invaluable role that NGOs and national human rights institutions play in the advancement of the framework of human rights—an attitude that has been instrumental in the development of the disability rights movement.

In the decades before the Vienna Declaration, the UN had slowly been turning its attention to disability rights, adopting various soft-law instruments. Thus, by the time the discussions on the treaty began in 2001, the UN had undertaken several measures, including passage of the 1975 Declaration on the Rights of Disabled Persons, which is the first rights-based international instrument on disability; declaring 1981 the International Year of Disabled Persons and 1983 the beginning of the UN Decade of Disabled Persons; and establishing the World Programme of Action Concerning Disabled Persons.

In 1993, the UN General Assembly adopted the Standard Rules on the Equalization of Opportunities of Persons with Disabilities, which gave impetus to the legal regulation of disability rights at the international level. Human rights treaty bodies of the core human rights conventions also started attending to the human rights violation of persons with disabilities; in 1994, the Committee on Economic, Social and Cultural Rights (under the ICESCR) adopted a comprehensive General Comment on "Persons with Disabilities."[7]

Nevertheless, challenges remain in establishing the human rights of persons with disabilities, not least because of the overwhelming power the medical profession has had over the issue of disability and complexities associated with defining what constitutes a disability.

Models of Disability

One of the most significant challenges for the disability-rights movement has been the medical approach to disability. The medical paradigm defines disability by strict categorization based on biomedical, scientific, and genetic causes. Persons with disabilities were viewed merely for their *inabilities* in comparison to an expected definition of "health." Industrialized societies have operated on a similar deficit model of functional performance, in which a disability is defined as the "limitation on the amount or kind of work" that one person can perform in lieu of the notion of economic profit.[8] Both views have seen disability as a personal trait in need of "correction." Consequently, public policies adopted a strong paternalistic approach based overwhelmingly on concepts of welfare and charity.[9] The goal was to "eradicate" the "disease" and create rehabilitation programs to encourage the assimilation of persons with disabilities into the "functional" society. Those who could not be "rehabilitated" frequently found themselves institutionalized or otherwise excluded from public view, with Darwinian notions of scientific survival, eugenic policies, involuntary sterilization, and medical experimentation of persons with disabilities frequently characterizing disability policies during the twentieth century.[10]

As a result of the activism of persons with disabilities and disability advocates, however, international concepts of disability, along with ideas about its proper diagnosis and treatment, have begun to shift. Instead of the medical approach, social models of disability have begun to take roots. Beginning in the 1970s, British activists argued that there is a need to distinguish between *impairment* (which reflects the biological condition) and *disability*, grounding one's limitations not in personal pathology (as the medical approach holds) but in *social* pathology. As Mike Oliver and Colin Barnes, among the leaders of the British social model, have argued, social oppression, inequality, discrimination, and prejudice are the predominant barriers persons with disabilities face, and these social and cultural conditions are what disable persons with disabilities from fully participating in various aspects of life.[11] Accordingly, their political strategy has been to call for the modification of barriers in the social, attitudinal, and built environment and the stereotyped perception of the "normal body and mind" (rather than the individual) that doom members with physical and mental difference to a disabling position.[12]

The British social model has been pivotal to the disability rights movement. It empowered persons with disabilities to mobilize themselves for social change and enabled them to forcefully challenge repressive societal norms.[13] But increasingly the British social model has also raised conceptual and practical difficulties both within and outside the disability community. The model's binary distinctions, foremost the impairment/disability one, have been viewed as "misleading and dangerous" as they prevented a proper reconstruction (rather than mere replacement of the medical model) of the concept of disability and its discourse.[14] The bifurcated approach of the British model and its increasing ideological definition of disability have also been charged with fixating on the individual experience of disability, thereby marginalizing other social-contextual approaches to disability and interrelated experiences of persons with disability who live with certain impairments.[15]

As Tom Shakespeare, a leading disability rights activist and scholar, contends, there isn't one universal social approach to disability, but "there was, and always has been, a plurality of social approaches."[16] Thus, for instance, the Nordic relational approach to disability focuses on the "principle of normalization," a mismatch between the individual and the environment, and unlike the British model it has been developed by persons with disabilities alongside many nondisabled researchers.[17] This principle was formulated in the 1970s, whereby welfare provisions and citizenship rights are extended to the entire population, and the solutions to disability are located in the environment and social contexts rather than in the individual and the therapeutic discourse.[18] As the Norwegian approach stressed, "Rather than expecting that disabled people one-sidedly shall adapt to society, we also need to adapt the environment to them."[19] According to this approach, disability is therefore contextual and relative.[20] Although widely adopted in the Nordic countries, this approach has nonetheless been faulted with its continued reliance on the medical approach and with lacking proper methods to operationalize the relational approach in regard to welfare provisions and to the issues of oppression and discrimination.[21]

North America's disability movement has also developed its own flavor, largely based on a minority group or identity approach to disability. Under this model, the means to overcome prejudice and discrimination against persons with disabilities are set by civil rights legislation, bearing in mind the social, cultural, and political dimensions of disability.[22] In addition, the struggle of persons with disabilities is framed in terms not merely of achieving equality and nondiscrimination but also of recognition as a separate minority group consisting of multiple subgroups, each with its own political identity, pride in its physical/mental characteristics, and sense of self-determination and self-identification. The Deaf community[23] in the United States is perhaps by far the most vocal proponent of this approach, as some of its members perceive efforts to eradicate the disabling condition as "cultural genocide."[24] Increasingly, however, this identity group model is being endorsed also by other subgroups of persons with disabilities, especially those with mostly sensory disabilities—persons who are deaf, blind, and deaf/blind—but also persons with mental disabilities and dwarfism (e.g., "Little People of America").[25] In the U.S., some have also discussed the obese identity of "big" people as another emerging subgroup of persons with disabilities.[26]

Regardless of their differences, the importance of social models of disability cannot be overstated. From a disability human rights perspective, these models share a significant approach to overcoming prejudice and discrimination: the view that disability is based on a social, structural, and contextual understanding. Indeed, this was the strongest unnegotiable element of the disability rights campaign at the UN, and probably the greatest success of the disability rights movement in the drafting of the CRPD. Yet a related obstacle that raised further considerable debate, both within and outside of the disability rights movement, was whether disability could and should be defined, and if so, how.

Disability and the Problem of Definition

While the organized disability rights movement has emerged only in the past few decades, disability is not in any way a new phenomenon. On the contrary, disability "is an integral part of common human experience,"[27] and it has existed throughout human history, cutting across time and space.[28] The universality of the phenomenon of disability should not be conflated with what counts as a disability nor for its causes, however. Indeed, the latter are complex questions, strongly contingent on one's background and cultural contexts.

In American culture and Western society more generally, the physical observation of bodily limitation has been a focal point in defining disability.[29] Consequently, perception of disability has often been associated with images of wheelchairs, crutches, guide dogs, and so on. These emphases are not universal, however. In some cultures disability applies only to psychological conditions, not to physical impairment.[30] Furthermore, the rationales and causes given for certain conditions differ. Unlike the Western obsession with scientific explanation, other cultures explain disability from a range of sources, particularly religious beliefs about one's sins, demand for collective restitution, imbalance in one's and the communal cosmos, and so forth.[31]

One good example of the different cultural meanings of disability is deafness. In the United States and in other Western countries, the Deaf community has increasingly been recognized as a separate linguistic or ethnic minority,[32] with a distinctive shared history, culture, and tradition.[33] This political pride is not necessarily shared by all people who are deaf, however. Asian communities in the U.S., for example, emphasize interdependency among family members and hold a holistic view as to medical treatment and disability, including deafness.[34] Among the Hispanic population in the U.S., not only is deafness viewed in terms of disability, but culturally the condition is also attributed to religious sources.[35] The conceptualization of deafness and the advocacy campaigns of the Deaf community have also been challenged by black deaf people in the U.S. who argue that cultural/ethnic subordination has silenced the voice of the black deaf people.[36] What counts as a disability thus depends on the perception of "normalcy" in any given society,[37] and it is strongly influenced by one's religious, ethnic, social, and cultural backgrounds.

From a human rights perspective, there are at least three implications of pluralism in defining disability. First, the size of the group that qualifies for protection under the CRPD is in question. Generally, persons with disabilities constitute one of the world's most vulnerable and largest minorities.[38] Current estimates categorize one billion persons as having a disability.[39] Many of these people have physical disabilities such as blindness, paralyzation, or lost or impaired limbs; others have mental, developmental, and intellectual disabilities. Some experience multiple disabilities. If we think about disability through the prisms of anthropology, sociology, and culture, however, the numerical estimate may be inaccurate and, most likely, low. Indeed, some languages, such as Masai and Somali, don't include a term for the category "disability."[40] How can disability be recorded if it is not classified? Furthermore, prejudices against persons with disabilities may lead to underreporting of a particular condition. In one study, for instance, no blind people were found to live in Egypt. The researchers found that fear of stigmatization prevented individuals from going on record as blind or having vision impairment.[41] Overall, the lack of accurate data about rates and types of disabilities is staggering.

A second implication concerns the scope of the "protected group" under the CRPD. In light of controversies that ensued about *how* disability should be defined, the international community has refrained in the operational part from providing a definition of the phenomenon. Instead, Article 1 of the Convention merely provides the targeted group for protection under the treaty, stating that "Persons with disabilities include those who have long-term physical, mental, intellectual or sensory impairments which in interaction with various barriers may hinder their full and effective participation in society on an equal basis with others." During the drafting process of the treaty it was agreed, however, that this statement is in no way a comprehensive or consensual definition for disability. The exact scope of who would count for the purpose of protection and under what circumstances will therefore be dependent on activism and continuing efforts of the disability rights movement.

Finally, as a practical matter, the disability rights movement had to unite itself on grounds other than the mere existence of a disability. For many activists, the shared experience of discrimination, as well as the overmedicalization and pathologization of disability, served as a common ground. Indeed, despite the increasing awareness of disability issues at the international level, as well as the ongoing efforts of disability rights activists to entrench the social model to disability (or at least to shift the exclusive focus from the medical approach), there was no question that persons with disabilities all across the world are still largely invisible from frameworks of international law that should otherwise provide them with dignity, autonomy, and equality. Structural discrimination, along with depersonalization of persons with disabilities, particularly for women and members of minority groups, has further created double and triple levels of invisibility and

sanctioned the continuing reign of the medical model of disability, locating
the "problem" merely within the person herself.[42]

Enshrining Disability Rights in the CRPD

As one might expect for such an international law process, the drafting of
the CRPD raised many questions, complexities, and disagreements about
the appropriate means to adopt and enforce disability rights. While the various authors in this book explore some of these controversies in depth, the
goal of the present discussion is more modest: it aims to sketch the key successes of the disability rights movement in this Convention and point to some
of the challenges ahead.

Five overreaching themes merit particular mention. First is the Convention's structure. Although the CRPD is modeled after other existing human
rights treaties, it also reflects in various ways, as described below, a more
contemporary understanding of human rights. First, in contrast to the original assertion of some states, especially the European Union, that a nondiscrimination treaty or an additional protocol to existing treaties would suffice,
the drafters of the Convention ultimately opted for a comprehensive, holistic instrument to address disability rights. In much the same way as did the
Convention on the Rights of the Child, the CRPD includes both sets of civil
and political rights, as well as economic, social, and cultural rights, in line
with the International Covenant on Civil and Political Rights and the International Covenant on Economic, Social and Cultural Rights, which are the
legally binding halves of the Universal Declaration of Human Rights. It
adheres to the universal and inalienable right to development as a comprehensive economic, social, cultural, and political process as expressed in the
1986 Declaration on the Right to Development and in the Vienna Declaration and Programme of Action,[43] and takes into consideration gender distinctions and the entire life span of persons with disability, from birth to
majority to old age and applies regardless of one's "race, colour, sex, language, religion, political or other opinion, national, ethnic, indigenous or
social origin, property, birth, age or other status (Preamble, para. (p))." Furthermore, as the chapters in the book illustrate, the Convention "tailors" the
stipulated rights to the specific needs of persons with disabilities to facilitate
overcoming the multiple and aggravated forms of discrimination that they
face.

Second, Article 1 clearly stipulates that the purpose of the Convention is "to promote, protect and ensure the full and equal enjoyment of all human rights and fundamental freedoms by all persons with disabilities, and to promote respect for their inherent dignity." As discussed above, the treaty includes neither a definition of disability nor of person with disabilities. However, the focus in the description of the targeted group for protection clearly takes an approach to disability that integrates factors of the physical impairment, the society, and the environment, rather than focusing on the alleged deficiencies of what a person with disabilities has or does not have.

A third overreaching theme is the notion of equality and nondiscrimination. This principle is reiterated throughout the CRPD, requiring equalization of human rights of persons with disabilities, regardless of sex, age, and other status. It is particularly emphasized in Article 2, which provides relevant definitions; in Article 3, which states the general principles of the Convention; and in Article 5, which delineates states' responsibilities to ensure the implementation of the principle of equality and nondiscrimination. Two important points should be highlighted in this context. One is the broad definition of "discrimination on the basis of disability," stipulated in Article 2 as

> any distinction, exclusion or restriction on the basis of disability which has the purpose or effect of impairing or nullifying the recognition, enjoyment or exercise, on an equal basis with others, of all human rights and fundamental freedoms in the political, economic, social, cultural, civil or any other field. It includes all forms of discrimination, including denial of reasonable accommodation.

This definition resonates well with the subparagraphs in Article 3, requiring among other things equality between men and women, equality of opportunity and respect for the evolving capacities of children with disabilities (in line with Article 5 of the Convention on the Rights of the Child) as well as with Article 5, which recognizes that all persons are equal before and under the law and are entitled to equal protection and equal benefit of the law; and obliges states to prohibit all discrimination on the basis of disability and to guarantee to persons with disabilities equal and effective legal protection against discrimination on all grounds.

The other important point in this regard is that the stipulation of reasonable accommodation as part of the definition of discrimination, reiterated also in Article 5(3), gives voice to the specific experience of discrimination of persons with disabilities, particularly discrimination experienced by children. Indeed, the concept of "reasonable accommodation" is built on the social model of disability. The assumption is that because society is designed with a bias toward the so-called "abled bodied" there is a need to reconstruct the social environment in order to overcome the bias and to "level the playing field" of persons with disabilities with the rest of the population. It should be noted, however, that although Article 2 includes a definition of "reasonable accommodation,"[44] questions remain as to what states' obligations would practically entail, for instance, in the context of access to justice. Can the effort to "mainstream" disability be universally applied, and how does it correspond with the various models of disability?

Article 3 moreover demands respect for inherent dignity, individual autonomy, including the freedom to make one's own choices, and independence of persons; full and effective participation and inclusion in society; accessibility (elaborated later on in Article 9); respect for the right of children with disabilities to preserve their identities; and, importantly, also respect for difference and acceptance of persons with disabilities as part of human diversity and humanity. Yet how far are we as a society willing to go with such a demand for independence and respect for difference? Among the more provocative cases in this regard are the claim of the Deaf community to be recognized as a linguistic minority and the demand for deinstitutionalization and demedicalization of persons with mental disability.

A fourth overreaching theme is the shift toward a more social and relational approach to disability, with greater social responsibility toward the inclusion of persons with disability in society. Paragraph (e) of the Preamble explicitly recognizes that "disability is an evolving concept and that disability results from the interaction between persons with impairments and attitudinal and environmental barriers that hinders their full and effective participation in society on an equal basis with others." The treaty also recognizes the interdependence between persons with disabilities and their families in the implementation of human rights. Accordingly, paragraph (x) states that "the family is the natural and fundamental group unit of society and is entitled to protection by society and the State, and that persons with disabilities and their family members should receive the necessary protection and assistance to enable families to contribute towards the full and equal enjoyment of the rights of persons with disabilities." Furthermore, aside from conventional methods of mainstreaming, such as adopting appropriate measures, legislations, policies, and programs to eliminate discrimination on the basis of disability and to protect and promote the human rights of persons with disabilities (Article 4), states are required to adopt immediate, effective, and appropriate measures to change negative public opinion, including within families, and to raise awareness as to the capabilities and contributions of persons with disabilities to society. Among the measures stipulated in Article 8, dealing with awareness-raising, are the initiation and maintenance of appropriate campaigns to nurture receptiveness to the rights of persons with disabilities; to promote recognition of the skills, merits, and abilities of persons with disabilities; and to foster an attitude of respect for the rights of persons with disabilities, including throughout all organs of the media. Thus, although, in line with previous human rights instruments, the provisions are generally stated in an "individualist" wording, the overall sense from the Convention is that disability rights are no longer merely conceptualized as a matter of an individual's trait in need of correction, but rather as an issue of social responsibility.

Finally, the last theme that has been strongly incorporated in the CRPD due to disability activism is the issue of representation and involvement of persons with disabilities. Although participation of NGOs and civil society organizations in human rights debates and enforcement has been on the rise, particularly in the past couple of decades, there is no doubt that the disability rights movement has taken it to a new level. For the first time in an international human rights treaty, the expertise of those to be protected under the Convention, including their representative organizations, is fully recognized. Importantly, the Convention establishes an explicit positive legal obligation on states to seek their input in all levels of development, monitoring, and implementation of disability rights. The groundbreaking provision is stipulated in Article 4(3), which deals with general obligations, and states that

> In the development and implementation of legislation and policies to implement the present Convention, and in other decisionmaking processes concerning issues relating to persons with disabilities, States Parties shall closely consult with and actively involve persons with disabilities, including children with disabilities, through their representative organizations.

The Convention further includes an array of other references recognizing and reinforcing the invaluable role persons with disabilities and their representative organizations play in the development and implementation of disability rights. These include mentions in the contexts of participation in political and public life (Article 29), of international cooperation (Article 32), and, important, also in the context of monitoring (Articles 33 and 34). In fact, persons with disabilities are explicitly recognized as partners in these latter processes. With regard to international cooperation, Article 32(1) requires states to "undertake appropriate and effective measures in this regard, between and among states and, as appropriate, in partnership with relevant international and regional organizations and civil society, in particular organizations of persons with disabilities." With regard to national and international monitoring, Article 33(3) stipulates that "Civil society, in particular persons with disabilities and their representative organizations, shall be involved and participate fully in the monitoring process." Moreover, while the members of the Committee on the Rights of Persons with Disabilities are to be elected by states parties, consideration should be given (along with other factors) to the participation of experts with disabilities. In this light and in the spirit of the Convention, the annual forum for states to discuss pertinent issues in regard to the implementation of the Convention as established in Article 40 is likely to be led by persons with disabilities. Persons with disabilities and their representative organizations will therefore remain hands on in all processes involving disability rights—as subjects, as partners, and as experts in their needs and in their lives. Indeed, there is no greater way to demonstrate the success of the disability rights movement and its motto: "Nothing About Us Without Us!"

CHAPTER 2

Our Lives, Our Voices: People with Intellectual Disabilities and Their Families

Anna MacQuarrie and Connie Laurin-Bowie

"This Convention can't just be about those of us here today. It has to be meaningful for the people who aren't in the room; to my friends who aren't always seen or heard by others because they don't communicate in the same way as us here. It has to protect their rights and speak about their lives as well." Robert Martin, a member of Inclusion International's Council and a self-advocate from New Zealand, first spoke these words in the very early stages of work on the Convention on the Rights of Persons with Disabilities. For people with intellectual disabilities and their families, the challenge of the Convention was and is to have state parties and other groups recognize that the Convention includes and must protect the rights of people who cannot always speak for themselves.

People with intellectual disabilities are among the most excluded groups in every society. Of the estimated 130 million people around the world with an intellectual disability, the vast majority live in poverty and experience exclusion and isolation; there is little to no support available to them or their families; less than 5 percent in developing countries are receiving any form of education; and it is estimated that about 26 million live on less than a dollar a day. Even among other disability groups there is little understanding of the issues and perspectives of people with intellectual disabilities and the role families play in supporting individuals to claim their human rights.[1]

Inclusion International's challenge in negotiating the Convention was ensuring that the voices of people with intellectual disabilities and their families were heard and that their particular perspective of inclusion was reflected in the text. For people with intellectual disabilities inclusion requires more than a simple adaptation, accommodation, or device. While many people with disabilities may participate and be included in their school, community, or workplace when provided with a ramp or other adaptation, for people with intellectual disabilities real inclusion requires that classrooms, workplaces, communities, and societies are organized in ways that enable their participation. For the Convention to be inclusive it had to reflect this approach, providing the right to accommodation while also creating an obligation on societies to change the way they are organized.

The development of the CRPD was an opportunity to entrench a progressive rights-based approach that respected this broad approach to inclusion and to develop an aspirational document with a vision for future generations, one that would stand the test of time and point the way toward progress. Anything less risked inadvertently institutionalizing the status quo. For Inclusion International this meant finding ways to ensure that the CRPD would be a relevant tool for its members all over the world that would recognize the very different legal, cultural, political, and economic context of member states but could simultaneously be used anywhere in the world to promote inclusion.

Inclusion International was represented in the negotiation process by its council members, families, self-advocates, and experts from its member organizations. Inclusion International was present at all major CRPD events from the Working Group meeting through all the sessions and the signing ceremony. Additionally, it was an active participant in the International Disability Caucus forum.

Developing the CRPD was not an easy process. The negotiations of the CRPD brought the world together to talk about disability. With that came stereotypes, assumptions, and outdated language use about disability—and not just from government delegations. While it was not unexpected that there would be tensions and differences between government delegations and civil society representatives, the tensions and differences among and within civil society organizations were, in many ways, more difficult and more important to overcome. It does not detract from the CRPD's status as a landmark achievement for disability rights to acknowledge that the negotiation process was fraught with differing ideology, differing priorities and tactics, and differing perspectives.

This chapter will tell the story of how Inclusion International sought to influence the formulation of the CRPD on behalf of people with intellectual disabilities and their families while balancing the different perspectives of its members around the world, building consensus with other disability groups, and prioritizing key issues that were important to its membership.

Background

Inclusion International is a global federation of family-based organizations advocating for the human rights of people with intellectual disabilities and their families worldwide. With more than 200 national member organizations in 115 countries throughout five regions, including the Middle East and North Africa, Europe, Africa, the Americas, and Asia Pacific, it represents a vast global network of people with intellectual disabilities and their families. In some countries national member organizations are large civil society organizations that have significant influence on their governments, while in many parts of the world they are small grassroots parents' groups simply trying to create better opportunities for their family members with an intellectual disability.

For more than fifty years Inclusion International has been a global leader for change, advocating for "A world where people with intellectual disabilities and their families can equally participate and be valued in all aspects of community life."[2] Inclusion International acts as an agent for change on the basis of four main principles: inclusion in all aspects of everyday society; full citizenship that respects individual human rights and responsibilities; self-determination in order to have control over the decisions affecting one's life; and family support through adequate services and support networks to families with a member with a disability.

Inclusion International was a founding member of the International Disability Alliance and has ECOSOC status with the United Nations. Inclusion International has many years of experience collaborating with UN agencies such as the United Nations Children's Fund (UNICEF), World Health Organization (WHO), and United Nations Educational, Scientific and Cultural Organization (UNESCO) as well as the World Bank and the Organization for Economic Cooperation and Development.

Inclusion International does not support labeling people but recognizes that its terminology may not be well understood by others. To this end, and for the purposes of this chapter, the term "intellectual disability" refers to people who have been variously classified as having a developmental disability, developmental delay, mental handicap, and, historically, "mental retardation." In the UK and some other countries the term "people with learning impairments" or "learning difficulties" is also used.

Breaking Down Barriers and Building Consensus

Throughout the negotiations Inclusion International had to balance two sets of tensions: first, the differences among its own membership in putting forward positions that reflected a broad spectrum of experiences and realities; and second, the specific issues and priorities of people with intellectual disabilities and their families in relation to the priorities and perspectives of other disabled people's organizations.

In the earliest stages of negotiations, many organizations (DPOs and other civil society groups) and member states, including Inclusion International, brought their issues, priorities, and perspectives to the table without any shared strategy or coordination. While this somewhat disjointed approach was necessary to highlight the depth and scope of the issues faced by particular groups, it risked developing a series of disability-specific entitlements. Such an approach would have resulted in the siloing of disability rights and would possibly have created a platform for parallel segregated systems. Overcoming this approach was challenging. There was a risk for the groups involved that, in stepping away from the traditional lines drawn in the sand, they could lose the hard-fought ground they had won over the years. There was not a history of collaboration and unity in the disability community that groups could have faith in; distrust and fear had to be addressed. The different groups were exposed to new ideas with which they were either unfamiliar or had had negative experiences. To give only two examples, for years key issues like inclusive education and the role of families had been divisive in the disability community. So long as the disability community was divided on positions and recommended courses of action, these divisions worked in favor of governments' inaction.

While disability groups realized quickly that a coordinated and strategic approach was required, international disability organizations still had a responsibility to bring the position of their members to the negotiations. For a large grassroots organization like Inclusion International this meant developing organizational positions that were responsive to and reflective of their diverse membership. Its members are at different stages in understanding disability as a rights-based issue, have various legislative and policy frameworks in place to support or promote inclusion, and have different socioeconomic factors impacting and influencing the lived experience of disability at a localized grassroots level. Inclusion International had to take the realities of its members into consideration and ensure that its positions were collectively progressive without risking alienation of those members who had not made as much progress toward inclusive practices. Inclusion International needed to address tensions among its own membership to achieve consensus on key issues like inclusive education, legal capacity, and living in the community. For example, on issues such as employment in sheltered workshops or other noncompetitive employment agencies that provide little or no remuneration for work by persons with disabilities, many members feared that if the Convention called for an immediate ban on these, people with intellectual disabilities in many places would be left with no services or supports at all. However, many members wanted the Convention to push for real inclusion in the regular labor market with a right to support and accommodation. In order to find a balance that worked for all its members wherever they were on a particular issue, Inclusion International developed its positions to be taken into the Ad Hoc Committee negotiations in a way that pointed to the future without explicitly denouncing the current state of affairs.

As a member of the IDA and the IDC, Inclusion International had a responsibility to work collectively and collaboratively without straying from the mandate it had been given by its members. It respected the positions taken by other disability groups but could not accept a common ground that risked the exclusion of people with intellectual disabilities and their families.

The success of the CRPD would depend on uniting the disability community and developing a shared perspective on articles. This was no small task. People with intellectual disabilities and their families have a unique perspective on issues affecting them. Inclusion International's inclusive approach has not always been supported by other disability groups. Additionally, it was the only organization representing families and calling for their recognition in the CRPD. At times, this division of opinion split into outright rejection of the ideas Inclusion International proposed. Strategically, Inclusion International turned to the power of personal stories to illustrate the positions of its members. It relied on the brave and courageous voices of self-advocates and family members to put a name and face to its position, to make real their lived experience and demonstrate the exclusion, isolation, and marginalization many people with an intellectual disability and their families face on a day-to-day basis.

During the negotiating sessions, Inclusion International brought self-advocate and family representatives from every region of the world to be part of its delegation in New York and supported those individuals to draw from their own experiences to illustrate the importance of key issues. Sharing the lived experience of disability also made clear that different groups and countries were in different places—philosophically, socioeconomically, and legislatively—and that the CRPD needed to be able to accommodate these differences in an overarching framework. The CRPD had to be able to articulate rights clearly and describe the conditions required to make these rights real. As such, the CRPD provided a road map for governments and communities to better understand where and how rights-based violations have occurred and the necessary steps to remedy that.

Having an Impact: Negotiating Inclusion International's Key Issues

From the outset Inclusion International believed that for the CRPD to be effective in advancing the rights of persons with intellectual disabilities and their families, the Convention must recognize inclusion as the means to achieving human rights. Rights are made real in our communities, and inclusion is the mechanism for communities to deliver on rights. Rather than seeing human rights only as a set of individual entitlements that a person may claim from the state, inclusion requires a broader collective social responsibility by all actors in society. The Convention as a whole needed to reflect the roles and responsibilities of society, communities, and families in realizing the rights of persons with disabilities. Inclusion requires a paradigm shift from viewing people with disability as people who require special conditions to one where people must be enabled and empowered to fully participate in society; one where disability is accepted as part of their unique humanity and our valued human diversity.

While Inclusion International's overall priority was to ensure that the structure and approach taken in the text of the CRPD reflected the concept of inclusion as a basis for realizing the specific rights articulated in the various articles, several important priorities were identified by its members that were seen as fundamental. These priorities were identified by a global process through which Inclusion International examined the economic and social exclusion and isolation faced by people with intellectual disabilities and their families and identified key strategies to promote inclusion. Inclusion International's 2006 global report *Hear Our Voices* was the culmination of three years of work and consultation by hundreds of families and self-advocates from more than eighty countries. Through that process, families and self-advocates identified four priority issues that require specific attention to address exclusion and discrimination: supporting families; securing legal capacity; ensuring that persons with intellectual disabilities are living and being included in their communities; and achieving inclusive education.

The issues identified by this global consultation would guide Inclusion International's priorities in the Convention negotiations, but understanding the sources of exclusion and general principles for inclusion were not enough to guide its involvement through nuanced negotiations and consensus building. Through ongoing consultation and collaboration with its members, Inclusion International developed positions that would be used as a basis for its contributions to the Convention articles dealing with these issues.

Throughout eight Ad Hoc negotiating sessions and an early Working Group meeting that produced the initial negotiating text, the articles developed and evolved. The negotiations ranged from formal to informal. As highlighted earlier, at times they were contentious. The following section will touch on the development and evolution of the articles related to the priorities identified by Inclusion International. This section will review the challenges and successes in negotiations and the development of a common position. It will also highlight the impact the voices of self-advocates and their families had in securing a progressive article.

Families

For Inclusion International, the inclusion of families in the CRPD was necessary to reflect the reality of the lives of people with intellectual disabilities. It has been estimated that 30 to 40 percent of household populations are affected by some form of disability and at least 25 percent of the entire population are directly affected by the presence of disability.[3] From our members we know that families are an essential bridge in the realization of citizenship in the daily lives of children, youth, and often adults, with intellectual disabilities. There is a need for structural and attitudinal change. Disability is not inherent to the individual, nor does it solely impact the individual.

Inclusion International believed the CRPD needed to recognize the unique needs of families supporting a family member with a disability. Children with disabilities are not the only persons with disabilities being supported by family members. The category may include spouses, grandparents, and siblings. We know that families, particularly in developing countries, provide the bulk of support to children, youth, and often adults with disabilities. Inclusion International called for the CRPD to recognize and promote the valuable roles and contributions of families.

The inclusion of families was one of the most contentious issues among civil society organizations. Other DPOs argued strongly that the Convention was about individuals, not about families. They rejected the notion that families were an essential bridge and told family members who Inclusion International brought to the negotiations to go home and let their sons and daughters come speak for themselves. These debates made Inclusion International return to Robert Martin's plea in the early days of the CRPD development: that the CRPD could not only speak to the people in the room. It had to go beyond the group of articulate, predominantly verbal communicators to include people with significant support needs. Inclusion International asked self-advocates and strong moms—like Sue Swenson from the United States, Susan Beayni and Zuhy Sayeed from Canada, Fadia Farah from Lebanon—and other family members to help demonstrate the need for families to be recognized in the CRPD.

A turning point was when Sue Swenson and Susan Beayni rose to the challenge of bringing their adult children to New York to be part of the negotiations. Rebecca Beayni, Susan's daughter, is a dancer and an artist; she helps children with their reading skills. She is also a woman with significant intellectual and physical disabilities. Rebecca does not communicate through traditional means. She does not make decisions the way many of us do. She relies on her family and friends—her circle of support—to help articulate her hopes and dreams, her decisions. Without her family she is powerless and voiceless. Rebecca, through her mother, made a powerful intervention to the AHC, at its sixth session, on the importance of family and the recognition of her interdependence.

Sue Swenson brought her son Charlie to the negotiations. A valued and loved member of his family—who is teased by his family that his only real disability is his love of opera—Charlie, like Rebecca, does not communicate in traditional ways and has significant support needs. His family and support team, based on their deep knowledge of who he is, what he likes and does not like, work together to articulate Charlie's decisions. Sue bravely talked about the risks of guardianship—of having one voice speak for Charlie—and the need for a collective approach to ensure that any one decision made is, in fact, Charlie's decision. She shared her story of how Charlie informed the family he was ready to move out on his own. Charlie, who uses a wheelchair to move around, had taken to wheeling himself to the front door and knocking on the back of it. People who do not know Charlie might not have understood what he was communicating—or that he was communicating at all. But the Swensons knew, and so began a long journey to find appropriate housing in the community for Charlie. Swenson talked about an opportunity that arose for Charlie to live with another woman. On paper it was a great match. The families knew each other, shared values and a commitment to inclusion, and the young adults knew each other and got along well. But there was a hitch. Charlie liked opera and he liked it loud. His potential housemate didn't and preferred a quiet living environment. Under guardianship, or if less care and consideration was given to Charlie's will, it would have been easy to have the two become housemates. However, through supported decision making and a dedicated family, the Swensons knew this would not be the decision he would make for himself. So they went on a new search until they finally found a house that Charlie can call home.

It was through these stories and meeting people with profound support needs that Inclusion International was able to garner support from the IDA and the IDC to include a preambular statement on families. The delegation from the United States, with support from the European Union, introduced a proposal that was eventually adopted as paragraph (x) of the CRPD (see Table 1). Inclusion International is proud of its contribution to securing this recognition and sees this as a real success for our movement and our participation in the CRPD negotiations.

Legal Capacity

Article 12 of the CRPD has been described as a cornerstone of the CRPD as a whole. The message from people with disabilities has been that when their legal capacity is questioned or compromised in one area in their life it affects all areas. In many regards, legal capacity was the most contentiously

Table 1. Summary of How Inclusion International's Priorities Were Treated in the CRPD

Families

Inclusion International's Position
Families play a critical role in the promotion of human rights of people with intellectual disabilities and they require supports to fulfill this role.

CRPD Preamble to the Convention recognizes the role of families:
"Convinced that the family is the natural and fundamental group unit of society and is entitled to protection by society and the state, and that persons with disabilities and their family members should receive the necessary protection and assistance to enable families to contribute towards the full and equal enjoyment of the rights of persons with disabilities."

What this means:
• Recognition of the role families play in supporting their family members with a disability
• Establishment of family supportive policies
• Assistance for families to enable them to support their family member with a disability—this could include tax breaks, respite, caregiver benefits, paid leave, employment security, and so on

---

Legal Capacity

Inclusion International's Position
All people, regardless of disability, have full and equal legal capacity. The right to make decisions in one's own life is foundational to all of our rights.

CRPD Article 12 recognizes
• that persons with disabilities have the right to recognition everywhere as persons before the law;
• Recognition of the role families play in supporting their family members with a disability
• that States Parties shall take appropriate measures to provide access by persons with disabilities to the support they may require in exercising their legal capacity.

What this means
• Recognition that all persons with disabilities have the right to make decisions for themselves and have those decisions respected.
• Recognition of the role of government(s) in securing legal capacity.
• Access to support where assistance in exercising legal capacity is needed.
• Establishment of supported decision-making legislation.
• Increased efforts to close down institutions.

Table 1. (Continued)

Living in the Community

Inclusion International's Position
All people, regardless of needed or perceived levels of support, can live successfully in the community. Institutions have no place in the lives of people with intellectual disabilities.

CRPD Article 19 recognizes:
"the equal right of all persons with disabilities to live in the community, with choices equal to others, and [States Parties] shall take effective and appropriate measures to facilitate full enjoyment by persons with disabilities of this right and their full inclusion and participation in the community."

What this means:
• The opportunity to choose where and with whom one lives.
• Increased efforts to close down institutions.
• Access to personal assistance and various community services to accommodate community living and to prevent isolation or segregation from the community.
• Supports are subsidized and accessible to all persons with disabilities regardless of location and economic status.

Education

Inclusion International's Position
Inclusive education is the basis for the full development of the person. All persons with disabilities should be able to choose inclusive education in their own community.

CRPD Article 24 recognizes:
"the right of persons with disabilities to education. With a view to realizing this right without discrimination and on the basis of equal opportunity, States Parties shall ensure an inclusive education system at all levels, and life-long learning."

What this means:
• Persons with disabilities are not excluded from education because of their disability.
• Persons with disabilities can choose education that is in their own community and is accessible.

negotiated article. There were differing perspectives on what the intent and outcome of the article would be. For Inclusion International, this wasn't a black-and-white issue. Inclusion International was prepared to challenge the traditional boundaries of competence and incompetence entangled in the notion of legal capacity—in particular the capacity to act. However, it had to recognize the very real challenges facing people with significant support needs—those who do not communicate traditionally or may be perceived by others not to communicate at all; those who are extremely isolated (possibly living in institutions); those who have no existing support network to draw on; those who are significantly vulnerable to abuse and exploitation. The CRPD could not leave them behind. Nor could outdated assumptions about decision-making capacity take away rights from people on the basis of disability. These are not simple issues that can be resolved in a short time frame.

From the beginning there was significant debate among UN member states about whether or not the concept of legal capacity included the capacity to act. The disability community stood in solidarity to oppose any understanding of legal capacity that did not include the capacity to act. Inclusion International, with support from its Canadian member the Canadian Association for Community Living, introduced to the disability community and to UN member states the notion of supported decision making that was developed in Canada in the late 1980s and early 1990s. It was designed to recognize that some people may need support to exercise their legal capacity but that they should not be punished for doing so.[4] A range of supports could be identified as part of a supported decision-making model, ranging from assistance in decision making (including communication supports like assistive technologies, interpretation, and translation); to assistance in expressing a person's will; and assistance in communicating to others someone's personal identity (including a person's hopes, expectations, and life plan).

During the negotiations about Article 12, Inclusion International, the WNUSP, as well as several key individuals had significant impact on the shaping of the article. While it supported a number of articulate and impressive self-advocates to participate in the negotiations for whom minimal support was required to enable their capacity to act, Inclusion International also had an obligation to ensure that the Convention reflected the realities of those who were unable to communicate in traditional ways. For this group, families, friends, and other supporters were essential to the realization of the capacity to act. Many other DPOs were suspicious of the role that families play in a person's decision making, fearing from their own experiences interference and an undermining of a person's autonomy. Again, the participation of Sue and Charlie Swenson and Susan and Rebecca Beayni was pivotal in establishing mutual respect and understanding between Inclusion International and other members of the IDC and IDA. At one side event on legal capacity during the sixth AHC session, Sue Swenson said, "You told me I should bring my son to speak for himself. This is Charlie, please ask him what he thinks about this Convention. When this meeting is over I invite you to take Charlie to lunch and to determine what Charlie would like to eat." This challenge and the reminder that the Convention was being developed for all people with disabilities helped to build some trust among members of the caucus and it helped to deepen the understanding of what supported decision making meant for people with intellectual disabilities. The model of supported decision making was able to garner support from the community and UN member states. It became central to the article and helped broker consensus. For the first time ever, the right to use support in exercising legal capacity has been secured.

Institutionalization

There was significant support from the IDA and the IDC that the CRPD had to be clear that people with disabilities have a right to live in the community and to choose where and with whom they live. It was critical that a new convention would not put people with disabilities at risk of institutionalization and that state parties do not interpret the Convention as a justification for the need for institutions.

The issue of institutions has been at the heart of our movement for decades. Many of our member organizations were formed by parent groups who had rejected that institutions had a role in the lives of their sons or daughters. Many of our members, however, still struggle with the provision of support and services outside of institutional settings, and many parents continue to support institutions as an option. While many countries, like Norway, Canada, and New Zealand, have successfully closed their institutions for persons with an intellectual disability, many more continue to invest in them or tie their services to them. In those countries, families who choose not to place their family member with a disability in an institution often receive no support of any kind and cannot access general services provided to others, such as education or health care. People with intellectual disabilities around the world are particularly vulnerable to institutionalization. They have been shut out of most societies around the world, or more accurately, they have been confined in institutions, quietly hidden inside their families' homes, isolated from public view, and prevented from achieving the full potential that every human being inherently has.

The Convention's article on living in the community was an opportunity to tackle these issues. Inclusion International worked very closely with Bizchut, an Israeli association also focused on people with intellectual disabilities, who were equally passionate and committed to securing a progressive article on living in the community.[5] The challenges in negotiating the article included assumptions by both member states and other DPOs that people with profound intellectual disabilities could not live in a community setting and that they were better "protected" by institutional settings. The title of the article, "Living Independently and Being Included in the Community," raised concerns among governments that the term "living independently" did not reflect cultural norms. Members of civil society groups warned that the term would be used as criteria for determining who would be supported to live in the community.

Similarly, the various attempts to have the article secure the provision of supports and services to facilitate living in the community drew concerns from states about the potential cost of these services and concerns from the community that the model proposed in early versions of the text were based on out-of-date models for supports and contained totally unacceptable references about the provision of services being "subject to existing resources." Such a qualification would never be considered in relation to the discrimination and exclusion of girls and women or members of minorities. We believed any reference to the need for institutions would be regressive and any interpretation of the responsibility of the state to provide support as justification for institutionalization must be eliminated.

It was, in part, the courage of people like Robert Martin and others who had experienced institutionalization that made a difference. Hearing people share their personal stories of the abuse and neglect they faced in institutions, the humiliation and powerlessness they lived with, was transformational. To meet and get to know people with profound disabilities who live successful lives in their communities demonstrated that institutionalization is an unacceptable outdated approach to supporting people with disabilities. Martin shared his story with bravery and humility. Revealing private information about himself and his history was not easy. Reliving the experience in retelling his story was, at times, trying and traumatic. Yet Martin and others persevered. They persevered because they knew that if states would listen they would agree that no one should ever live in an institution.

In a lobby sheet developed by the IDC, Martin reflected:

> For me, living in an institution meant my life was taken over by a service. The doctors seemed to have a lot of power but I was not sure who was really holding me there against my will. In the institution I slept in a bed alongside strangers, often ten people in the same room. I saw no value in myself as a person and did not understand the idea of choice. I learnt to eat quickly or my food was thrown out or taken by others.
>
> Like everyone else I became a slave to routine, my day was measured by the routine of the institution, not the time of day. I never left the institution, everyone came to the institution and I never got to go out. I seldom saw my family as my sister was also placed in care in another institution. I personally experienced the sexual, physical and emotional abuse that goes on in institutions.
>
> I came to understand what happens to the staff, how they also become victims of the institutionalisation process and become institutionalised as well. How the institution develops a life of its own which is far removed from life in the community. It has its own values and ways of doing things. People are no longer an individual, they are part of a system and the system always wins. I quickly learnt not to challenge authority. When we are forced to live in an institution we never know if or when we will be able to leave. You look around and see people who have lived their whole life in an institution. It is the only life they know and are often scared to leave when this becomes a possibility.
>
> I believe that all institutionalisation does at best is to put a person's life on hold and at worse it makes their needs even more profound.
>
> What are the alternatives?
>
> There is really only one and that is life in the community.
>
> Locking people away from their family or friends or denying them the right to be part of the community, taking over another

person's life and trying to say it is their best interests or forcing people to live in an institution and being institutionalised can never be justified.

I became the person I am today because I finally got the support and assistance I needed to live in the community. My friends with a disability who are still being institutionalised or being forced to live in institutions deserve the same opportunity.

Regardless of their need for support or assistance a person with a disability can live a full and useful life in the community.

The key is providing the support and assistance they need to achieve this.[6]

Article 19 of the CRPD, for the first time anywhere, recognizes that people have a right to live in the community and to choose where and with whom they live. While it stops short of saying all institutions must close, it provides the road map that will move us closer, in time, to this goal. Additionally, it places an obligation on states to ensure that supports and services are available in communities to facilitate successful community living and commits states to ensuring that community services and facilities are available for people with disabilities, equal to those in communities for the general population. This represents a significant step forward in our efforts to combat marginalization and isolation within communities. Additionally, it reinforces the principle of inclusion as necessary for true and meaningful participation in communities.

Inclusive Education

Article 24 of the CRPD on education is a clear example of the type of compromise required in developing the CRPD. From the outset, there were strong opinions about what the article should—and should not—contain. It would have been easy to follow a path that prescribed the necessary conditions to provide education to particular groups of learners. In its initial formulations, the article on education provided a right to "choose" inclusion and provided significant loopholes for segregated learning by referencing "where the general education system does not adequately meet the needs of persons with disabilities special and alternative forms of learning should be made available." This formulation and language was indicative of the struggles and tensions related to education. For UN member states there were concerns about resources required to operate an inclusive system. For the disability community there were concerns about only providing for inclusive options. Even within Inclusion International's membership this was an issue. Many of its members are organizations created by parents in order to start segregated schools as their sons and daughters were not welcome in mainstream schools. Over the years many saw that segregated schooling led to further segregation in the community and in adult life. Many others recognized that there are not enough resources to adequately fund two separate systems. Many Inclusion International members began to believe that inclusive education was the way forward but still wanted choice.

Through research and lived experience the positive lifelong outcomes and benefits of inclusive education have been demonstrated. Inclusive education plays a role in providing shared public spaces for children with disabilities to grow and develop alongside their nondisabled peers. Studies have also shown that lifelong patterns of inclusion are established in early childhood education programs, preschools, in the classroom, and on the playgrounds of neighborhood schools. Social inclusion in schools is therefore foundational for social inclusion in society.[7]

It is for these reasons that it was critical that inclusion form the foundation of the article on education. Certainly, there are very real challenges of delivering an education system in overcrowded, inaccessible schools that lack adequate staff or trained teachers. However, the concern for Inclusion International, based on the experience of people with intellectual disabilities and their families, is that where segregated options are provided for, students with intellectual disabilities are disproportionately represented. This demonstrates a risk that students with intellectual disabilities are particularly vulnerable to being excluded from regular classrooms. Thus, while Inclusion International respected the position taken by other disability groups (as well as states' concerns), it could not accept a common ground that risked the exclusion of students with intellectual disabilities.

For years the issue of inclusive education had divided the international disability community. From different understandings of what inclusive education means, to different disability-specific educational needs, to "purists" who subscribed to one vision or one approach, finding a common voice on education required a respectful deliberative dialogue among CRPD stakeholders. It meant talking about what inclusive education really is and what a framework for inclusive education could look like in various parts of the world with various levels of development. It was thus important to be clear on what inclusive education was not. Inclusive education is not simply inserting students with disabilities into traditional classrooms. Inclusive education cannot happen in overcrowded classrooms that lack trained teachers. Inclusive education does not mean a one-size-fits-all approach or that all students are in the regular classroom all the time, regardless of support needs. It does not mean that the educational needs of blind, deaf, and deafblind students could be ignored in the name of inclusion. Inclusive schools put into place measures to support all children to fully participate. Where barriers exist, inclusive schools transform the way they are organized to meet the needs of all children.

Mia Farah of Lebanon shared her story about being excluded from public school because of her disability. Her teacher thought she would not be able to learn in a typical classroom or learn Arabic—the language of instruction at the school. At information sessions during AHC sessions and on the floor at the UN, Mia Farah shared with people how this made her feel. And that, although she may learn differently, she wants to be included and respected. To demonstrate how wrong her public school teacher had been, Mia Farah shared her story in English, in Arabic, and in French. Her lived experience demonstrated that we all belong and we can all achieve things others see as impossible when we and our families are supported.

Through the lived experience of people with intellectual disabilities and through dialogue with other disability groups, Article 24 was crafted to reflect a carefully constructed compromise among disability groups. The article would secure a right to inclusion but would not prohibit alternatives. Having a common voice and standing in solidarity with each other meant the development of an article on education that is based on inclusion but respects the specific needs of blind, deaf, and deafblind students; an article that ensures all learners benefit from a general education system. As a result, the first legally binding statement on inclusive education has been established in the CRPD.

Outcomes

By coming together with one voice and a common position, the disability community was able to achieve successes that had previously eluded us. We were able to achieve a level of solidarity and as a result a newfound level of credibility within governments, the UN, and its agencies. We removed the key barrier—division—that had enabled governments to benefit from a divide-and-conquer approach.

The results were nothing short of dramatic. For the first time ever, the IDA developed a common position on inclusive education. For the first time ever, international law recognized that people with disabilities have a right to live in the community and to choose where and with whom they live. For the first time ever, international law recognized that all people have an inherent right to legal capacity—including the capacity to act as well as the right to use support in exercising that capacity. For the first time ever, people with intellectual disabilities and their families felt respected and heard.

This was the power of our stories, of our voices.

Next Steps

Over the course of six years the CRPD was negotiated and adopted by the UN. While this was a long, and at times arduous, journey, the real work, the tough work, has only just begun. The challenge will be to interpret the CRPD at local levels in ways that are meaningful for people with disabilities. To be successful as a consensus document the CRPD had to speak in generalities. As the work now turns to focus on implementing, monitoring, and reporting, the CRPD is open, and vulnerable, to wide interpretation. The carefully crafted, and often fragile, common ground developed among the disability community is also vulnerable as the more detailed work of implementation gets under way. The challenges the disability community faced in coming together during the negotiations are just as challenging now. Transitioning from the generalities of the CRPD to the detail of implementation action plans will test the bonds and solidarity developed during the negotiating process. The IDA will play a critically important role in maintaining and fostering the solidarity of the disability community. Inclusion International is committed to working as a part of the IDA to ensure that the CRPD is implemented in ways that reflect the intent of those who contributed to its development.

Inclusion International has launched a strategy to support its members to work with their governments and community stakeholders in the implementation of the Convention in each of its priority areas. At the Fifteenth World Congress of Inclusion International held in Berlin (June 2010) almost

3,000 families, self-advocates, and community stakeholders came together to share and build strategies to use the Convention as a tool for developing inclusive practices in education, legal capacity, living in the community, and family support. The General Assembly of Inclusion International adopted a new strategic plan that has as its basis the Convention and these key priorities for implementation. Inclusion International will draw on the expertise of its members around the world to support innovative practices at the country level in each of its priority areas, provide a platform for global knowledge exchange and research, support its members to contribute to the monitoring process, develop litigation strategies, and develop information tools and resources.

For people with intellectual disabilities, their families, and for Inclusion International, the central challenge in implementation of the Convention remains the same as the challenges of negotiation: to ensure that state parties, other DPOs, and community stakeholders understand that this convention includes people with intellectual disabilities and particularly that people who cannot speak on their own behalf are not left behind as we move forward with a new global agenda.

CHAPTER 3

Living in the Community, Access to Justice: Having the Right Makes All the Difference

Tirza Leibowitz

The right of all persons with disabilities to live in the community is central to the Convention on the Rights of Persons with Disabilities. Yet this right was only incorporated into Article 19 at the last possible negotiating session in January 2006, as a result of extensive groundwork spanning one-and-a-half years and four negotiating sessions.

Why was this right almost left out, and why was it finally incorporated? What are the implications of this right for persons with disabilities, and what may we learn from the process that will aid in its implementation? This chapter explores these questions from the perspective of Bizchut, the Israel Human Rights Center for People with Disabilities. The following account reflects my experience as legal counsel to Bizchut and one of its representatives at the treaty negotiations.

The story of how the right to live in the community made its way into the CRPD is closely linked with the broader issue of making the Convention relevant in cases where persons with disabilities experience the most acute marginalization. It is precisely such marginalization that prevents those affected to speak up and challenge it, particularly persons with psychosocial and intellectual disabilities. Communities around the globe still question the entitlement of these individuals to enjoy the basic rights of personhood and inclusion in the community. Eliminating discrimination against them necessitates a fundamental change in social structure, including changes in deep-seated legal constructs.

A common thread in Articles 12, 13, and 19 of the CRPD is their profound impact on personhood in both a legal and physical sense. Article 12 addresses the long-standing practice of denying legal consequences to decisions and actions taken by persons with disabilities. It restores legal personhood by proscribing limits on legal capacity and requiring that support be provided to enable its exercise. Article 13 eliminates barriers within the justice system that prevent individuals from accessing justice in order to counter the negation of their legal personhood. Finally, Article 19, which requires providing support to enable independent living and inclusion in the community, is the antithesis to segregation either by the absence of support to partake in the life of the community, resulting in people geographically located in society but effectively isolated, or by the practice of placing individuals in institutions, which effectively removes the individual from society.

Interestingly, Article 12 was the most debated article of the CRPD negotiations, taking center stage throughout the negotiations and beyond, while the more subtle drama around Articles 13 and 19—the story told here—took place largely behind the scenes. The formulators took a major step when they embedded these rights in the framework of the CRPD; the next step is to upgrade their prominence in the arena of implementation. Society still has a long way to go to make Articles 13 and 19 key components of basic compliance with the CRPD.

Disability Rights in Israel

Bizchut (literally "by right") is the leading advocacy organization in Israel for the rights of persons with disabilities.[1] By the time negotiations on the actual CRPD text began in 2004, multiple developments in the field of disability rights were already underway in Israel. In 1996, the Supreme Court issued the first precedent addressing disability from a human rights perspective and requiring that accessibility accommodations be made in schools.[2] Israel's disability rights law, initiated and supported by Bizchut, was passed in 1998.[3] After the legislation of the disability rights law, additional cases were argued and decided: polling stations and voting procedures were to be made accessible,[4] and import of inaccessible public buses were halted.[5] The first cases challenging discrimination in employment were brought before the court beginning in 2001.[6] In 2000, the Commission for Equal Rights of Persons with Disabilities was formed.[7] Also that year, a law was implemented that detailed the entitlement of persons with psychosocial disabilities to community-based rehabilitation services.[8] In 2002, the Special Education Law was amended to create an explicit entitlement to support services enabling inclusive education, and gaps in the law's implementation were challenged in court.[9]

One highlight in the progress was in the area of access to justice. As in most, if not all countries around the world, investigative and judicial procedures in Israel did not previously meet the needs of persons with intellectual, psychosocial, or communications disabilities. The police did not know how to question people with such disabilities, and the courts lacked the tools to enable them to testify. Evidence was not properly collected, and with little knowledge of the barriers faced and how to overcome them, the validity of complaints and testimonies was too easily challenged at the investigative stage and in the courtroom. Abusers of persons with disabilities easily avoided being charged and brought to trial. Suspects and offenders returned to the streets, perpetuating the vicious cycle of violence. Consequently, though persons with disabilities are more vulnerable than others to violence and abuse, the majority of cases in which they were victims were closed. Additionally, the risk of extracting false confessions from suspects with disabilities was high, at times leading to wrongful convictions.

In 2003, Bizchut initiated the Due Process Project, which provided guidance on accommodations that must be made to existing procedures. Bizchut offered this service to courts, the state prosecution, the public defender, police investigators, and other law-enforcement agencies. The goal was to enable fair investigation, testimony, and trial in cases where persons with disabilities are complainants, victims, witnesses, suspects, or defendants. The crowning success of the project was the 2005 Law on Accommodations to the Investigative and Testimonial Processes for Persons with Intellectual or Psychosocial Disabilities.[10]

Throughout this period, little progress was made in another key area of concern—the right to live in the community. Rather than close institutions for persons with disabilities, the government supported creation of new ones.[11] Although programs existed for supported living in the community, making them available as a matter of policy to individuals with high support needs was a constant struggle. According to ministerial policy, individuals in need of intensive support in everyday lives were denied entitlement to that support if they chose to remain in the community rather than enter an institution.[12]

Bizchut's first petition on the matter, in 1994, was rejected by the court and did not result in policy change.[13] It did lead, however, to the establishment of the first framework of supported living in the community for individuals with high support needs. (A later petition, which cited Article 19 and Israel's signature of the CRPD, took this framework a step farther by striking down the policy that contravened this right.)[14]

When Bizchut joined the CRPD negotiation process at the UN in mid-2004,[15] the Working Group established by the Ad Hoc Committee negotiating the Convention had already submitted a draft that served as the basic text for the negotiations.[16] After reading the Working Group draft, Bizchut discerned that it could contribute to the process by offering Israel's experience of progress made in some areas and impasse reached in others. Access to justice fell into the first category—a field in which Israel had made a breakthrough that could be shared by translation into appropriate treaty language. Living in the community fell into the second category, as an area of impasse. Here, too, the Israeli experience could serve as an example to inform treaty formulation. Since discriminatory policies on living in the community do not characterize Israel alone but are in place in most countries around the globe, such language would help counter discriminatory policies worldwide.

Access to Justice

The right to access to justice is familiar from other UN treaties, most notably the International Covenant on Civil and Political Rights. Article 14 of the ICCPR affirms the right to fair and public hearings by independent and competent courts, the presumption of innocence unless proven guilty, and guarantees for due process. Access to justice is also understood as a principle ensuring that social and economic factors do not hinder individuals from accessing the system. As negotiations progressed, it became evident that this concept warranted explicit mention also in the CRPD. However, access to justice did not appear as a stand-alone issue in the Working Group draft or other early drafts. Though it was discussed as a subtopic of legal capacity, liberty, and security of the person, and freedom from exploitation, violence, and abuse (now CRPD Articles 12, 14, and 16), in none of these cases was it translated into specific treaty text.

During the fourth ad hoc session (August 2004), some states, most notably Costa Rica and Chile, suggested that access to justice be addressed in a separate article, due to the importance of access to courts as a main pillar of citizenship rights and its denial from persons with disabilities owing to the particular barriers they face. Chile suggested a separate article that would require states to "guarantee adequate access to courts for persons with disabilities, facilitating their effective role as direct or indirect parties to contentious and noncontentious legal proceedings."[17]

Interestingly, these proposals went beyond physical or communications barriers experienced by persons with disabilities due to inaccessible infrastructure or lack of accommodations in imparting information (such as sign language translation). A separate article was not needed to redress physical and communications, as these were already comprehensively addressed in the articles on accessibility and access to information (which became CRPD Articles 9 and 21).

Costa Rica followed with a proposal that for the first time mentioned accommodations to *procedures*, stating that "equality before the law shall require the modification, adjustment and flexible application of legal procedures, practice and rules, including rules of evidence."[18] At the end of the session, however, it remained to be seen whether these proposals would resonate with the negotiating states and receive the necessary support for incorporation into the evolving treaty.

From Bizchut's perspective, this move toward procedural accommodations was crucial. Rules that limit or void the capacity of persons with disabilities to testify had to be abolished. Even when such rules were no longer in existence in a given system, or had never been in existence, the possibility for accommodations had to be incorporated into the judicial process. Such accommodations were necessary in order to neutralize any embedded barriers in systems that had never previously accounted for persons with intellectual, psychosocial, or communications disabilities as participants.

By the time Bizchut became involved in the CRPD negotiations, it had helped promote the accessibility of investigations and the testimony process for individual victims and offenders with disabilities in dozens of cases in Israel. Bizchut staff had also conducted training programs and hands-on workshops on adapting investigative and judicial procedures to meet the needs of people with intellectual or psychosocial disabilities. The programs were offered to the police, state prosecutors, legal aid attorneys, judges, and rape crisis centers. Recommendations based on this experience had been presented to the Ministry of Justice and served as the basis for the comprehensive law passed in 2005.[19] The law provides illuminating examples of procedural accommodations, including but not limited to allowing the individual to be accompanied by a chosen support person; the use of alternative and augmentative communication (AAC) aids (such as pictures and communication boards);[20] having investigations performed by individuals with experience and expertise in communicating with persons with disabilities, instead of by standard police investigators; the participation of experts to eliminate any misinformation regarding the disability that might hinder courts from accepting the testimony, and to assist in understanding the witness's method of communication; and the opportunity to testify without official attire, or in camera (in private) through video links or in the judge's chambers.

As the CRPD draft evolved, two articles came close to addressing the issue of procedural accommodations. The guarantee of freedom from exploitation, violence, and abuse (which became Article 16) includes providing support to persons with disabilities, families, and caregivers on how to recognize and report instances of exploitation. Under this article, facilities serving persons with disabilities must be monitored for instances of abuse by an independent authority; rehabilitation must be made available for persons with disabilities who were victims of abuse; and identification, investigation, and prosecution must be promoted. However, on this last point the draft CRPD remained nebulous. What must be done differently to combat the scant instances of prosecution in cases involving persons with disabilities as victims, and over-representation of persons with disabilities in prisons? The article on liberty and security of persons (which became CRPD Article 14) went as far as mandating that if persons with disabilities were deprived of their liberty, this should be done on an equal basis with others, including by providing reasonable accommodations. However, neither of the articles touched the heart of the barriers that deny equal access to justice specifically for persons with disabilities, and thus could not pave the way toward dismantling them. Bizchut recognized that linking the existing Chilean and Costa Rican proposals with its experience on the ground could help the proposals gain traction and become treaty language. That is what it set out to do.

Living in the Community

From the start of negotiations, living in the community was formulated as a separate article and linked with the obligation of party states to provide access to support services in the community, enabling inclusion in the community. The first formulations affirmed the aspect of choice, such as the Working Group draft from January 2004, which stated that

States Parties to this Convention shall take effective and appropriate measures to enable persons with disabilities to live independently and be fully included in the community, including by ensuring that:
(1) Persons with disabilities have the equal opportunity to choose their place of residence and living arrangements;
(2) Persons with disabilities are not obliged to live in an institution or in a particular living arrangement.

In subsequent sessions, a proposal was made to add reference to liberty of movement, in addition to choice, as a fundamental principle of living in the community. New Zealand suggested aligning the language with that of Article 12 of the ICCPR, which addresses freedom of movement and liberty to choose one's residence.[21] However, still missing was the right at the core of the article. This stood in contrast to most other substantive articles, which began with the affirmation of a right—whether the right to recognition as persons before the law, to life, to liberty and security, to freedom of expression, or to education, among others.

As mentioned, Bizchut had been struggling for years with this very issue, in the form of a ministerial policy that recognized the entitlement of persons with intellectual disabilities and high support needs to receive support only within institutions. An individual who could not demonstrate a minimum level of independence would not receive state support to live in a community framework.[22] Persons with disabilities and families had to fight a system that was heavily biased toward institutionalization. Living in an institution was the result not necessarily of outside coercion, that is, by overriding a choice made by the individual, but rather of the absence of support to enable community life. Thus in Israel, the vast majority of persons with intellectual disabilities living outside their family home are in institutions and group homes. Only about 25 percent live in scattered apartments and homes in the community.[23] The underlying assumption in Israeli society that Bizchut had to challenge was that persons with disabilities and high support needs cannot or are unable to live in the community; in other words, that living in the community is not a right, but rather a privilege subject to threshold conditions. Bizchut looked to the evolving CRPD draft to provide tools for resolving the deadlock on such a fundamental right.

Bizchut's experience revealed that the responsibility of making community living happen could not be placed on the individuals alone. The *system* had to be modeled around the obligation to support a community-based way of life. This required adding the core right to the article—the right of all persons with disabilities to live in the community.

Getting Involved and Securing the Rights

Bizchut joined the International Disability Caucus as a national organization promoting the rights of persons with disabilities. Within the IDC, Bizchut established a strong alliance with organizations representing persons with intellectual and psychosocial disabilities, primarily Inclusion International and affiliated self-advocates (with strong representation from New Zealand), the Canadian Association for Community Living, and the World Network of Users and Survivors of Psychiatry.[24]

Collaboration did not come free of debate. While the original draft on living in the community addressed forced institutionalization, Bizchut argued that insufficient reference was made to noncoerced institutionalization as the result of a biased system and absence of services in the community. Through a productive exchange among the various organizations, the IDC spelled out its positions on both aspects more clearly. Its final position challenged institutionalization per se on the basis of the nonnormative character of institutions, even if residing in them was not coerced. The IDC position also bolstered the element of choice by emphasizing the need to guarantee that support services respect the autonomy and choice of the individuals.

Working from within the IDC enabled doubling and tripling the power of the message. For example, while Bizchut, Inclusion International, and the Canadian Association for Community Living coordinated IDC efforts on the article on living in the community, each organization also spearheaded its own interventions that strengthened the IDC's message. Advocates were also able to enlist each of their country's delegation, so that New Zealand, Israel, and Canada stood at the forefront of discussions on upgrading the language of the article on living in the community.

Despite the formal stance of maintaining independence from the Israeli governmental delegation, the delegation's dominant rights-based streak made for an outstandingly productive partnership. Bizchut was able to gain the delegation's support for its central proposals on access to justice and living in the community. This support was critical, for in order to gain traction a proposal by civil society had to convince a state delegation to incorporate it into an official proposal. Then both sides had to work to garner significant support by other governments.

Although at that time internal policies in Israel curbed the right to live in the community when it came to individuals with high support needs, Israel's delegation took up Bizchut's proposal for upgrading the article and inserting the right of all persons with disabilities to live in the community.[25] The IDC suggested a similar proposal.[26] Both proposals argued that nonrecognition of this right left a loophole for maintaining many persons with disabilities in institutions.

The turning point was reached at the seventh session, during which Israel and the IDC submitted written proposals that asserted that persons with disabilities have "the right to live in the community and to live independently";[27] citing the reality of continued placement of persons with disabilities in institutions, the Ad Hoc Committee chair posited the premise "that is fundamental towards the goal of a paradigm shift" according to which persons with disabilities have the right to live independently and be included in the community.[28] Kenya, New Zealand, Canada, Chile, Jamaica, and others supported Israel's proposal and provided further clarification. Bizchut and Mental Disability Rights International (MDRI) supported it as well.[29] Efforts were successful. The final language adopted in Article 19 opens with the right — "States Parties to this Convention recognize the equal right of all persons with disabilities to live in the community . . ." It reflects the notion that living in the community is a right, not an entitlement one merits by fulfilling any threshold conditions. It also establishes states' duty to "take effective and appropriate measures to facilitate full enjoyment by persons with disabilities of this right and their full inclusion and participation in the community."

As with the right to live in the community, the right of persons with disabilities to equally access the justice system was a new frontier. In the name of learning from experience, state delegations and civil organizations set aside customary boundaries. They collaborated openly, keeping formalities to a minimum. The evolution of Article 13 on access to justice is a telling example of the extraordinary level of collaboration between states and civil society. It also reveals how this collaboration helped push the language in place at the starting point of negotiations to an even higher level.

At the opening of negotiations, a number of states suggested devoting a separate article to access to justice, instead of its original "home" in the article on equal recognition before the law. But states were not yet unified into a critical mass of support, nor did they have a concrete proposal for treaty language. Even among states that did promote a separate article, positions diverged about the focus. Should it be on removing physical barriers? Or was it about communications or procedural barriers? What exactly *are* procedural barriers, and how should they be surmounted? After an initial discussion at the fifth session, in January 2005, the coordinator "encouraged all delegates interested in drafting language to confer."[30] Involved delegations, including Chile, Costa Rica, Mexico, Canada, Australia, Bosnia-Herzegovina, and Russia, met and composed an initial draft. Bizchut was invited to participate and shared its experience from legislative advances in Israel. Bizchut also reported on its Due Process Project for making accommodations to enable fair investigation, testimony, and trial in cases where persons with disabilities are victims, witnesses, suspects, or defendants.

A number of parallel developments at the negotiations substantiated the growing consensus. The IDC presented a position paper and lobbied governments on the need for a separate article and what it should include.[31] As part of the informal program, Bizchut conducted a side event on access to justice, which included a concrete demonstration of the impact of communication-related disabilities on the ability to give testimony in the absence of accommodations justice.[32] Bizchut presented a number of Israeli cases in which accommodations were made to enable investigation and testimony, and a discussion ensued on the appropriate content of an article on access to justice.

The conferral among state delegations and civil society organizations bore fruit. Representatives reached a consensus draft, based on Chile's original proposal, but with an important addition. The new draft emphasized enabling participation in legal *proceedings*, including in *investigative and other preliminary stages*,[33] signaling the extension of the article beyond physical barriers. As explained above, the inaccessibility of the justice process profoundly limits access to justice for persons with communications barriers on account of intellectual, psychosocial, or physical disabilities. The IDC proposal in that session complemented the consensus reached by the conferring states, by adding the component of *accommodations to the process*.[34] Bizchut had demonstrated that this was the answer to procedural barriers.

One final push was needed from the parties involved to make the seventh session decisive for the article on access to justice. Both Israel and the IDC presented proposals that expanded guarantees to accessing legal proceedings.[35] Again, the chair's introductory remarks indicated the close collaboration between the sectors: "The Chair noted that Israel had submitted a proposal to add two additional subparagraphs, both of which mirrored the IDC's proposal."[36] Slowly, states concurred. The IDC concluded with an illuminating example of barriers to persons with disabilities in accessing the justice system and how treaty language can guide states to eliminate these barriers. In one particular case described to the participants, a young Israeli woman with an intellectual disability had her testimony regarding abuse she had suffered disregarded because under cross-examination she could not correctly answer basic questions such as how many weeks are in a month, or months in a year, resulting in discrediting of her testimony and acquittal of her abuser. On appeal, however, an expert witness provided the court with tools to identify the reliable aspects of her testimony even when certain questions were answered wrongly.[37]

This time the proposals elicited a critical mass of support. At last the need to devote a separate article to the matter was clearly recognized, and the place of procedural accommodations to enable equal participation in the justice system at all stages and in all forms, including as witnesses, was secured. The final formulation of Article 13 incorporates these components, including the "provision of procedural and age-appropriate accommodations, in order to facilitate their effective role as direct or indirect participants, including as witnesses, in all legal proceedings, including at investigative and other preliminary stages." It moreover calls for appropriate training for those involved in the criminal justice system.

The unprecedented collaboration between governments and civil society and level of involvement of civil society in formulating the treaty is often described as a unique contribution to human rights. The process of formulating and negotiating Article 13 is a clear example of that.

In Retrospect

The journey toward recognizing the right to access to justice culminated in success. Yet some aspects did not make it into its final formulation. Both Israel and the IDC had proposed that the treaty language include examples of procedural accommodations, such as communications assistants and devices, use of experts to enhance communication, and advice on the disability's effect on the process.[38] The chair expressed valid concern that the article should not turn overly prescriptive.[39] But pressing for a more detailed formulation also had its clear merits, particularly considering that the meaning of access to justice for persons with disabilities was yet unchartered territory. The examples proposed for the text were eventually dropped, and the article remained in its general formulation.

It has taken time for Article 13 on access to justice to gain traction. States are struggling with the basic task of understanding its intent. Access to justice in the CRPD is commonly taken to refer to ensuring legal aid, legal representation, or legal remedies[40]—certainly critical components of achieving access to justice. Yet these do not exemplify barriers typical to persons with disabilities; rather, they are faced by all marginalized groups. Slowly the opportunity is seized to use this article as a frame for identifying and removing barriers encountered specifically by persons with disabilities in accessing justice. Fortunately, due to the hard work and successes of the negotiation process, the treaty language contains the necessary basic components, including emphasis on participation of persons with disabilities in all proceedings and on procedural accommodations. Momentum is building toward bringing to light the full significance of the article.[41] It is hoped that this momentum will be picked up not only by disability rights organizations and state agencies addressing the rights of persons with disabilities, but also by national and international organizations dealing broadly with criminal justice and access to justice issues, such as advocates challenging violence against women or ensuring rights are upheld for those caught up in the criminal justice system.

Similarly, the challenge of turning Article 19 into a reality remains before us. The article could have been stronger by clarifying the nonnormative nature of institutions and requiring that plans be established to enable the transition into the community for the many persons with disabilities who are currently institutionalized. Reallocation of budgets by global donors and international agencies, who have until now supported the establishment of new institutions or refurbishing of old ones, is also a conditio sine qua non for any significant change.[42] But although the treaty language omits explicit detail on these steps, they are implied in the fundamental principles recognized in Article 19. Incorporation of both the right of all persons to live in the community and the obligation to provide services to prevent isolation or segregation from the community negates institutional life, even if not formally coerced. Moreover, the article can serve as a powerful advocacy tool in the many contexts where the main barrier is not institutions so much as it is the lack of community-based support to address the isolation many persons with disabilities experience even if physically located in their communities.[43] The onus is now on society—both governments and civil society—to breathe life into these words, thereby ending some of the most marginalizing practices humankind has known. Speaking from the perspective of civil society, we have yet to live up to at least the same collective commitment that was demonstrated during the negotiating phase.

CHAPTER 4

Inclusion or Choice? Securing the Right to Inclusive Education for All

Belinda Shaw

> Hope, in this deep and powerful sense, is not the same
> as joy that things are going well, or willingness to invest
> in enterprises that are obviously headed for early
> success, but rather an ability to work for something
> because it is good, not just because it stands a chance to
> succeed. . . . Hope is definitely not the same thing as
> optimism. It is not the conviction that something will
> turn out well, but the certainty that something makes
> sense, regardless of how it turns out.
> —Vaclav Havel, *Disturbing the Peace*

Securing the right to inclusive education for all in the Convention on the Rights of Persons with Disabilities involved a struggle between perspectives on what it means to honor a human right to education for persons with disabilities. According to one perspective prevailing early in the negotiations, education for persons with disabilities should be about free choice between opportunities for learning, including specialized education in separate settings. However, another position became increasingly dominant and eventually prevailed: that inclusive education for all with specialist support in mainstream settings should be the core value underpinning education rights in the Convention.

This controversy meant that a plethora of arguments and questions were raised and debated as Article 24 on education was negotiated at the United Nations. Was separating people for their education on the basis of impairments or health condition, social, emotional, or educational needs a form of discrimination that hurt individuals and society? Did so-called "special" education guarantee human rights or perpetuate the very discrimination, devaluation, stigmatization, stereotyping, prejudice, and isolation in the lives of persons with disabilities, which the Convention aimed to tackle? In order to uphold human rights, education needed to focus not only on skills, accomplishments, and qualifications but also on enabling all people to live together on the basis of nondiscrimination and equality, and the development in every individual of a sense of worth and dignity and a respect for the worth and dignity of others.[1] How could such aims be achieved by separating students for their education? Should all education be inclusive and states be prohibited from setting up segregating educational institutions for students with disabilities because of the harm they caused?

The need for the Convention's education article to apply to both children and adults, for whom human rights are interpreted differently, created further tensions. And a further level of complication in reaching a resolution arose because of different understandings about what it means to be a free citizen in a democratic society. Was the removal of obstacles and barriers in society in order to facilitate the general good—the common weal—at the heart of ideas about freedom for citizens? Or was it more about maximizing individual choices and protecting autonomy, status, and ownership of private property and wealth?

After much soul searching and deliberation, inclusive education for all was accepted as the basis for Article 24 on education. An agreement was reached between governments around the world that they should take responsibility for ensuring "an inclusive education system at all levels" and that "persons with disabilities are not excluded from the general education system on the basis of disability" (Article 24(2)(a), CRPD). At the same time, there was no agreement for an outright prohibition on separate "special" education on the basis of disability.

This chapter tells the story from the point of view of one civil society activist representing the Centre for Studies on Inclusive Education (CSIE), a small UK NGO, of the struggle for inclusive education and how persons with disabilities played a key role in refusing to allow choice for some to undermine freedom for all.

Getting Involved

Since its inception in 1982 as a lobby group for inclusive education, CSIE has been closely associated with disability and human rights.[2] The reason CSIE became involved in the Convention, and what kept us going in the nearly three years leading to its final adoption, was the pressing human rights considerations at stake for children with disabilities and young people. The fact that they are routinely denied the same basic human rights enjoyed by others is an injustice CSIE challenged daily in the UK in trying to get proper support and accommodations for students with disabilities in mainstream settings and to phase out separate "special" schools. Because we identified so strongly with the Convention's purpose we felt that although we were not constituted as an organization of persons with disabilities (DPO), we had an important contribution to make.

When CSIE first heard about the CRPD, we had little idea of how to become part of the discussions. Until then CSIE's main involvement in human rights conventions and other international instruments had been through research, publications, and conferences on the human rights framework and arguments for educating all children and young people together with appropriate supports and adaptations for individual learning needs—the process we called "inclusive education." Inclusive education is a radically different approach to the prevailing practices in most of the world of placing students with disabilities in separate "special" settings to obtain necessary help; failing to provide them with appropriate support and adaptations in mainstream or general settings where most students go; or excluding them from school and colleges altogether.

It was through the Internet early in 2004 that we became aware of the contents of an early draft on education issued by a working group comprising government and nongovernment representatives. While the draft article on education (then Article 17) called for inclusive education, it also emphasized choice in education, including choice of separate, "special" settings. From CSIE's perspective, choice of segregated schooling on the basis of disability could never be a human right. Segregated schooling was itself discriminatory and perpetuated the very stigma and prejudice against persons with disabilities that the Convention aimed to overcome. Although our basic position was that as a human right, inclusive education required implementation—not proof—we were nevertheless able to call on an expanding body of research documenting the benefits of inclusion, examples of good practice, and the problems of labeling and segregating students into separate "special" settings for their learning.[3] With both rights and research on our side—as we saw it—CSIE began work in earnest to get choice removed from the text and inclusive education strengthened as an entitlement for all.

Over the next months, several other UK organizations joined the struggle, including the Alliance for Inclusive Education,[4] the Children's Rights Alliance for England,[5] British Council of Persons with Disabilities, now United Kingdom Disabled People's Council,[6] Disability Equality in Education, now World of Inclusion,[7] and Enabling Education Network,[8] among others. We issued press releases and other statements and held meetings to enlist support and agree on the wording to amend the WG draft on education. We also began posting what became a series of position statements and proposed amendments on the UN website for the Convention (see below). Most importantly we made contact with representatives of the WG and others already taking part in the meetings of the Ad Hoc Committee, asking them to endorse our point of view. Links made with the UK delegation, especially the member representing persons with disabilities, proved invaluable at this point by providing contacts as well as vital information about the workings of the AHC and the progress of negotiations. As a small voluntary organization, we also needed to address budgetary concerns. In January 2005, I made the first of four trips to New York to attend the AHC sessions; from August that year, I was joined by colleagues from other UK organizations similarly concerned about Article 24.

During that first visit, CSIE was very much on its own challenging the idea of choice of segregated "special" education—I was one person from an organization *for*, not *of* persons with disabilities, putting forward what was then seen, in public at least, as a highly unpopular if not a downright risky and heretical point of view. Some organizations of, and for, persons with disabilities had more than thirty representatives attending. CSIE's biggest critics were the World Blind Union, the World Federation of the Deaf, and the World Federation of the Deafblind . They insisted that the so-called "twin-track" approach to education for persons with disabilities of both inclusive education and separate "special" education had already been settled. More-over, they warned that this twin-track approach was unchallengeable because of an agreement within the International Disability Caucus that the views of those specific impairment groups should be deferred to because of their position as key stakeholders on the issue.

Fortunately this proved not to be so. The attempt to shut down discussion was not sustainable. During a major debate on education at the sixth AHC session in August 2005, a number of governments, DPOs, and NGOs argued strongly for abandoning choice and making inclusion for each and every student the central principle of the education article. Subsequently, the WG text promoting "a free and informed choice between general and 'special' systems," which had been the basis for discussions so far, was removed from the draft convention. An amendment to give blind, deaf, and deafblind children "a right to choose education in their own groups and settings" based on suggestions from the IDC also failed to gain sufficient support at the sixth session and was not included in the revised text for Article 24.[9]

An Ongoing Struggle

Although choice of separate "special" education was removed from the Convention's draft text in 2005 it was necessary for efforts to continue into the last days of the eighth and final meeting in August 2006 to get other draft text removed that could have been equally damaging. Language creating exceptions and alternatives in cases "where the general education system cannot adequately meet" needs would have created a huge hole in the Convention and permitted segregated education whenever the general education system felt unable to be inclusive because of prevailing attitudes and barriers. At these sessions it seemed that some governments were changing their minds about supporting inclusion while others entered the debate for the first time in favor of choice. At times, it felt as if the Convention were going backward—a highly dispiriting experience compared with the optimism at the sixth session.

However, at the final count, sixty state delegations as well as the IDC supported an amendment proposed by Panama that led to an entitlement to inclusive education for all students with disabilities being enshrined in Article 24 without qualifications or alternatives. There were no objections.

The now much revised and strengthened education article that was subsequently adopted by the UN General Assembly and entered into force in May 2008 contained provisions for, among others, a government responsibility to ensure an inclusive education system at all levels; no exclusion from the general education system (primary or secondary) on the basis of disability; access to inclusive education (primary and secondary) on an equal basis with others in local communities; reasonable accommodation of individual requirements; support in the general education system to facilitate effective education; and effective individualized support measures. In a compromise to satisfy the needs and wants of those desiring separate educational facilities, the provisions also called for governments to ensure that education for blind, deaf, or deafblind students is delivered in the most appropriate languages and modes and means of communication for the individual in environments that maximize academic and social development.

Although clear progress had been made during the course of the negotiations to remove text justifying separate "special" education and to strengthen inclusive education for all, it had not been possible to secure an outright prohibition in the Convention on segregated education on the basis of disability in state-provided education. CSIE advocated for this position, but no government delegation was willing to take up the cause and table an amendment to the draft Convention on these lines. Since the question of prohibition did not reach the stage of public debate at the UN, it is difficult to analyze the reasons behind the lack of support. Perhaps the need for a safety net was considered important, or perhaps prohibition was thought unnecessary, since the phasing out of separate special schools and/or their transformation into resource centers was an inevitable development of implementing the inclusion provisions in Article 24.

The shifting of opinion at the negotiations to support inclusion rather than choice in education was connected with much debate that arose with regard to the nature of disability, the "appropriate" educational system, and the limited resources of governments. Hopefully, people changed their minds on the basis of the strength of the arguments put to them or were encouraged to speak up with views already held but not expressed. It is also possible, however, that the support for inclusive education arose as individuals felt pressured to take positions about which they were not fully convinced for the sake of concluding the Convention, or perhaps they were persuaded on a personal level to reach an agreement beyond their remit. The British government's delayed ratification of the Convention with reservations on Article 24 unfortunately suggests possibilities of this kind.

Disagreements and Resolutions

As explained earlier, major debates over inclusive education continued into the sixth, seventh, and eighth AHC sessions. The sticking points behind the ongoing disagreements centered on four issues:

(1) Did the specific nature of some students' impairments make it necessary for them to be separated on a full-time basis in order for them to receive an effective education?

(2) Did not persons with disabilities, as the subject of the Convention, have the right to choose the type of education they wanted, particularly if they had been let down by education systems so far?

(3) Was separate "special" education required as a safeguard in case of inadequacies in the general education system?

(4) How could governments with limited financial and human resources be expected to meet obligations to provide fully inclusive education?

There were no principled objections to inclusive education itself—indeed many expressed support for inclusion and had in fact already endorsed it as a fundamental freedom of the CRPD. A misunderstanding about the nature of inclusive education and concerns about inadequate support seemed to be at the center of the difficulties. It required repeated efforts to explain and clarify the position before agreement could be reached.

The key arguments and explanations put forward at the negotiations to support the struggle for inclusive education for all might be summarized as follows.[10] Inclusive education is not about placing children with disabilities without adequate support in an unchanged mainstream. That situation—best described as poor integration—is just as much discrimination as is segregation. Moreover, inclusive education involves the transformation of general education to accommodate the needs of all learners, so that education rights for students with disabilities, which had been denied for so long, could at last be realized. From this perspective, the CRPD provides an opportunity to build a better future for persons with disabilities by being an aspirational document about how general education should be further developed in order to achieve rights for all. It cannot offer lower standards for persons with disabilities by improperly turning choice of segregation in education into a so-called right. To achieve the realization of rights, the Convention needs to build on progress already achieved to develop better support for students with disabilities in mainstream settings.

The language of choice and of "special" education recognized and legitimized the provision of education for some persons with disabilities in settings segregated from general education. A human rights convention enshrining the goals toward which governments are obliged to strive is undermined by provisions not fully compatible with those goals, even if they are seen as some form of "safety net." This self-defeating exercise to create choice was probably unfeasible in most parts of the world given the costs to governments of creating and maintaining incompatible systems of both inclusive education and separate "special" education for students with disabilities. On an everyday, case-by-case basis, choice between "special" education and inclusive education would not be made by persons with disabilities, by parents of children with disabilities, or children with disabilities themselves for whom in fact choice was strictly limited. It would be made by professionals and administrators on the basis of expediency and what was already in place.

Taking into account the history of discrimination faced by persons with disabilities, choice in terms of autonomy and self-determination for persons with disabilities, including the right to make decisions about their own lives, was a welcome part of the CRPD. However, choice by any adult—disabled or not—should not usurp the rights of children to inclusive education with all appropriate supports and accommodations. Rights of parents to choose education for their children in international law referred only to the right to remove a child from state-provided education, not to choice within it.

Deaf, blind, and deafblind people had reason to suspect general education's willingness and capability to include students with disabilities because of poor integration. However, this does not have to be the case where mainstream schools have been restructured to meet their needs. Increasingly there are indeed examples around the world of inclusive education working for these students. The CRPD should be setting standards for the continuing development of inclusive education, not justifying segregation.

The changes to general education in Article 24 to include students with disabilities by providing necessary supports and accommodations are expected to be achieved on a progressive basis. This allows states to move forward with improvements to an agreed timetable taking account of their human and financial resources and with international cooperation. Overnight closure of "special" schools is not expected. The way forward, as suggested by South Africa and others, was to transform "special" schools into resource centers to support the development of inclusive education. Countries that have not yet set up separate "special" schools would not be required to do so under an Article 24, which provides the right to inclusive education for all, without exception or choice. Proposals for developing inclusive education systems and phasing out education for students with disabilities in separate "special" settings focus on state-provided education.

Getting the Message Across

The messages, outlined above, were conveyed to governments and to colleagues in numerous ways on an almost daily basis at the Ad Hoc meetings and in the weeks leading up to the meetings. Getting the message across involved time-consuming searches on the Internet to identify delegates attending the AHC sessions and others with influence. We also had to find out the protocol for getting papers posted on the Convention website and in other forums. With our limited capacity in terms of staff and resources, lobbying would have been impossible without access to e-mail, the Internet, and photocopying facilities. Materials, such as petitions suggesting amendments to the draft text and proposals on particular issues, often had to be prepared at short notice and were sometimes handwritten.

In addition to circulating written, printed, and electronic communications, civil society representatives enthusiastically took up the opportunities provided by the AHC chair, Ambassador Don MacKay of New Zealand, to make statements in the main debating hall in the presence of government delegations. Because of the developing nature of the draft convention and the need to be relevant and up to date these were invariably delivered from speedily prepared notes, if there was time to make notes at all.

Generally, it seemed that government representatives and others at the AHC were very willing to be approached directly to learn as much as they could from people involved in disability to guide their deliberations. Many government representatives were not familiar with topics of disability and inclusive education. In the interests of better understanding, a number of countries had already included persons with disabilities and parents of children with disabilities in their official government negotiating teams. Engaging with governments in a constructive way involved making sure approaches were relevant and focused by carefully following the Convention negotiations as they progressed, both "live" in the main negotiating hall and through online reports. There were always opportunities before negotiations opened each morning to speak with government delegates. The regular lunchtime presentations on the Convention also provided an opportunity to talk with people and ask them to consider matters from different perspectives.

Among the most serious worries in deciding approaches for lobbying were concerns over whether a particular action would do more harm than good. The dilemma hinged on the following logic. When activists make approaches about a particular point of view there is no guarantee they will be successful and influence proceedings in their direction. By displaying their views they risk provoking opposition that might undermine their cause. This insecurity can be exacerbated when activists are being advised by supporters to take different directions about the best way forward. This was the case, for example, in the deliberation over whether to strongly advocate for an outright and uncompromising prohibition on separate "special" schools, even though it was seen by some as unachievable and risked undermining the progress already achieved, not only in education but for the Convention as a whole.

If the unpredictability of outcomes was a constant dilemma so was the impossibility of escaping personal responsibility and the need to make choices. Situations like the one described above require personal judgment. Similarly, one might rightly ask to what extent activists rely on good will, good faith, straight talking, and the integrity of their arguments. To what extent do they hope to achieve success through holding back, hedging bets, maneuvering and bargaining in the hope of gaining advantage? To what extent do they go ahead despite insufficient information and perhaps even misinformation?

Being convinced that efforts to place inclusive education at the heart of Article 24 were worthwhile in their own right, regardless of outcomes, the good-faith route seemed the best. It involved careful research, observation, and listening, trying to be as open as possible, and sorting out misunderstandings, rethinking and revising while not betraying principles and values. Having people with diverse backgrounds and with different languages and communication systems made the need for honesty and flexibility even more important. Perhaps the greatest difficulty was deciding if and at what point to drop CSIE's call for an end to segregated education as an active lobbying position at the Convention.

Our decisions were greatly influenced by the warning from AHC chair MacKay during the later stages of negotiations, that continued lobbying for provisions that had not already commanded widespread support might undermine all the good work achieved so far and might put the Convention at risk. He appealed to delegates not to let the perfect be the enemy of the good and only to press objections if they felt it was impossible for them to live with text that had been agreed on over several years of negotiations. The standard for agreement of the Convention at the AHC was no less than consensus—nothing could be agreed unless everything was agreed; if everything could not be agreed, the Convention was lost.

Consequently, during the final AHC session, CSIE put all efforts into further strengthening the right to inclusive education and securing as strong a convention as possible, rather than pursuing a complete prohibition on separate education.

During the last week of negotiations, chair MacKay created many opportunities for colleagues to leave their seats in the main debating hall and talk with each other face to face to try to reach agreement. In such circumstances, although doing their best to represent their organizations and countries, all were on their own in taking responsibility for their words and actions. It seemed that those present rose to the challenge, counting on trust, respect, and each person's innate integrity to see us through to consensus. The agreement reached on Article 24 did not achieve everything CSIE and others wished, but, no doubt, it was the best that could be reached at the time.

Implementing Article 24

Putting the CRPD into practice in a way that honors the text and the struggle of persons with disabilities for their rights calls for development across the globe of inclusive education in mainstream, general settings that provide support and accommodations for all students with disabilities. In practice, a fully inclusive education system at all levels, accommodating and supporting all students with disabilities, whatever their impairment, health condition, social, emotional, or educational needs, would render "special" education in separate settings unnecessary. As the Convention is progressively implemented such settings can be phased out and transformed into resources to support inclusive education. The Convention does not prohibit separate "special" education settings on the basis of disability but neither does it demand them, as it does inclusive settings.

Because inclusive education is necessarily about development and requires progressive realization, it also seems inevitable that in those countries where separate "special" educational settings exist, there will be a transitional or interim period in which these settings are phased out and governments fulfill their responsibilities to "ensure an inclusive education system at all levels" (Article 24(1)). This is most likely to be the case in countries like UK with developed—though waning—systems of separate "special" education. In effect this means that some segregation may have to be tolerated for an interim period in some situations. This will require decisions to be made about such issues as who decides which students are segregated, how to ensure that governments do not delay implementing inclusive education, how to make sure that the rights of students with autism or other emotional, social, and health needs are not denied opportunities for retreat and respite without undermining their rights to inclusive education, and how to ensure that segregation does not reoccur in either general or "special" settings on the basis of disability.

For the CRPD to fulfill its promises, these issues will require monitoring arrangements and mechanisms for reporting and reviewing countries' progress toward implementation. Resolving these matters will be as important—and achievable—as the original struggle for inclusive education.

CHAPTER 5

An Eye Toward Effective Enforcement: A Technical-Comparative Approach to the Drafting Negotiations

Tara J. Melish

The Convention on the Rights of Persons with Disabilities is a historic achievement on many levels. Hard-fought and comprehensive, it promises to change the way the rights of persons with disabilities are understood and socially claimed by a broad range of stakeholders for generations to come. This is as true for the rights of persons with physical and sensory disabilities as it is for those with psychosocial, intellectual, and other developmental or learning disabilities.

It may be noted in this latter respect that a fairly high degree of confidence existed from the beginning of the negotiations that the final drafted treaty would offer important and significant protections for persons with physical and sensory disabilities. What was far less clear was the level of protection the new treaty would offer persons with intellectual and psychosocial disabilities. Such persons have long faced a particularly abusive and deeply embedded set of social stereotypes regarding competency that have functioned in practice to institutionalize and legitimize structures that often deny their very capacity to act and make free decisions as recognized human beings. These widely held attitudes have served historically to justify, both legally and socially—and hence to render invisible from a mainstream human rights lens—such stark abuses against such persons as their forced segregation and warehousing in institutional facilities, relegation to separate educational, housing, and employment settings, subjection to long-term restraints and forced interventions in the name of treatment, and enforced loss of legal capacity. Such abuses would provoke an immediate and sustained international outcry by the global human rights community if committed against persons without mental impairments, either real or perceived.[1] To ensure that the acceptability of such abusive and discriminatory practices was not transposed into the new treaty, either directly or indirectly, explicit strategies of socialization, awareness raising, and legal framing would need to be a major focus of the negotiation process.

Disability Rights International—then Mental Disability Rights International—entered the negotiations with this problematic in mind, intent on ensuring that the substantive and procedural protections in the treaty were as effective and meaningful for persons with mental disabilities as they were for persons with physical and sensory disabilities. It is thus useful to highlight DRI's substantive mission and how it calculated that it could most effectively pursue this mission through the CRPD negotiation process, especially in coordination with the many other members of the disability rights movement present in the negotiations who, while differing at times in approach, were equally committed to this important goal.

This chapter is accordingly divided into three parts. The first part seeks to explain the strategic approach DRI took to the CRPD negotiation process, highlighting its methodology, the guiding principles it embraced, and the resulting strategies of engagement it pursued. The second part turns to some of the key substantive issues DRI focused on in its interventions and advocacy before the Ad Hoc Committee. The chapter concludes with a brief reflection on the Convention, the ultimate efficacy of DRI's approach, and the road ahead.

DRI's Strategic Approach to the Drafting Negotiations

Authorized to participate in the very first session of the AHC, DRI understood early on that it had a potentially important strategic role to play in the CRPD negotiation process. That role derived primarily from its institutional status and operational expertise as the leading international human rights organization dedicated to protecting the human rights and full participation in society of persons with disabilities worldwide. That is, unlike most international disability rights organizations, which have taken up the human rights framework only more recently in their global work, DRI had assumed an express human rights identity from its inception in 1993; it was founded precisely to make visible the human rights violations against persons with disabilities that the mainstream human rights community had long chosen to ignore. Correspondingly, with a substantive focus on ending the institutionalization of persons with disabilities and promoting their social integration into community settings where they could live with dignity and human rights on an equal basis with others, DRI's methodological focus has, since its founding, been rooted in the strategic use of international human rights treaties and their corresponding monitoring and enforcement mechanisms to achieve its advocacy objectives.

DRI thus came to the CRPD negotiating process with significant first-hand experience using existing regional and international human rights treaties, including the International Covenant on Civil and Political Rights, the International Covenant on Economic, Social and Cultural Rights, the Convention on the Rights of the Child, the Convention Against Torture, and the American and European conventions on human rights. Together with other disability rights instruments, these treaties have framed and structured the human rights methodologies and advocacy tactics DRI has employed over the last two decades. Such methodologies have ranged from detailed investigative reporting and global shaming campaigns, to grassroots training and institutional staff education, to human rights advocacy before supranational policy-making and technical forums, to regular use of UN human rights oversight mechanisms and strategic litigation before the world's regional human rights bodies.[2]

DRI's work program and institutional profile had two significant implications for its strategic approach to the CRPD negotiating process. First, based on the practical lessons learned from its long-term work using the existing international human rights architecture, DRI came to the process with a priority concern for maximizing the operational effectiveness of the CRPD's provisions from an institutional enforcement or implementation perspective. DRI appreciated that achieving this important objective would require close attention to the details of the treaty's technical and structural drafting. Second, and closely related, DRI was particularly alert to ensuring that the treaty contained not only strong substantive norms, but also strong procedural safeguards and independent monitoring guarantees. Such safeguards and guarantees, DRI recognized, served essential instrumental roles in the implementation process, especially as enforcement "hooks" before domestic and supranational supervisory tribunals and as necessary external checks on the substantive protection of rights. Such checks were particularly important for monitoring institutional policies and practices related to legal capacity, supported decision making, medical treatment, and any form of institutionalization or incarceration, all primary issues in DRI's global human rights work. Both concerns, each core to DRI's understanding of how rights are most effectively enforced in practice, affected how DRI approached its role in the negotiation process. Each is addressed more substantively below.

The Treaty's Operational Effectiveness

DRI's first strategic priority, as noted, centered on ensuring that the CRPD was technically drafted in a way that would maximize its operational enforceability before a range of domestic and international policy-making forums and legal tribunals. DRI's experience had taught it that, although a great deal can be done through purposive interpretation of human rights texts, the precise formulations through which a treaty or treaty norm is drafted can have tremendous impact on the possibilities for institutional and legal oversight. DRI thus came to the negotiation process with a priority concern not just for the recognition of critical concepts in the Convention, but also for *how* those concepts were technically framed and structured inter se. Accordingly, DRI saw a major part of its role in the negotiation process as seeking to improve the CRPD from a technical or operational perspective, ensuring that the treaty did not repeat mistakes or recreate normative inconsistencies that have served in practice to impede the effective enforcement of human rights under the existing international human rights architecture. This was true both for the treaty text itself and for its optional protocol.

DRI's approach was correspondingly calculated to complement that of many of the other NGOs and disabled people's organizations (DPOs) engaged in the process. Given deeply entrenched social stereotypes and the invisible status of many of the most regularized abuses committed against persons with disabilities, the majority of these civil society groups had found it necessary to focus their oral interventions and advocacy efforts on emphasizing the *experiential* and *lived* aspects of human rights abuse in the disability context. This was most frequently done through powerful personal testimonials by persons with disabilities themselves about their own experiences with societal and institutional discrimination, interventions that were vital to the negotiation process.[3]

DRI did not seek to replicate these powerful testimonials. Rather, it sought to complement and reinforce them by placing them in technical context wherever possible, especially by emphasizing their legal basis and justification within the existing international human rights law architecture and jurisprudence. It thus sought to place DPO calls for recognition of certain rights and concepts within the context of other major human rights treaties and the evolving jurisprudence of the European Court of Human Rights, the inter-American human rights bodies, the African Commission, and the many UN treaty bodies, including their general comments and observations. At the same time, it sought to expose dangers in delegate-proposed treaty language, especially with respect to the recognition of explicit exceptions to rights-based rules in the treaty text and the creation of other kinds of "let-out" clauses that would enable states to avoid taking on real legal responsibilities with respect to systemic institutional and policy reforms. In this way, DRI saw its primary role as attempting to ensure that, in substantively addressing the rights of persons with disabilities, the Convention text did not create incompatibilities with other instruments of international and regional human rights law, that it in fact strengthened existing legal protections rather than diminishing or simply repeating them, and that it was structurally well designed from a technical-operational perspective—getting the law qua law right.

DRI's particular technical-comparative approach to the drafting negotiations was, in turn, reinforced by its choice of organizational representative. For this role, it hired an international human rights attorney and legal expert in comparative human rights systems with significant experience studying and working before regional and UN human rights monitoring systems. Although this representative had worked closely with DRI on deinstitutionalization litigation and advocacy in the inter-American human rights system and had personal connections to disability, she was known to DRI as a human rights comparativist with a particular technical-legal bent. The expectation was thus that she would monitor the drafting process from the perspective of ensuring the draft convention's technical and legal compatibility with other international human rights instruments and the jurisprudence developed thereunder by the respective supervisory bodies. At the same time, DRI's representative was not new to the CRPD negotiation process. She joined DRI's legal team immediately after leaving a technical position in the CRPD drafting committee's substantive secretariat. She thus possessed a close working knowledge of the negotiation process from its inception, the work of the AHC over its prior sessions, and the evolving negotiating positions of the varied participants. Indeed, in her earlier position she had been tasked with preparing daily summaries of the key issues and points of conflict for the AHC chair, maintaining transcript notes of the proceedings, preparing background conference papers and briefings (on such issues as comparative national approaches to reasonable accommodation), and attending intersessional Bureau meetings of the Committee.

Consistent with this technical focus, DRI adopted a particular methodology of engagement in the negotiation process. First, following its representative's practice as UN social affairs officer, DRI maintained a close-to-verbatim transcript of all delegate interventions in the AHC. Shared on a daily basis with all requesting state delegations, national human rights institutions, UN officials, and civil society participants, this unofficial transcript was used to keep track of how many states supported or opposed each issue as well as the specific arguments or justifications used to defend those positions.[4] By scrupulously recording and monitoring the precise positions of all parties, DRI sought to make its interventions as targeted and value additive as possible. Interventions were structured in particular to do five principal things.

First, DRI aimed never to make abstract or merely conceptual points. Rather, it sought to respond directly to technical issues raised in debate that suggested misinterpretations or misapplications of international human rights law. It would, accordingly, begin each intervention by recognizing its satisfaction or significant concern with the positions taken by specific sets of states on a given issue or draft article. Briefly expressing its support for the substantive positions already highlighted by other DPOs, NGOs, and Committee members, it would then focus its observations on two to four technical issues that had not yet been raised in the discussion that could nonetheless shed light on the text under debate.

Second, in raising these technical issues, DRI sought explicitly to situate its responses to delegate proposals within the context of recognized international law principles, both substantive and interpretive. It accordingly frequently sought to allay delegate concerns as to specific language choices or textual terminology by explaining their foundational basis in or consistency with authoritative interpretations of UN and regional human rights bodies in their evolving jurisprudence. DRI's interventions thus cited broadly to the provisions and interpretations of other treaty texts as a way to ground and substantiate the proposals of civil society groups and friendly states. It did so even while insisting on the need not to fall into the trap of merely reconstituting existing norms in the CRPD; indeed, the treaty's very raison d'être was to relate existing norms to the specific experience of persons with disabilities and the distinct ways their rights are impacted by widespread social, attitudinal, institutional, and architectural barriers.

In this respect, DRI's interventions sought to mediate two of the dominant thematic tensions running throughout the drafting process, constantly reminding states of the early decisions that had been made thereon. The first related to the treaty "model" the CRPD was to follow. A major debate in the first two AHC sessions involved whether the new treaty was to follow a narrow "nondiscrimination" model (like the Convention Eliminating All Forms of Discrimination against Women and the Convention on the Elimination of All Forms of Racial Discrimination), a "comprehensive" model (like the CRC), or a "hybrid" model that combined elements of the two. The general consensus arrived at by the AHC in authorizing the Working Group to proceed with a draft text was that the CRPD should follow a hybrid model. This approach was vital, it was agreed, given the recognized failure of existing treaty language to ensure in practice the rights of persons with disabilities worldwide. Accordingly, explicit substantive specification of the precise ways in which the human rights of persons with disabilities were regularly violated was indispensable to the treaty's instrumentality and purpose. In floor debate, states nevertheless repeatedly tried to return to a mere nondiscrimination model, simply repeating rights already recognized in existing treaties and hence losing the distinctive quality of the disability-specific text.

This tendency was reinforced by a closely related thematic tension, one that continues to raise challenges in the post-adoption ratification and implementation stages. That tension arises from the interpretive friction between two assertions regarding the CRPD, both correct and each raised consistently throughout the drafting process. First, the CRPD *creates no new rights* in international law. Second, in affirming the substantive equality of existing rights in their application to persons with disabilities, the CRPD recognizes the *distinct ways* that those rights are lived and experienced by persons with disabilities on a daily basis—experiences that often differ quite substantially from those of persons without disabilities. Indeed, it is precisely because of this differential treatment, and particularly the justificatory assumptions underlying them, that the rights of persons with disabilities have for so long remained invisible from the mainstream human rights lens. DRI thus repeatedly found itself affirming the basis of textual provisions in existing international human rights law, while defending textual wording that departed from existing treaty language in its recognition of the distinct ways those rights are experienced by persons with disabilities.[5]

Third, in relating its technical points to the specific proposals raised in floor debate, DRI made an express point of specifying by name each of the individual states that had offered positions on the issue, identifying those positions as either consistent or inconsistent with international law principles. It did so not only for situational and legitimation purposes, but also for reasons of peer-based persuasion and socialization. The interventional tactic was thus directed toward recognizing and affirming as international norm leaders those states supporting pro-persons with disabilities positions, encouraging them to continue taking such positions. Correspondingly, by expressly naming states taking positions inconsistent with international law principles or harmful to the equal rights of persons with disabilities, DRI sought to identify them before their peers as human rights outliers, situated outside the mainstream human rights consensus. It was hoped that a dynamic would be promoted through which state delegations would seek to take public positions that grouped them with international norm leaders.

At the same time, on a more direct tactical level, because DRI often raised narrow technical issues that might not independently generate direct floor debate, it sought to identify its positions with specific proposals already raised by identified state delegations. The purpose was to make it easy and natural for those delegations to make the points their own, directly incorporating them into their own proposals, advocacy, and peer-based consultations with other states. This was particularly important given the relative lack of time DRI's representative had for broad-based consultations with state delegations, given the corresponding need to maintain a detailed record of delegate interventions and to prepare DRI's own article-by-article oral interventions.

Fourth, DRI sought to avoid repeating points raised effectively by others or for which there was already a clear consensus in the Ad Hoc Committee. Rather, it sought to "add" to what other civil society and state actors had said by focusing on points not yet raised in floor debate and/or by providing a perspective or explanatory approach that differed from, but complemented, that which had already been taken by state delegations and other DPO and

NGO leaders, especially the International Disability Caucus. As explained below, DRI was not able to join the IDC given certain tactical differences in approach regarding the most effective way to protect key rights related to legal capacity and institutionalization. It nonetheless sought to support IDC positions in all other areas of substantive advocacy.

Finally, and relatedly, DRI used the technical focus of its interventions to try to find consensus positions or "ways through" substantively divisive or otherwise difficult issues.[6] The offer of a "neutral" technical perspective was frequently very helpful in this regard, especially when participants appeared to be talking past each other on the underlying substantive issue or as a way to explain principled text to skeptical delegations in ways they might be more inclined to comprehend. This was particularly important on such issues as inclusive education and the lack of need, from a practical or legal perspective, to recognize specific exceptions or qualifiers to rights in the text of the treaty. In this latter regard, recognizing the basis of a provision in another treaty or underscoring the practical methodologies used by human rights bodies to interpret distinct norms, especially those that created significant positive obligations for states, often helped to quiet concerns that treaty language was creating impossible standards for states to meet and hence needed to be explicitly qualified in the text.

DRI thus sought to articulate major points in ways that could be "heard" both by skeptics on state delegations and by the more technically minded participants in the negotiations. The utility of this perspective was often apparent in the relative quieting of the committee room when DRI made its oral interventions and in the number of delegations asking for written copies of the same. This neutral technical focus was also used to mediate certain disagreements within the disability community itself. Indeed, by underscoring the international law basis of discrete components of competing interest-based positions, DRI sought to identify textual pathways that could meet the core interests of all affected constituencies.[7]

Strong Procedural Safeguards and Independent Monitoring Guarantees

DRI's second priority concern in the negotiating process lay in ensuring that the Convention's substantive norms were accompanied by strong procedural safeguards and independent monitoring guarantees. DRI was convinced that the Convention would provide little protection for persons with disabilities if it did not provide expressly for independent monitoring of the treaty's substantive protections by civil society groups and persons with disabilities themselves. At the same time, it was alert to the fact that international human rights supervisory bodies often mediate their subsidiary role as guarantors of rights vis-à-vis domestic authorities by relying preferentially on procedural safeguards and other procedural hooks as a way to leverage the substantive protection of rights. This is particularly true where such bodies must balance competing rights and/or legal duties held by the state and where substantive agreement as to the scope of the underlying norm has not yet been sufficiently concretized in the circumstances at issue, necessitating a certain margin of appreciation for local authorities. Accordingly, ensuring the existence of strong procedural safeguards and enforceable process commitments throughout the text of the treaty was a particular priority for DRI in ensuring the treaty's operability in post-adoption implementation processes.

This principled priority concern nevertheless had an important implication for DRI in the negotiating process: it prevented the organization from being able to join the IDC. The IDC had been created to coordinate the positions of the vast number of civil society groups participating in the negotiation process, allowing them to advance a common platform and speak with a single voice, thereby amplifying their presence, persuasiveness, and authority as equal negotiating partners. A "consensus" program, the IDC platform nonetheless incorporated certain "nonnegotiable" positions that not all organizations could accept. In particular, at the urging of key groups in the psychosocial disability community, such as the World Network of Users and Survivors of Psychiatry (WNUSP),[8] the IDC had adopted a nonnegotiable position on the issues of institutionalization and legal capacity. That position would accept nothing less than a full and express prohibition in the treaty on both civil commitment and forced treatment. To underscore the absoluteness of the dual prohibitions, the IDC had taken the negotiating position that it would accept no legal safeguards in the text of the treaty with respect to either. DRI, it is important to emphasize, agreed unreservedly and categorically with the IDC on the underlying substantive issues: as a matter of principle, DRI opposes forced treatment and believes that all institutions can be closed.[9] Nonetheless, as a tactical matter, it recognized that there are many ways to achieve these ends, and an absolute prohibition might not be the most effective way of doing so.

Indeed, from a pragmatic perspective, the achievement of a direct prohibition in the treaty appeared largely unrealistic with respect to what states could politically be expected to adopt in a legal instrument at the present time. Far more important, by forfeiting some of the most effective treaty-based tools for ensuring the protection of the critical underlying substantive rights, the position appeared shortsighted and even counterproductive from an operational perspective. Given that every country we know of today permits institutionalization and forced treatment, DRI believed that *indirect* ways of pressuring and incentivizing governments to change practices may be the best strategy for achieving the disability community's shared objectives.

To be able to freely advocate this tactical position in the negotiation process and to offer specific language proposals with respect to procedural protections, hard process commitments, and independent monitoring guarantees designed to promote participation, oversight, and transparency, DRI was accordingly compelled to remain formally outside the IDC.[10] This is true even as it supported IDC positions on virtually every issue in the negotiation process—including the IDC's evolving position on procedural safeguards by the end of the negotiations.

Guiding Principles for DRI Interventions

All the above led DRI to approach the CRPD drafting process with a certain set of guiding principles in mind. These principles reflect the primary thrust of DRI's interventions and advocacy in the AHC, including with respect to the key issues in the negotiations highlighted below.

DRI's first priority, as already underscored, was to ensure that no language included in the treaty was weaker than or inconsistent with that found in existing international human rights law instruments. It thus structured its interventions around existing norms of international law, explaining in as accessible language as possible why distinct state drafting proposals were either consistent or inconsistent with recognized international law principles and the evolving jurisprudence thereon. This was as true with respect to substantive norms—such as attempts to dilute international human rights standards on the rights to health, work, and education, and on state duties to ensure against discrimination in private settings—as it was with respect to the inclusion of paternalistic language and inappropriate qualifiers on rights such as "endeavor to" and "to the extent possible."[11]

Second, DRI's interventions repeatedly insisted that the Convention must be one of broad principles, not detailed exceptions. DRI thus constantly challenged state proposals seeking to insert express exceptions to rights norms or their correlate duties in the draft treaty, especially where the rights of persons with mental disabilities were at issue and with respect to resource commitments. A prominent cohort of states even tried to insert a footnote into the Convention—a dangerous practice followed in no other human rights treaty—that would exempt them from any obligations relating to the guarantee of legal capacity for persons with disabilities, citing the lack of separate words for "legal capacity" and the exercise thereof in their national languages. "In Arabic, Chinese and Russian," the footnote would have read, "the term 'legal capacity' refers to the capacity for rights, rather than the capacity to act." Allowing exceptions such as these and others into the text of the treaty, DRI insisted, would significantly undermine its very object and purpose as an instrument to ensure the equal rights of persons with disabilities. Indeed, as Liechtenstein's delegate had aptly observed, doing so would be like enumerating all the ways child discipline is permitted under the CRC, or that persons can in fact be treated differently under the ICCPR. This is decidedly not the purpose of a human rights treaty, a key point to which DRI consistently returned in its interventions.

At the same time, DRI believed it equally imperative that the treaty not overly detail or predetermine the content of rights. The treaty would be most effective, DRI believed, if its guarantees were recognized in broad, open-textured ways, contoured by the overarching principles of dignity, inclusion, social agency, and participation. This was true over both space and time. Indeed, such texture would allow interpretation and implementation strategies to vary as necessary over distinct geographies, allowing the treaty to be maximally responsive to the varied contexts, realities, imaginations, and changing priorities of affected communities around the globe. On the other hand, it would ensure the interpretive elasticity necessary for treaty norms to evolve progressively with time and comparative experience—a quality of particular import as the world disability community gathers strength, social consensus shifts, and new opportunities and barriers present themselves. Indeed, because all rights are bounded by social expectations and evolving context, such normative elasticity is crucial for the long-term relevance and responsiveness of all rights-based strategies, platforms, and creative discourses.

A third principle guiding DRI's interventions was the insistence that the CRPD's substantive norms must be framed and recognized *as rights*, not merely as state duties or general undertakings. As experience with other treaties has shown, this technical framing is important for ensuring that human rights treaty provisions can in fact be effectively claimed as rights by individuals before international tribunals and other supervisory mechanisms.[12] DRI was thus highly vigilant to attempts by delegations, whether intentional or unintentional, to remove references to rights in the course of redrafting provisions.[13] It specifically challenged such attempts, for example, with respect to the draft norms on accessibility, access to justice, inclusive education, reasonable accommodation, and habilitation and rehabilitation.

Similarly, DRI paid close attention to the evolving structure of the draft treaty and, specifically, to where norms were placed therein. For example, the treaty was long divided substantively into separate parts. Part I encompassed the treaty's purpose, general principles, and general obligations, while Part II included the treaty's substantive rights. When the Australian delegation thoughtfully called for the movement of the provision on accessibility to a higher position in the Convention to reflect its central importance thereto, the provision was nonetheless moved from Part II to Part I. DRI intervened to insist that Australia's well-intentioned objective was not served, and in fact was undermined, by the provision's movement into Part I where it would no longer be interpreted as an autonomous right, but rather as a general obligation. This was important from an operational perspective, DRI believed, as the norm would now need to be affirmatively paired with a substantive norm from Part II for its direct enforcement, at least by an international tribunal. (The same was true, DRI argued, with respect to the recognition of nondiscrimination exclusively in Part I, rather than as a norm that should appear in both parts, as in most other human rights treaties. It conversely applied to the AHC's failure to include a duty to provide effective remedies in Part I to accompany the late-added guarantee of effective access to justice in Part II.)

In direct response to these technical arguments, the Committee agreed to remove all textual references to structural "parts" from the treaty. It thereby sought to obviate any interpretive inference that the referenced norms were intended to be understood exclusively as duties. As with many issues, this was not the ideal technical solution from DRI's perspective. It was nonetheless an important technical modification that would be highly consequential for the treaty's post-adoption interpretation under general principles of international law.

Fourth, DRI was consistently guided by the precept that the treaty's individual norms should directly and textually reflect the principles of social inclusion, community integration, participation, and individual development, as was generally done in the Working Group draft. Inclusion of such language was operationally important at the implementation stage, DRI believed, for ensuring a broad, relevant, and evolving interpretation of the treaty's norms in distinct national and disability contexts. It was particularly important for avoiding interpretations based on "formal equality" reasoning alone and, specifically, for preventing the conversion of treaty norms into "benefits traps," that is, interpreted to allow services to be provided in ways that lead to further segregation of persons with disabilities. Such separate systems are often expressly justified in national systems under "equality" rationales—frequently with explicit exemptions for minimum wage requirements and other labor protections for persons with disabilities in employment contexts and through the offer of mere busywork, rather than work that promotes individual dignity, development, and social inclusion.

At the same time, DRI was highly sensitive to the loss of key language from individual provisions when norms were split apart or other drafting modifications were made, often in an attempt to simplify language or to accord the CRPD provisions with existing human rights treaty norms, especially those of the International Covenant on Civil and Political Rights. The result of this "simplification," or streamlining process, was often to lose the very specificity and relevance of the CRPD to the disability context. The draft norms on freedom from torture and personal integrity, for example, were not only needlessly divided into separate articles, but were streamlined to repeat almost verbatim the text of the ICCPR.[14] There were likewise strong, but ultimately unsuccessful, efforts to remove references to free and informed consent from the norm on the right to health. As indicated previously, the effect of removing the disability specificity of such norms largely obviates the need for a separate disability convention. Accordingly, while DRI acknowledged the benefits of streamlined text for the clarity and elegance of the treaty, it repeatedly underscored the necessity of not allowing important conceptual elements of rights to get lost in the streamlining process.

Finally, as already noted, DRI's interventions were closely attuned to the inclusion of strong procedural safeguards for ensuring substantive rights norms and hard process commitments for achieving rights-based outcomes. It was thus a strong advocate of independent international monitoring, as well as robust and mutually reinforcing procedural safeguards for any form of intervention in the freely decided life choices of persons with disabilities.

Key Issues in the Negotiations

The methodologies and guiding principles described above governed DRI's interventions with respect to all substantive norms of the Convention. Below, a few of the key substantive issues focused on as part of DRI's participation in the AHC are likewise described. Although many of the important arguments and issues DRI advanced are not captured here, a taste is offered.

Legal Capacity and Procedural Guarantees for Supported Decision Making

For DRI, as a human rights NGO focused primarily on ending human rights violations committed against persons with disabilities as a result of abusive civil commitment procedures and guardianship practices, forced institutionalizations and treatment, social and residential segregation, and lack of available support for living in the community on an equal basis with others, the level of protection the CRPD would offer against these practices was the organization's top priority in the negotiation process. The question of legal capacity and the ability of persons with disabilities to make free and informed decisions about where and with whom they live, what medical interventions they consent to, and other basic personal decisions about their bodily integrity and private lives were particularly central to DRI.

To DRI's satisfaction, the final text of the CRPD provides multiple layers of protection with respect to many of these issues, including in Articles 14, 15, 17, 18, 19, 22, and 25. DRI made substantive interventions with respect to all of these provisions, consistently affirming the need for strong safeguards on and guarantees for ensuring decision-making autonomy and the availability of real options for inclusion and participation in the community. Article 12 was nonetheless vital to DRI's organizational principles and priorities. It enshrines the right of persons with disabilities to recognition of their legal personality and to the enjoyment of legal capacity on an equal basis with others in all aspects of life.

It is important to highlight in this regard that substantial agreement existed in the AHC on the need for recognition in the treaty of this broadly phrased right. Far less consensus existed on questions involving the *exercise* of that capacity. Indeed, the issue was volatile, threatening at times to undermine the entire negotiation process. The volatility revolved specifically around the following question: To what extent and under what conditions, *if any*, can the exercise of legal capacity lawfully be limited or even fully denied?

Large numbers of participants in the process took opposing positions on this important question. At one extreme, a sizable number of states rejected the idea that persons with disabilities, especially those with intellectual and psychosocial disabilities, could in fact make decisions on their own or live in the community independently. Accordingly, they rejected the idea that civil commitments and substituted decision making could be prohibited outright, arguing that involuntary institutionalization and forced treatments are at times both necessary and beneficial, especially to protect the safety of persons with disabilities themselves or others in the community. They correspondingly sought to enshrine specific exemptions into the treaty to recognize the right of states to civilly commit, provide nonconsensual treatment to, or assert guardianships over persons with mental or other impairments in such situations. At the other extreme, the IDC, pressed by vocal and powerful groups like the WNUSP, had adopted the converse stance as one of its nonnegotiable positions: it refused to accept the legitimacy of any treaty that authorized or permitted the civil commitment, institutionalization, or involuntary treatment of persons with disabilities under *any* conditions, even under limited circumstances and with significant due process protections.

For DRI, getting this issue right was crucial for the Convention. As noted, given present realities in the world, including the number of institutions operating in all regions of the globe, it did not believe that inclusion of an outright prohibition on institutionalization or forced treatment in the Convention was politically feasible. Nor did it believe the final treaty would allow for no permissible limitation of any kind on the autonomous exercise of legal capacity. More importantly, given reservation, nonratification, and other legal "exit" options open to states, it was not convinced that the textual inclusion of such absolute prohibitions in the treaty would necessarily constitute the most effective way of achieving the two priority objectives it unequivocally shared with the IDC leadership—ending the institutionalization of all persons with disabilities as quickly as possible and maximizing individual autonomy in all personal decision making about life choices.

Accordingly, DRI took a position in the negotiation process that aimed toward three complementary objectives. Each directed at promoting a pro-active dynamic of progress and protection at the implementation stage, they included: (1) ensuring the strongest possible state commitments and legal duties with respect to the affirmative right of all persons with disabilities to live independently in the community with the support services they need (that is, not in institutions); (2) supporting overlapping protections for choice and autonomous decision making in as many treaty provisions as possible (that is, not limited to a single prohibitory provision); and (3) ensuring that any assistance lawfully provided to persons with disabilities in exercising their legal capacity was governed by the principle of *supported* (not substituted) decision making and, likewise, was surrounded by strong and multiple procedural safeguards. Taken together, DRI believed these positions would not only promote the strongest state buy-in and participation for ending institutional warehousing and nonconsensual or abusive treatments, but would also create the greatest number of implementation hooks and entry points for independent monitoring, participatory oversight, and effective enforcement.

DRI's interventions supported this three-prong approach. With respect to the third prong, DRI played a particularly active role in ensuring that the text of Article 12 expressly included multiple legal safeguards, substantive restraints, and review requirements for any possible limitation on the exercise of legal capacity. Citing the extensive safeguards already developed in international human rights jurisprudence and in relevant disability instruments, DRI was particularly insistent on textual inclusion of three requirements, each viewed as necessary for preventing abuse and ensuring respect for the rights, will, and preferences of the person: (1) strict proportionality and tailoring to actual individual need in the circumstances; (2) application of any limitation or restraint on autonomous decision making for the shortest time possible; and (3) regularized review by independent judicial authorities. In achieving the inclusion of these essential safeguards, it sought to work with and support friendly state delegations strongly committed to a similar approach, such as New Zealand and Israel. The final text of Article 12(4) correspondingly reads:

States Parties shall ensure that all measures that relate to the exercise of legal capacity provide for appropriate and effective safeguards to prevent abuse in accordance with international human rights law.

Such safeguards shall ensure that measures relating to the exercise of legal capacity respect the rights, will, and preferences of the person, are free of conflict of interest and undue influence, are proportional and tailored to the person's circumstances, apply for the shortest time possible and are subject to regular review by a competent, independent and impartial authority or judicial body. The safeguards shall be proportional to the degree to which such measures affect the person's rights and interests.

By providing key leverage points for supervisory enforcement, the operational effectiveness of this "safeguards approach" for preventing unjustified institutionalizations and arbitrary deprivations of legal capacity has already proven itself in practice. Indeed, the European Court of Human Rights has found express violations of the European Convention on Human Rights where persons have been deprived of their legal capacity without the provision of appropriate, proportional, and strictly tailored safeguards, including regular review.[15] As an interpretive tool, Article 12(4) will undoubtedly continue to be a vital enforcement hook for issues of institutionalization, civil commitment, and guardianships before courts and human rights supervisory bodies around the world.[16]

A second key issue in Article 12—one that is central to the entire treaty in shifting the disability paradigm toward a social model—is its codification of the principle of supported decision making in place of substitute decision making. It recognizes in this regard that there may be times in a person's life in which he or she needs assistance in making certain personal life decisions. The practice in such circumstances has historically been to appoint a guardian or substitute decision maker, often a family member or the director of an institutional facility, who then becomes the exclusive decision maker for the person. Such substitute decision making is effected even where persons with disabilities can express their own will and preferences with respect to a given decision or decisions (with or without support) and even where guardians possess substantial conflicts of interest with those persons. Article 12 seeks to end this abusive practice, one that lies at the core of so many other regularized abuses committed against persons with disabilities. It does so by requiring that states ensure that persons with disabilities have reliable access to the support they may require in exercising their legal capacity and, correspondingly, by expressly constraining the level of support that can be provided to that which is strictly necessary for the individual at the moment the decision is taken. Where support exceeds this level, Article 12 is implicated.

Both of these aspects of Article 12 will prove vital for protecting persons with disabilities from the regularized abuse they have experienced both in institutions and at home. This is especially true with regard to their ability to decide where and with whom they will reside and what medical interventions they will consent to, to own and inherit property, to control their own financial affairs, to have equal access to financial credit, and to decide the number and spacing of their children as well as other personal life decisions at the core of being human.

Living Independently in the Community

Closely related to Article 12, a second core priority for DRI in the negotiation process was Article 19, "Living Independently and Being Included in the Community." Indeed, in its day-to-day work, DRI has mounted concerted international human rights campaigns against building or rebuilding institutions for persons with disabilities worldwide, insisting that government and donor funds be used instead to invest in safe and dignified community-based services and appropriate supports so that persons with disabilities can live independently in the community on an equal basis with others. Correspondingly, its top institutional priority is its Worldwide Campaign to End the Institutionalization of Children, a campaign directed against both governments and donor agencies that continue to fund the building or rebuilding of institutions for persons with disabilities.[17]

A provision in the treaty expressly guaranteeing the right of persons with disabilities to live independently in and be included in the community—and creating correlate duties for ensuring access to the resources and support services necessary for the enjoyment of that right—was thus central to DRI's political priorities. As highlighted above, such a provision would serve as a positive and proactive way to achieve the ultimate goal of ending the institutionalization of persons with disabilities. The key challenges DRI faced to such a provision came in the form of two widely repeated arguments by states. The first was that the draft provision created a *new* right not recognized in other human rights treaties; it thus exceeded the Committee mandate and could not be included in the treaty as a right. Second, and related, a large number of states argued that they lacked the resources as a practical matter to ensure that all persons with disabilities could live independently in the community and that, accordingly, the referenced norm could not be recognized in the Convention as a legal right, but only as a programmatic goal.

DRI used its oral interventions to respond from a technical-comparative perspective to each of these arguments. With respect to the former, DRI underscored that the "right to live in the community" was simply a straightforward articulation of the widely recognized international norms to non-discrimination and freedom to choose one's residence, rights expressly recognized in the ICCPR and all three regional human rights treaties. Correspondingly, just as a state may not restrict a person's options to reside in any particular section of a country, city, or town on account of racial, religious, or political grounds, neither may it limit the options of a person to live in the community on account of his or her disability—by, for example, restricting a person's residential options to an institution or other particular living arrangement, either directly or indirectly. Such limitations constitute unambiguous discrimination under international law. Just as in other settings where societal discrimination has functioned to create segregated social environments, states have clear affirmative legal obligations to take all appropriate and necessary measures to ensure that persons with disabilities can enjoy freedom of living arrangement on an equal basis with others.

With respect to the second argument, DRI underscored a similar legal point to that which it had made throughout the negotiations: ensuring the effective enjoyment of human rights on an equal basis by all is an expensive and resource-intensive undertaking with regard to *all rights*. It is precisely for this reason that states undertake the conduct-based obligation to take all "appropriate" measures to ensure the enjoyment of rights, with the definition of what is "appropriate" necessarily responsive to local realities. All major human rights tribunals and supervisory bodies take this distinction into account in their individual-rights jurisprudence. Accordingly, the fact that enjoyment of a right cannot be achieved in full immediately for all rights-holders is not a legitimate or credible justification for not recognizing it as a "right." Indeed, if it were, we would recognize no human rights in international treaties, including the right to equal treatment on grounds of race, gender, or religion—the full enjoyment of which has not yet been achieved in any national community.

The right to equal treatment, then, is a work in progress with respect to all grounds of discrimination. The instrumental purpose of international human rights law, DRI insisted, is to create legal duties for states to take all appropriate and necessary measures to ensure, without delay and on a targeted basis, the enjoyment of rights by all rights-holders on an equal basis. Such conduct-based measures include reviewing and revising national legislation and policies, training officials in their human rights obligations, creating benchmarks and plans of action to achieve specified human rights targets, closely monitoring progress and setbacks, constantly measuring and evaluating performance, and correspondingly changing policy and practice as necessary. In this respect, the distinction between "legal rights" and "programmatic goals" is a false one, long used as a smokescreen for avoiding positive obligations for rights in the social field that are fully and unquestioningly undertaken with respect to rights in other fields.

Inclusive Education and Work Environments

As a human rights NGO committed to ending the segregation of persons with disabilities in all institutional settings and environments, DRI was likewise highly motivated with respect to ensuring the treaty's guarantees on inclusive education and inclusive work environments, enshrined in Articles 24 and 27, respectively. With respect to the former, DRI played an active advocacy role in a number of the very technical aspects of Article 24. Its most important contribution, however, lay in helping to ensure the deletion of a very strongly supported textual exception to the principle that education should always be inclusive.[18] That exception would have expressly provided that "separate education *shall* be provided" in those circumstances where the general education system cannot adequately meet the educational needs of persons with disabilities. Together with other NGOs and DPOs, DRI argued that this exception would effectively swallow the rule, providing an explicit "let-out" for states to justify maintaining separate educational systems for persons with a wide range of intellectual, physical, and sensory impairments. The Convention, DRI insisted, should not be one of exceptions— no international human rights treaty is—but rather one of strong principles and commitments to work toward systematically on a targeted and tireless basis.

Revealingly, the states supporting this provision argued explicitly that the individualized needs of persons with intellectual disabilities cannot be met in the general education system, and thus the Convention needed to recognize the appropriateness or acceptability of separate education for persons with mental disabilities. In the end, the provision was bitterly fought over, with China serving as the holdout until the very last, eighth session. With consensus unable to be reached in floor debate, the final text had to be negotiated privately in state-to-state consultations and informal small group settings. Within this struggle, Australia, the principle state supporter of deleting the offending phrase on separate education, expressly requested assistance from DRI on how most effectively to frame the legal issues for China's delegation.

DRI likewise attempted to offer a technical perspective drawn from comparative human rights law to help mediate a significant conflict on the point of separate education within the disability community itself. That is, groups supporting the rights of persons with intellectual disabilities tended to support vigorously the inclusion of an unqualified "right to inclusive education" in the treaty, accompanied by a correlate "prohibition" on separate education systems.[19] By contrast, the deafblind community preferred a "twin-track" approach that would expressly recognize the right to separate education systems or state-financed "special" schools for the deaf and blind. In deference to the deafblind community, the IDC had adopted the latter view as one of its principle platforms, emphasizing the right to "choice" between separate or inclusive education by persons with disabilities themselves.

DRI sought to mediate this conflict by recognizing two distinct but complementary points from international human rights doctrine. First, in insisting on the removal of the general reference to "choice of inclusive education" for persons with disabilities in favor of a textually unqualified right to inclusive education for all,[20] DRI underscored that the "right to educational choice" in current international law is in fact highly limited. Parents and guardians do not enjoy a general right to choose a specific type of public educational system for their children. Rather, they enjoy only the liberty to remove their children from the general public education system, "choosing" to place them instead in a *private* system or home-schooling environment that nonetheless conforms to minimum educational standards laid down by the state. A broad reference to "choice" within the general education system therefore lacks support in international human rights law at present and should be replaced, DRI concluded, by a focus on ensuring the right to an inclusive education system at all levels and access to such education *in the communities* in which persons with disabilities live.

At the same time, however, DRI underscored that international law does recognize that certain defined subgroups *with their own cultural identity* and specific needs may be entitled to state funding to establish their own educational institutions. Grounded in the internationally recognized right to culture, major international instruments enshrining the rights of indigenous persons, for example, recognize their right to establish and administer their own educational institutions and facilities, accompanied by a correlate state duty to provide appropriate financial resources, assistance, and training in administering them.[21] Accordingly, just as textual recognition of a broad "right to educational choice" would lack an established international law basis, so too would a "prohibition" on separate education systems.

DRI made these technical points in the sixth session, recalling them in the seventh and eighth, to underscore the international law basis for supporting *both* positions within the disability community: the imperative of recognizing a broad and unqualified "right to inclusive education" for all, while not in the process undermining the right of certain *culturally self-identifying* groups, such as members of the deaf, blind, and deafblind community, to establish their own educational institutions if it is their choice. The final text of Article 24 reflects this doctrinally grounded "compromise" position. It also reflects the caution that should, in DRI's view, generally be exercised in any human rights treaty drafting process with respect to the codification of absolute prohibitory language. In most cases, positively worded guarantees to affirmative conduct or outcome-based results not only will open a greater diversity of creative and multileveled enforcement options, but may also avoid significant unintended consequences for differently situated social groups that are negatively affected, including those not well represented in the negotiation process.

Monitoring and Enforcement Mechanisms

Finally, with its focus on post-adoption implementation processes and based on its on-the-ground experience working with states to ensure deinstitutionalization and community integration, DRI actively intervened on questions of monitoring and enforcement at both the national and international levels throughout the negotiation process. In this respect, it strongly agreed with Senegal's observation that the CRPD provisions on monitoring and enforcement would serve as the "soul" of the Convention, determining how it would be implemented on the ground.

With respect to national-level mechanisms, DRI was particularly insistent on ensuring that the Convention include strong independent monitoring provisions, especially for service provision in both closed institutions and community settings. Thus, in addition to systems for general monitoring, it emphasized that the Convention should provide for *specialized, independent monitoring* to protect the rights of people who are especially vulnerable, including but not limited to those receiving services in institutions or other closed environments. DRI could not close its eyes in this regard to the fact that millions of children and adults around the world remain segregated from society in closed institutions, within which they often lack the means to publicize abuses or claim their own rights. At the same time, as countries move away from institutions toward community-based services and supports for persons with disabilities, more and more abuses are found in the community. Often, what are called "community services" are actually small, isolated institutions located in physical proximity to what could be called the community. Thus, any oversight and monitoring system must also monitor rights protection in community-based services.

While highlighting numerous comparative models of effective rights oversight and monitoring bodies from around the world, DRI focused in particular on the standards adopted by the Council of Europe in 2004 with respect to mental health institutions.[22] These standards specify that, to avoid a conflict of interest and to ensure that abuses by an institution can be challenged, oversight and monitoring must be conducted by a body that is "organizationally independent from the authorities or bodies monitored" and should include not only mental health professionals and laypersons, but also persons with disabilities and those close to them.[23] Importantly, they likewise provide that regular visits and inspections should be able to be undertaken *without prior notice* and that systematic and reliable statistical information and information on implementation should be made available to the public.[24] At the same time, following the UN Standard Rules on the Equalization of Opportunities of Persons with Disabilities, which explicitly recognize the rights of persons with disabilities to be involved in monitoring and implementation of human rights that affect them, DRI strongly supported the early proposals of Sierra Leone and Yemen to expressly incorporate the guarantee of direct participation by persons with disabilities and civil society organizations in the treaty monitoring process. This proposal was explicitly incorporated into Article 33(3), decidedly one of the most important provisions in the treaty.

DRI was also successful in ensuring that a provision on effective monitoring *by independent authorities* of all facilities and programs designed to serve persons with disabilities was directly included in Article 16 of the Convention, which guarantees "freedom from exploitation, violence and abuse."

With regard to an international monitoring and enforcement mechanism, DRI strongly supported the emphasis of Costa Rica and Liechtenstein on the importance of a *proactive treaty body*, one that does not only respond to state reports but also—and perhaps principally—is able to react effectively and promptly to information and complaints of violations presented by persons with disabilities themselves and those who work with them. Indeed, DRI's experience has shown that situations on the ground rarely change until persons directly affected force that change. Such action nevertheless inevitably requires the support of international oversight bodies empowered to accompany the process of contestation, settlement, reform, follow-up, and supervision. In this regard, DRI underscored three essential elements it believed critical to any international enforcement mechanism: (1) an individual complaints mechanism; (2) precautionary or urgent interim measures; and (3) on-site visits.

With respect to the former, DRI questioned the view of others in the process that collective complaints procedures are preferable to individual communications because they allow structural inequities to be addressed. Indeed, DRI has been highly successful in promoting structural reform in national mental health systems through the use of individual case-based procedures.[25] Such procedures have the decisive advantage of allowing the concrete specificities and contours of abusive situations to be detailed, allowing for the crafting of more targeted and responsive remedial measures than are generally available through collective complaints processes. Offered within the framework of an "effective remedy," such measures—which include structural guarantees against nonrepetition—can then be the focus of longer-term implementation processes, promoted jointly by international monitoring and on-the-ground civil society mobilization campaigns.

At the same time, DRI sought to respond to concerns about institutional duplication at the international level by proposing that the Committee might consider endowing the CRPD treaty body with the capacity to refer individual complaints to the corresponding regional human rights system where jurisdictional overlap existed (that is, the Inter-American, European, and African systems)—preferably with its continued participation in an expert advisory capacity. This would simultaneously serve to lessen the workload of the Committee—allowing it to focus on individual complaints in those regions that lack judicial and quasi-judicial human rights bodies—while also helping to mainstream disability rights protections into human rights treaties that are not disability specific. Because the regional systems are well developed and have generally strong dispute settlement, follow-up, and supervisory procedures, this might have been one innovative step forward for international enforcement.

In emphasizing the need for the new treaty to innovate with respect to international enforcement mechanisms and to avoid the weaknesses of the current treaty-body system, DRI likewise underscored the need for the treaty-body complaints process to be closely linked with processes for integrated follow-up and continual supervision by monitoring bodies, especially given the fact that certain structural reform processes take significant time. Simple recommendations, without a follow-up procedure, would be insufficient and a tremendous lost opportunity for persons with disabilities. At the same time, because international complaints procedures inevitably involve significant delay, DRI believed it essential for the treaty to provide for urgent interim measures to protect persons with disabilities from grave and irreparable harm that can occur while a complaint is being processed. On-site visits, DRI believed, also serve as a critical implementation tool to allow members of the monitoring body to see abuses firsthand, to consult and negotiate directly with decision makers, to hear directly from persons affected, and to put remedial action plans in place in cooperation with responsible governments and in consultation with civil society.

In supporting these positions and others, DRI put forward detailed amendments to the drafting proposals in circulation, seeking to ensure that the treaty body created under the new Convention would indeed innovate beyond the current treaty body structure. Unfortunately, in the end, this did not come to pass. The CRPD treaty body, in its composition and functions, looks almost identical to those of the other major UN human rights treaty bodies. The one innovation in the human rights field was a Conference of

States Parties, borrowed from the Land Mines Treaty, the effectiveness of which is still to be seen.

Final Reflections

As pointed out by others in this volume, the final CRPD is not perfect. It contains provisions that could have been better drafted and it omits protections or concepts that some stakeholders would have liked to have seen included. At the same time, significant opportunities for creating new and creative mechanisms at the international level to promote national-level compliance with the CRPD were unfortunately not taken up. Overall, however, the CRPD is a comprehensive and highly useful tool for promoting the rights and dignity of persons with disabilities, and it will have an important impact on the way the rights of persons with disabilities are fought for both domestically and internationally for generations to come.

In contributing to the final treaty outcome, DRI won many of its battles and lost many others. It nonetheless believes that it played an important role in the process, especially in providing a consistent technical perspective on the drafting proposals as they evolved and in maintaining a principled focus on the long-term operability of the treaty text in post-adoption implementation processes. As highlighted earlier, this role served to complement the advocacy role taken by many other DPOs and NGOs in the negotiations and, in the end, strengthened, we believe, the overall civil society presence in the drafting process. At the same time, it is important to recognize that the arguments DRI advanced and the principles it fought for will continue to play a vital and central political role in the much harder implementation work ahead of transforming the substantive norms and process commitments of the CRPD into concrete, meaningful change for affected communities worldwide.

CHAPTER 6

Children with Disabilities

Gerison Lansdown

Children with disabilities, like adults, experience widespread violation and neglect of their human rights. Despite the unique provision in the Convention on the Rights of the Child, which explicitly includes disability as a ground for protection from discrimination, as well as a dedicated article introducing government obligations to ensure services for them, children with disabilities continue to face extreme forms of discrimination in most countries around the world. When children's rights are considered, children with disabilities tend to be forgotten. When the rights of people with disabilities are considered, children with disabilities tend to be forgotten. Their rights, therefore, are at risk of being marginalized. An analysis of government reports and the Concluding Observations of the Committee on the Rights of the Child undertaken between 2000 and 2003 found that governments consistently failed to give appropriate recognition to the violations of disabled children's rights.[1] Except where expressly mentioned in the CRC, in areas of education, training, health, and rehabilitation services, rights for children with disabilities were disregarded.

Children with disabilities, and the challenges they face in realizing their rights, remain largely invisible. It was imperative, therefore, that the new treaty for persons with disabilities extended to children as well as adults in imposing obligations on governments to ensure that all people are afforded equal respect for their rights. This chapter discusses the positions developed on children with disabilities through the involvement of Save the Children, an international NGO with a strong record of protecting the rights of children. Although neither a DPO nor a specifically disability-focused NGO, it does have programs working on the rights of children with disabilities in a number of countries.

Making a Case for a Dedicated Article
for Children with Disabilities

The initial draft text of the Convention on the Rights of Persons with Disabilities did include a specific article on children with disabilities, modeled largely on the text of Article 23 of the CRC. It was, however, soon recognized to be unsatisfactory. Its limitations lay in the fact that Article 23 was drafted with a focus on the special needs of children with disabilities. The philosophy of the new Convention, in contrast, focused strongly on a social model of disability and the need to remove the barriers impeding the realization of rights. Beyond the specific article on children with disabilities, and an article on education, the Working Group text included little recognition of their rights at all.

It moreover soon became apparent that a significant number of governments were resistant to the principle of including any explicit focus on children. A range of arguments were proposed in support of this view, including the idea that additional protections for children with disabilities in the CRPD were unnecessary because of the existence of the CRC; that including children would set a precedent for a "shopping list" of special pleading (that is, a case would also be made for women, older people, indigenous people, people living in rural communities, and so on); and that such provisions might risk undermining the CRC and lead to a lowering of the protections it provides.

It was evident that considerable work was needed to challenge these arguments if the final text of the CRPD was to include appropriate protection for the rights of children with disabilities. Action was needed at two levels. First, it was necessary to undertake a detailed analysis of the CRPD draft text, and determine what amendments and additions were needed for children with disabilities, in light of both the best available knowledge of their experiences of discrimination and exclusion and the impact of the CRC in serving to challenge violations of their rights. Second, a comprehensive strategy was needed to overcome the arguments being posed against the inclusion of children with disabilities in the final text of the CRPD and to lobby for the proposed amendments to be accepted.

Clearly, almost all the articles in the draft text could have been argued to have implications for children and could, in principle, have made reference to them. However, the approach adopted was to propose amendments, keeping four points in mind. (1) A dedicated article on children would lend explicit recognition to the fact that the treaty extended to children as well as adults with disabilities, and would also give force to the understanding that they face particular challenges in the realization of their rights. (2) Where there were rights violations experienced by children and not adults, not acknowledged in the current text, additional provisions would be drafted. (3) Where it was likely that a provision would only be interpreted as applying to adults, but should also extend to children, the text should be amended to make this clear. (4) Where a provision needed special adaptation to acknowledge the particular status and vulnerabilities of children, an amendment would be drafted to accommodate their circumstances.

The aim of the dedicated article was to profile children with disabilities in the text, ensure their visibility, and establish an overarching framework for the realization of their rights. To this end, it needed to affirm the obligations of governments to ensure that children with disabilities enjoy all rights and freedoms on an equal basis with other children. It also needed to reaffirm the general principles of the CRC and ensure that these principles were recognized as applying to the implementation of all other rights in the CRPD.[2] The principle of nondiscrimination and the right to life were already well established in the text. The other two—the best interests of the child and the right of the child to be heard in all matters affecting him or her and to have those views taken seriously—were not included elsewhere. It was necessary, therefore, to include them in the dedicated article. Furthermore, in light of the experience of the CRC, and the difficulties faced by children with disabilities in getting their voices heard, it was important to include additional obligations on governments to ensure that these rights were protected equally for children with disabilities, and that the necessary assistance was provided to make that possible.[3]

Issues Specific to Children

It should not be assumed that by addressing the rights of adults, all the issues facing children will be addressed. Children cannot be subsumed within an adult agenda. Some rights violations are unique to children. Analysis of the draft text indicated that the following issues needed to be added if children with disabilities were to be adequately recognized and protected.

BIRTH REGISTRATION

Although in many developing countries, overall rates of birth registration remain low, particularly for poorer children, the problem is especially acute for children with disabilities, although it is difficult to gather accurate data. The CRC does include the right to birth registration for every child, but does not call for the necessary measures to ensure that it is implemented for children with disabilities. In many countries, where there is strong stigma and blame associated with the birth of a child with disabilities, parents can be reluctant to pay the required registration fee. Without registration, parents can and do deny the child's very existence; and such a child can face difficulty in accessing health care, education, and citizenship. It was proposed that the CRPD should include a specific obligation on governments to take the necessary measures to address this particular form of discrimination. This could include more effective mapping of children with disabilities, parent education and awareness, community support measures for birth-registration campaigns, and incentive schemes.

RIGHT TO FAMILY LIFE

The focus of the first draft text of the CRPD in respect to family life centered almost exclusively on an adult agenda. It dealt with the right to intimate relationships, to marriage, and to found a family. However, the issues for children with disabilities are different. Many experience abandonment, neglect, and concealment. Many are institutionalized as a matter of government policy, because of a lack of any community-based support services, because of stigma and discrimination, or as a result of poverty and inadequate social protection.[4] Their families lack support, education, and understanding as to the nature of disability. Provisions were needed to introduce obligations on governments to take all the necessary actions to protect the right of children to family life, including obligations to ensure that where families were unable to care for a child, every effort was made to provide an alternative home within the wider family or local community, and not within an institution.

RIGHT TO PLAY

In the original text, there was an article addressing the right to participation in cultural life, recreation, leisure, and sport. Notably, its adult focus resulted in no provision on the right to play. However, for children, play is a fundamental right. It is probably in the field of play, recreation, and leisure activities that children with disabilities experience the most acute sense of social exclusion and marginalization. Consultations with children repeatedly reveal the importance that they all attach to their relationships with their peers. Children with disabilities are no different. They, too, want opportunities to be with friends, to play, to have fun, to "hang out." However, for them, physical, attitudinal, cultural, and social factors can place almost insuperable barriers in the way of the daily activities that other children are able to take for granted. It was important, therefore, to incorporate this right into the article, placing obligations on governments to take the necessary action to remove these barriers.

Provisions Needing Affirmation of Their Application to Children

Many key provisions in the draft text could, in principle, be understood to extend equally to children as well as adults with disabilities. In reality, the relative invisibility of children rendered it likely that without explicit affirmation these rights would not be extended to and implemented for them. It was not appropriate, nor would it have been acceptable to the Ad Hoc Committee, to seek the addition of references to children in every relevant article. Proposals were, therefore, limited to those issues where it was likely that, without mention that the provision explicitly included children, governments could seek to interpret the article as applying only to adults. Two particular issues were identified: consultation and sterilization.

CONSULTATION

The draft text included a general obligation on governments to consult with and involve persons with disabilities and their representative organizations in the development of laws and policies to implement the CRPD. However, although the wording did not exclude children, it was extremely unlikely that it would be applied to include them. Very few, if any, governments throughout the world have traditions of involving children in any such consultative processes. Yet children's experiences and concerns cannot be adequately represented by adults. They have their own unique expertise and perspective to contribute. Experience demonstrates that without an explicit entitlement, children will not be listened to. Furthermore, since the right of children to be heard and taken seriously was introduced by the CRC, it has become evident that the involvement of children in such processes, is not only a right, but also of significant benefit in producing better outcomes (Article 5, CRC). It was proposed, therefore, that the text should be amended to make it absolutely clear that this provision applied to children with disabilities as well as adults.

STERILIZATION

The draft text provided for the right of persons with disabilities to the equal opportunity to retain their fertility. In other words, forcible sterilization was prohibited for a person with disabilities on exactly the same basis as for a nondisabled person. The difficulty for children, with and without disabilities, arises in that decisions relating to medical treatment are made by parents, not by the children themselves. Sterilizations are often undertaken on children with disabilities, with their parents' consent, before they have either the capacity or the legal right to make such choices for themselves. The CRPD, therefore, needed to be clear that the right to fertility applies from birth, not just from the age at which the choice to have a child becomes relevant. It was important that children were protected from decisions made by their parents on their behalf. The provision, therefore, needed to state explicitly that it extended to children with disabilities, and thus limited the powers of parents to make such decisions.

Provisions Needing Adaptation for Their Application to Children

Children, both with and without disabilities, have a different legal and social status from adults in all societies, and in many situations, they do also face greater challenges in the exercise of the rights because of their youth and consequent vulnerability. Scrutinizing the CRPD draft text was important, therefore, to review where there was a need to amend proposed provisions to ensure they reflected the particular legal status and circumstances faced by children with disabilities.

AUTONOMY

Respect for the autonomy of persons with disabilities on an equal basis with others in any given society is central to recognition of the inherent dignity of individuals. It is therefore included as a fundamental principle that must underpin the implementation of all other rights in the CRPD. However, it is not possible to argue for autonomy for all children, with or without disabilities. Rather, parents are afforded rights and responsibilities to make decisions and act on their children's behalf in accordance with the children's capacities to exercise their rights for themselves (Article 5, CRC). In other words, parents do have a protective role. Accordingly, if the CRPD demanded respect for autonomy without reference to children's protected status, its provisions would, de facto, have appeared to apply exclusively to adults. This was clearly not the intention. Conversely, an additional challenge arises for children with disabilities. They experience far greater difficulties in gaining recognition of their capacities for independent decision making. They are commonly overprotected, infantilized, and denied opportunities for their emerging autonomy. This overprotection limits their capacity to develop fully and can undermine confidence and deny them respect for privacy and personal integrity.[5] It was therefore necessary to add to the general principles a provision requiring respect for the evolving capacities of children with disabilities. Such a provision would ensure that the concept of autonomy was understood as a principle that cannot be applied without qualification from birth, but must be respected for children with increasing effect as they acquire the capacities to exercise their rights.

PROTECTION FROM VIOLENCE

The original draft included a provision on the right of persons with disabilities to protection from exploitation, violence, and abuse, and the introduction of measures to ensure that protection. However, it made no specific reference to children. Without doing so, there was a real risk that they would continue to fall through the safety nets provided to address violence. A growing number of countries now have specific child-protection laws and policies to address violence and abuse of children. However, although children with disabilities are disproportionately vulnerable to both sexual and physical violence, very few governments currently address the need to develop child-protection services accessible or appropriate for children with disabilities.[6] Hotlines and keep-safe programs, for example, are largely irrelevant to many children with disabilities. They are less likely to have access to information about their rights and, therefore, lack knowledge of what they are entitled to challenge. And even if they have that knowledge, they are denied opportunities to report or challenge the abuse. Conversely, legislation and policies to address violence against adults are dealt with in the main criminal justice system, quite separately from children. What this meant was that, without specific requirements to focus on the right to protection for children with disabilities, a situation would continue in which both child-protection frameworks and adult criminal justice systems would serve to exclude children with disabilities. It was imperative, therefore, that the article dealing with violence made explicit reference to the obligation to take measures to prevent, avoid, recognize, and report violence that were sensitive to children with disabilities. Additionally, it was important that measures to support rehabilitation and recovery of people who have been victims of exploitation, violence, or abuse take account of their needs. In other words, dedicated laws, policies, and services have to be designed that are appropriate and accessible for children with disabilities.

ACCESS TO JUSTICE

Many persons with disabilities face challenges in realizing their right of access to justice. Accordingly, the draft text included a provision requiring their access to justice on an equal basis with others, together with an obligation to facilitate their effective role as direct and indirect participants in all legal proceedings. However, additional measures are needed if children with disabilities are to gain access to justice. It is hard for all children to demonstrate competency or to be able to participate effectively in respect of legal proceedings. Children with disabilities experience a double jeopardy in this regard. Their childhood status, combined with their disability, serve to render it almost impossible for them to be judged competent as a witness or to bring a case. Assumptions of incapacity, prejudice about disability, and failure to provide appropriate interpretation or other forms of support mean they are unable to seek or gain justice—and in consequence, many abusers achieve impunity.

Accordingly, the text needed to include an obligation to ensure that any accommodations to render legal processes disability sensitive should also take account of the accommodations needed for children. This might include, for example, support to render legal processes accessible, interpretation where appropriate, information about the nature of proceedings and their rights in relation to those proceedings, and counseling and advice, to enable them to use the courts to achieve justice at all stages of proceedings. Additionally, all staff in the field of administration of justice need training on the rights of children with disabilities and how to ensure that they fulfill their obligations in this area.

Developing a Strategy to Achieve the Changes Needed

Having undertaken an analysis of what was needed, the next challenge was to convince the government delegations of the case for including our proposed amendments. We were prepared to adopt a pragmatic approach as to how our changes should be incorporated. Ideally, we were pursuing what became known as a "twin-track" approach—a dedicated article on children with disabilities, alongside the mainstreaming of specific amendments to individual articles. However, if governments were more likely to be persuaded by either full mainstreaming, and the deletion of the dedicated Article, or, alternatively, for all children's issues to be drawn together in one Article, we were willing to be flexible. We were also willing to accommodate alternative formulations in the language adopted and to consider different locations for some of the amendments where there was not an obviously appropriate article. What we were determined to pursue, however, was that all the issues we were raising did get included somewhere in the text, without any watering down. The various strategies we adopted are discussed below.

Collaboration with the IDC

Although there were many DPOs and disability NGOs actively involved in the International Disability Caucus, there were few with a particular capacity to advocate on behalf of children. However, the IDC fully endorsed the need for action if the rights of children with disabilities were to be addressed adequately. Accordingly, it agreed to the introduction of a coordinator with responsibility for taking the lead on advocacy for children with disabilities who would also be represented in the IDC Steering Group. Responsibility for supporting this role was undertaken by Save the Children. Collaboration through the IDC was vital for a number of reasons. It had the respect of governments who were far more willing to listen to proposals if they were seen to have the backing of the IDC. It also provided a sounding board for proposed amendments, their possible location, and alternative forms of wording.

Suggested additions and changes to the text were subjected to scrutiny before being given approval, thus providing a degree of rigor to the process. Finally, the very considerable body of expertise and experience within the IDC provided an invaluable source of knowledge about which governments to approach, in terms of both their likely levels of support and their strategic importance in influencing others in their region.

Active Participation in the Ad Hoc Committee

In order to have access to government delegations and influence their decisions in respect of children with disabilities, it was necessary to be present throughout each of the AHC meetings in New York. Action was needed to draft amendments and briefings on all issues planned to be debated in that particular session. Concentrated efforts were then needed to talk with key government delegations to seek their support for the amendment. Often it was also necessary to work with regional groups in order to try to build a regional position for the proposed change.

Enlisting the Support of the Committee on the Rights of the Child

It was decided to enlist the support of the Committee on the Rights of the Child to challenge the arguments posed against explicit recognition of children with disabilities in the text of the CRPD on the basis that it might serve to undermine existing rights in the CRC and that it was unnecessary in any case as the CRC already provided adequate protection. Accordingly, the proposed amendments were shared with by Committee chair Professor Jaap Doek, to seek his views. He strongly endorsed all the proposed amendments. Save the Children then requested his participation at an AHC meeting to make a statement on behalf of the Committee on the Rights of the Child to lend strength to the proposed amendments. In his subsequent presentation in August 2005, further reinforced in a separate meeting with the AHC chair, he made a strong case arguing for the fundamental importance of inclusion of children with disabilities. He stressed that the fact that the inclusion of children with disabilities in two different treaties would not lead to duplication and overlap in the monitoring process, emphasizing that the Committee on the Rights of the Child would coordinate its monitoring activities regarding children with disabilities with the body in charge of monitoring CRPD implementation to avoid duplication. Indeed, he argued that such coordination should result in better, more consistent, and frequent monitoring of the protection and promotion of the rights of children with disabilities.

Enabling Children with Disabilities to
Make the Case for Themselves

The motto "Nothing About Us Without Us" represented a fundamental principle underlying both the process of drafting the CRPD and its overall objectives. However, children with disabilities were not there to speak for themselves. Prior to its direct involvement with the IDC, Save the Children had sought to facilitate the active and direct involvement of young people with disabilities in the negotiation process. However, lack of both financial support and an organizational infrastructure for the young people rendered it impossible to achieve this goal. Instead, it was decided to bring a group of young people to one session in New York in order to ensure that the AHC had an opportunity to hear, firsthand, their views and experiences. Again, the chair was approached and he agreed to offer fifteen minutes to the young people to present their statement to a plenary session of the AHC.

Save the Children then brought six young children and young people with disabilities to New York—two each from Bangladesh, China, and the UK. They spent two days sharing life experiences and identifying the rights violations they wished the attention of the AHC. Interestingly, despite the huge cultural, social, and economic differences between the six young people, they converged very quickly around four common themes they highlighted as the top priorities to present to the AHC for inclusion in the CRPD—the rights to inclusive education, to be consulted, to support for families, and to nondiscrimination. In a widely circulated written statement, they also highlighted the need for recognition of the importance of ending institutionalization, challenging violence and abuse, ensuring access to services, opportunities for friendships with peers, and access to information. In addition to the formal presentation, the young people held a lunchtime meeting at which they encouraged participants to share childhood experiences of abuse, discrimination, social exclusion, and isolation associated with disability. This well-attended session provoked a stimulating and often extremely painful exploration of the challenges facing children with disabilities, prompting some participants to acknowledge emotions, memories, and fears repressed since childhood. The young people also attracted a high level of media interest, which provided them with further opportunity to disseminate their ideas and perspectives.

Their participation in the process was important, serving to challenge the argument for excluding specific provisions on children. It brought home to the government delegations that children with disabilities are a distinct constituency who had a right to recognition, yet who had, to date, been given very little consideration. It affirmed that children with disabilities can be effective advocates for their own rights and are entitled to be involved in decisions that affect them. It affirmed that adults have lessons to learn from children with disabilities, and it highlighted the principal concerns faced by children with disabilities, many of which required specific additional provisions in the draft text.

Collaboration with the Facilitator on Children with Disabilities

In all areas of the draft convention where there were significant unresolved issues of dispute, the chair appointed a facilitator to try to reconcile differences in advance of the matter coming before a plenary session of the AHC. In August 2005, the chair appointed a facilitator, Josephine Sinyo, a member of the Kenyan delegation, to try to produce a reasonable consensus on proposed amendments to the draft text of the Convention in respect of children with disabilities. The IDC worked extremely closely with the facilitator to press for our amendments on children, to find common language that would reconcile differences, to provide her with briefings, and to undertake joint lobbying of government delegations.

During the August 2005 session, the facilitator requested submissions from NGOs and government delegations highlighting the key issues that needed to be addressed in respect to children. The IDC submitted detailed proposals. The facilitator then produced a paper outlining the major recommendations for amended text. The IDC proposals were not only fully included, but formed the major basis of her paper. Two meetings were held to discuss the proposals. Unusually, both governments and NGOs were permitted to participate in these meetings on an equal basis. However, there was little consensus, either as to the case for a stand-alone article on children or the need for specific reference to children in substantive articles throughout the text. Accordingly, the chair decided that it would be inappropriate to try to bring a discussion on the issue to the plenary at that session. He wanted to provide more time for discussion and accommodation toward an agreed position.

In the following AHC meeting in January 2006, the two facilitators for children and women, at the request of the chair, held a meeting at which a joint paper was presented that incorporated the issues relating to both constituencies. This time, NGOs were not allowed to speak, although they undertook extensive briefings of government delegations prior to the meeting. Two subsequent separate meetings were held, one each for women and children, to try to reach an overall consensus on the proposed amendments. Following these meetings, the two facilitators then produced an integrated report, comprising their proposals to be added to the draft text. This report still included most of the proposals on children initially put forward by the IDC, which by now, although initially strongly contested, were commanding significant support by delegations. Accordingly, the chair agreed to place the issue of children with disabilities on the agenda of the plenary session.

Impact of the Advocacy on Behalf of
Children with Disabilities

Given the very considerable resistance by some government delegations to any references to children and by others to some of the specific proposed amendments, a very significant level of advocacy and persuasion was required in order to achieve the IDC goal of both a stand-alone article and the mainstreaming of children with disabilities. However, through the multifaceted approach described above, we did begin to see a shift in the attitudes of many delegations. Indeed, by the end of the January 2006 session, the chair's overall analysis of the mood of the Committee was that there was support for several measures, including a preambular statement on children; inclusion of respect for the evolving capacities of children in the general principles; inclusion of reference to children in the obligation for governments to consult with persons with disabilities and their representative organizations when developing legislation and policy; inclusion of reference to age-appropriate accommodation to facilitate access of children with disabilities to the justice system; measures to ensure birth registration of children with disabilities; reference to the need for protection services to be age, gender, and disability sensitive;

and inclusion of provisions providing for support for families. The inclusion of a provision on play in the article on cultural life, recreation, leisure, and sport had already been adopted at the previous session.

Despite these agreements, there still was no consensus on a stand-alone article on children with disabilities, although there did appear to be broad agreement that if the article was not included, then the proposed text of such an article would instead be included as a separate paragraph in the article on general obligations. Nor could delegates reach agreement on an explicit prohibition on sterilization of children with disabilities or on institutionalization of children.

Overall we had made very significant progress, although there was still some way to go. The chair was strongly committed to finalizing the text at the following meeting, scheduled for August 2006. It was clear that considerably more work would be needed to ensure that these issues gained sufficient support by that stage. We also needed to ensure that the in-principle support for the other changes was sustained and formally voted on at that final session.

Our work at this final stage involved seeking to persuade governments that were either hostile or indifferent, of the value of our proposals, while also encouraging those governments already in support to speak from the floor of the AHC. In the event, we gained support for all the proposals, although not always in wording as explicit as we had originally sought. A stand-alone article on children with disabilities was adopted. Our attempt to introduce a ban on sterilizations of children on nonclinical grounds was successful in that the provision on the right of persons with disabilities to retain their fertility was amended to state that this included children. Although no express prohibition on institutionalization of children was drafted, the emphasis in the article on family life on the obligation to make every effort to provide alternative care within the wider family or, failing that, within the community in a family setting makes clear that institutions should always be avoided as a placement for children.

Conclusion

Children with disabilities experience many of the same rights violations as adults with disabilities. However, they are a distinct constituency entitled to be represented as such. The challenge during the drafting of the CRPD was how to ensure that representation and that the measures needed to address the rights violations they face were argued effectively during the negotiations. The strategy that was evolved during that process indicated that there were a number of pieces in the jigsaw puzzle, all of which were critical in achieving a successful outcome.

The role of the IDC was clearly vital. Its emergence as a coordinated forum, which commanded the respect of governments, provided the key platform for advocacy, as well as a huge source of expertise and experience. It created a sense of solidarity, offered support, and stimulated intellectual debate. A dedicated focus on children with disabilities was also essential and without the continued support and backing of Save the Children would not have been possible. There is a real danger that in an adult-orientated environment, children's issues are given insufficient consideration, sidelined in favor of other priorities, their importance unacknowledged. The pressure of time, the huge range of issues to be addressed, and the limited number of people available to undertake the work meant that children would inevitably be marginalized without focused attention. Expertise in respect of both disability and children's rights was important: only with an understanding of the rights embodied in the CRC, together with the extent to which its provisions had been implemented for children with disabilities, could there be clarity as to how the CRPD could serve to complement and strengthen its provisions to ensure greater protection of their rights. The presence of children and young people at the AHC served as a catalyst for change—it rendered children and their perspectives visible and made it harder for them to be disregarded. A willingness to combine flexibility with principle was crucial. In order to help delegations accommodate their governments' positions, it was often necessary to find different solutions to the problem being identified. The challenge was to demonstrate a willingness to cooperate with their parameters, while holding fast to the central objective of a proposed amendment.

Finally, without persistence and investment of time, little would have been achieved. Government delegations did not, in the main, have children on their agenda. Many were highly resistant in principle to the inclusion of children in the text, others were hostile to, or unsupportive of, the specific proposals being advocated for. There was a need for a constant presence throughout the process—a commitment to making the arguments over and over again, to keep talking, persuading, lobbying and bringing evidence to bear in support of those arguments. However, what became apparent was that it was possible to convince those delegations; we were able to change their minds and sensitize them to the issues. We did place children on the agenda. Through the broad range of strategies employed, we achieved a successful outcome. All the changes proposed were included in the final draft of the CRPD.

Of course, inclusion in the Convention is just the first rung of the ladder to be climbed. Nothing will change for children unless and until its provisions are implemented. However, we do now have the architecture in place from which to enter into the next stage of advocacy. What we must remember is that the struggle for implementation will require even more commitment, time, and energy. And as it moves to the national level, it must be undertaken not just for but with children and young people with disabilities themselves.

CHAPTER 7

Women with Disabilities: The Convention Through the Prism of Gender

Mi Yeon Kim

Starting with the UN premise that of the world's population of seven billion at least 15 percent have a disability, persons with disabilities make up the single largest marginalized social group. Considering that women constitute 51 percent of the world's population, there are consequently at least 510 million women with disabilities around the globe. Despite this staggering figure, laws and policies accommodating the needs and desires of women with disabilities are largely nonexistent both at national and international levels. Regulations and policies that exist are frequently extremely limiting and often fragmented, which has often jeopardized meaningful practical application. Reflecting this bleak reality, the UN at one point referred to women with disabilities in the Asian and Pacific region as "hidden sisters" to underscore the multiple discriminations that most of them face.

Women with disabilities are doubly or triply invisible—facing discrimination as women and as persons with disabilities, other distinctions adding to the risk of being marginalized, excluded, and pushed into oblivion.[1] Forced sterilizations, violence, abuse, rape, exclusion from services, particularly health, lack of education, and therefore high illiteracy rate are only some of the consequences. Women with disabilities are poorer and more isolated and generally have lower social status.[2] As the first UN special rapporteur on disabilities, Bengt Lindqvist observed,

Women with disabilities face triple discrimination daily because of their poverty, their disability, and their gender. Women with disabilities are denied equal access to education—their literacy rate as a group, worldwide, is probably under 5 percent. Women with disabilities do not have equal access to the labour market—less than a quarter, says the UN, are in paid employment, though the majority contribute significantly to their families and communities through cooking, cleaning, caring for children of relatives, and carrying out daily chores. Women with disabilities receive only about one-fifth of the rehabilitation in the world.[3]

It is believed that 80 percent of women with disabilities acquired their impairment or disability through diseases, abuse, accidents—including complications stemming from obstetric problems during labor—and environmental factors.[4]

This chapter examines the challenges, successes, and pitfalls in the inclusion of gender in the text of the Convention on the Rights of Persons with Disabilities. It reflects my experience as an individual, an expert of a disabled people's organization (DPO) who worked closely with her country's delegation to ensure that the needs and rights of women with disabilities were properly addressed.

The Challenges

In addition to the challenges faced by all persons with disabilities, women with disabilities face particular obstacles in drawing attention to and obtaining support for their needs. These particular challenges are outlined below.

The Invisibility of Women with Disabilities

Women with disabilities have been rendered invisible in discussing not only female issues but also disability issues. It is extremely hard to find concerns related to women with disabilities in most government policies and laws in the world. Surprisingly, there is little difference between the developed and developing world when it comes to women with disabilities. This shows that there is a strong need to reflect the gender perspective and the reality of women with disabilities being triply discriminated against in disability policies due to deeply rooted social stereotypes, including those related to sexuality. The public's perception of women with disabilities as asexual further compounds patriarchal practices in disability policies aggravating the gender-based discrimination of women with disabilities.

The Sexual Discrimination of Women with Disabilities

Aristotle once said, "the only stable state is the one in which all men are equal before the law." Since the beginning of history, the term "men (male)" has been effective in distinguishing men and women. Historically, although equality is entangled with spiritual, materialistic, economic, sexual, and political problems, feminism emerged demanding that men and women should be treated equally. Sex-based discrimination is discrimination against persons or groups on the basis of their gender, meaning that one gender has more privileges, resulting in limitations for the other. When the attribution of impairment or disability, respectively, is added to the equation, chances of discrimination accelerate, also when compared with men with disabilities. Equality does not necessarily mean that men and women should be equal; rather, it implies that equivalent rights, responsibilities, and opportunities are given to a person regardless of the sex he or she is born with. And while sexual equality is not restricted to women, given the status quo, women tend to be the ones to emphasize the importance of gender equality.

The Perceived (A)Sexuality of Women with Disabilities

As the Committee under the International Covenant on Economic, Social and Cultural Rights observes, "Persons with disabilities are sometimes treated as genderless human beings."[5] This genderlessness and perception as asexual beings compounds discrimination and exclusion further. In addition to frequently being denied the right to family, including the right to have children, both girls and women with disabilities are regularly denied access to basic services such as health services, in particular sexual and reproductive ones. The stereotype of asexuality of persons with disabilities, however, does not mean that women with disabilities are saved from rape and other forms of sexual violence, exploitation, and abuse. On the contrary: as if the stereotype were nonexistent, women with disabilities are frequently subjected to sexual violence and abuse, including rape.[6]

Importantly, girls and women with disabilities are more in need of sex education in order to protect themselves against the various forms of violence, exploitation, and abuse.

Implications of the Gender Perspective

The gender perspective is essential to eradicate gender-based discrimination at the most fundamental levels, not just a demand to pay extra attention to the special desires of women with disabilities. Unlike biological sex, gender identity is a social quality, a code, with wide-ranging implications. In the human rights context at the international level "gender" has been used in place of the term "sex" since the Fourth World Conference on Women in Beijing in 1995.

Gender connotes a wide set of characteristics, ranging from the biological sex to the social role as well as the identity determined by gender, all of which are intertwined with the roles constructed within society and differences emerging from that (non)distinction. In Korean, for example, "gender" and "sex" are both translated as "sexuality." While sex is more associated with sexual desire, gender indicates difference of sexuality apart from sexual desire. In English, and as is widely used in many countries including the European Union and the United States, in contrast, the distinction differs: the concept of "gender" implies the achievement of gender equality, rather than biological sex. Moreover, the gender perspective implies the assessment based on a female and a male perspective. Given the marginalization based on the attribution of impairment or disability respectively, the gender aspect has to be added to understand the structural and institutional exclusion girls and women with disabilities face and to pave the way for inclusion and equal participation.

Disability and Women: Intersectional Discrimination

It is indeed not enough to describe the gender inequality of women with disabilities as simply a problem within the disability community. The "disability" surrounding women with disabilities—facing social barriers due to impairments—intersects with gender inequality and, therefore, produces a more severe form of discrimination. In order to understand the situation of women with disabilities better, understanding the gender perspective as well as disability is paramount. It does not just mean adding a "disability" factor to a "gender" factor; rather, it is a distinct and far more complex form of discrimination, which is more difficult to overcome. Therefore, disability or gender should not be used as a category to separate the experiences of women with disabilities; rather, they should be understood as a compounded form of discrimination. Furthermore, considering that the concept of a so-called "normal" and "complete" human being originates from physical, mental, and social suppression, women with disabilities often also suffer discrimination from nondisabled women. Disability thus becomes a necessary prerequisite of any suppression.

EXCURSUS: WOMEN AS MAIN CAREGIVERS OF PERSONS WITH DISABILITIES

Discussing gender and disabilities requires a brief side step: If a member of your family has an impairment or disability, the role of caregiver is usually assigned to the women in the immediate family. The concerns of these women have not been taken up adequately anywhere—neither in the disability nor in the women's movement.[7] My mother, for example, has borne a heavy burden for forty-two years since I got poliomyelitis when eleven months old. Her whole life has been devoted to my survival and development. She has basically lived as a woman with disabilities, just like me. One may also note that many women who have a child with disabilities suffer under misconceptions derived from superstition, sorcery, and related "beliefs." Frequently, mothers of children with disabilities are assumed to have some sort of "defect," and in many cases they face physical and mental violence in their families.

Most of the people working in the social service industry, "caring" for the aged and persons with disabilities—in place of family members—are women. They are asked to work hard for low pay. In developed countries, jobs related to persons with disabilities are often done by immigrant women who have few other options and as a result suffer from unfair treatment. Therefore, the interests—and therewith rights—of women as primary caretakers have to be part of a holistic assessment of the situation of persons with disabilities.

The First Steps Toward Highlighting the Rights and Needs of Women with Disabilities

As in most areas of society, persons with disabilities, including women with disabilities, have been largely absent from mainstream human rights discourse.[8] The Convention on the Elimination of All Forms of Discrimination against Women—despite being a milestone on gender equality upon its adoption in 1979—was no exception to the invisibility of women with disabilities in mainstream human rights in that it did not address issues of women with disabilities. Undoubtedly, since women with disabilities are also women their rights are legally protected by the treaty, which protects "all" women. However, with no specific mention in CEDAW, women with disabilities have also not been on the receiving end of the benefits generated by its related policies.

In the years after CEDAW was adopted, the pertinent committee established under the treaty started to highlight the absence of national action plans on gender equality in many countries, requesting modification of laws that contradict human rights and urging governments to increase efforts in enhancing the rights of women with disabilities. However, references to women with disabilities in the reports of states parties remained scarce to nonexistent.[9] While one could reasonably argue that the absence of women with disabilities from these provisions is to be expected, given that it is unusual to refer to interest groups in the context of international law, CEDAW does have a provision that specifically refers to rural women. Thus, each government reports on the reality of women in rural areas on a regular basis. Leaders of women with disabilities hoped that a disability rights treaty might similarly require governments to report on the status of women with disabilities within their borders. It was held that without a provision that explicitly defines the responsibility of each government in terms of women with disabilities, it would be difficult to make claims for action.

The UN Third World Conference on Women in Nairobi (1985), which reviewed the achievements of the UN Decade for Women,[10] highlighted the situation of women with physical and mental disabilities. The Conference Report observed that the "human dignity and human rights and the full participation by disabled persons in society is still limited, and this presents additional problems for women who may have domestic and other responsibilities."[11] It also demanded that "opportunities for the participation of such women in all aspects of life should be provided."[12]

Picking up on these demands, the CEDAW Committee in 1991 reflected on the reports it had received from more than sixty states parties, noting that they provided "scarce information on disabled women." In turn the Committee recommended that information on women with disabilities be provided in periodic reports as it was "concerned about the situation of disabled women, who suffer from a double discrimination linked to their special living conditions."[13]

The above-mentioned 1994 General Comment by the CESCR,[14] which focused on persons with disabilities, highlighted the need for dramatically increased attention to the exclusion of persons with disabilities generally, and emphasized the need for upholding gender equality. Starting from the notion that persons with disabilities are frequently perceived as "genderless human beings," the Comment underscored the "double discrimination suffered by women with disabilities," which is often neglected. The Committee urged states to make the inclusion of women with disabilities a high priority.

The UN member states, in adopting the Standard Rules in 1993, concluded: "special attention should be given to women and children with disabilities."[15] The Declaration on the Elimination of Violence Against Women, adopted that year, highlights the special vulnerability of women with disabilities to violence among "women belonging to minority groups, indigenous women, refugee women, migrant women, women living in rural or remote communities, destitute women, women in institutions or in detention, female children, elderly women, and women in situations of armed conflict."[16]

The Convention on the Rights of Persons with Disabilities Negotiations

Following the third session of the Ad Hoc Committee, the delegation of the Republic of Korea submitted a proposal to include a specific article on women with disabilities, as gender equality is a priority issue at both the national and international levels. The proposal called for a separate reference to the rights of women with disabilities, data collection disaggregated by gender, policies and programs for the reproductive needs of women with disabilities, access to the right to work for women with disabilities, and protections from sexual exploitation, abuse, and violence.[17] In putting forward this proposal, the Korean delegation stated that "The plight of women with disabilities is not simply the sum of the barriers faced by persons with disabilities and the barriers faced by women; it goes beyond to utter neglect. . . . The aim of the AHC should be to lift women with disabilities out of invisibility."[18]

This proposal, together with a specific article on children with disabilities,[19] quickly turned into a hot potato. On the proposed reference to women with disabilities, every government extensively acknowledged that women with disabilities face difficulties and multiple, complex discrimination that places them on the bottom tier of the society. Those governments also agreed that the human rights of women with disabilities should be vastly improved. However, the way to include the issues of women with disabilities within the CRPD, especially the demand that there should be a single, specific article, caused a heated dispute among delegations.

The Key Issue: Twin-Track or Mainstreaming?

If women and girls with disabilities were to be explicitly included in the Convention, how should this be done? Those who saw merit in making a specific reference to issues of gender quickly settled into a debate of whether to mention gender-related aspects throughout the text or to have one stand-alone provision highlighting the need for increased attention to gender-related issues. The two concepts are referred to as mainstreaming and twin-track respectively.

Mainstreaming a gender perspective denotes that men and women's concerns will be addressed simultaneously, a strategy that aims to end the perpetuation of gender inequality.[20]

First introduced to UN commitments at the Third World Conference in Nairobi in 1985, the concept originates in the social development of the community. It was later formally introduced at the Fourth World Conference of Women in Beijing (1995). In addressing the issue of education, for example, the Report of the Conference notes that a policy of mainstreaming a gender perspective into all policies and programs should be promoted, "so that, before decisions are taken, an analysis is made of the effects on women and men, respectively."[21]

The AHC discussed the possibility of mainstreaming, particularly in light of the growing experience with gender mainstreaming, which has had a positive impact on a range of policies and programs, effectively enhancing equality between women and men. Mainstreaming policies, particularly those with a focus on gender, are utilized by many European states. Therefore, the European Union particularly favored an approach that would resemble its mainstreaming efforts in the gender realm—although its support was not straightforward.

The twin-track approach, on the other hand, recommended the combination of a specific article, focusing on equality of women with disabilities, and specific references to women's issues in various relevant articles of the Convention: one track of action and legislation would focus on the particular needs through a stand-alone provision, whereas the other would seek to highlight the needs throughout the Convention by way of mainstreaming.

The aim was thus to have a stand-alone provision on women with disabilities but to also include specific references throughout the Convention text, wherever appropriate.

The Emergence of a Stand-Alone Provision

Following Korea's proposal at the third AHC session, the discussion of the pros and cons of a provision on women and girls with disabilities and gender started to grow; the debate over mainstreaming the issue or following the twin-track approach grew in equal measure.

Opposition to the provision was originally comparatively large and included the EU, New Zealand, Australia, Serbia (and Montenegro), Mexico, Japan, Norway, and Jordan, mainly based on the inadequacy of the proposed wording. Additionally, the debate was conjoined with the debate over children with disabilities: in a stereotypical nod to patriarchal patterns, women and children were conflated issues. While there were some overlaps in the arguments made in favor of a specific provision, there were clearly separate reasons underlying the need for specific regulation.

After it became clear that gender and women would have to be addressed in one way or the other, the arguments became more nuanced. Three main reasons were provided in opposition to a specific provision on women and gender. (1) No group should be singled out due to the risk of creating further demand for special mentions, a stern warning that becoming too specific would increase the likelihood of leaving someone or something out. (2) A specific reference would, some—mainly the EU—contended, weaken the overall text and distract from broad and general provisions, such as the ones on violence and abuse. The UK delegation—which held the presidency of the EU at the time—warned of a risk that men with disabilities would face increased vulnerability if a provision on women with disabilities were introduced. (3) It would create uncertainty vis-à-vis the provisions in CEDAW. The final argument failed to acknowledge that impairment and disability, respectively, are not featured in CEDAW. The EU made a counterproposal, suggesting a cross-cutting provision as part of the CRPD general obligations (Article 4) and in the Preamble.[22] Furthermore, it was held that it would be impossible to cover the necessary ground in just one provision. This, it was held, would subsequently lead to limitations in protecting the human rights of women with disabilities. While similar objections were made vis-à-vis the provision on children with disabilities, the women's caucus of IDC underscored the importance of separating the concerns of women and children.[23]

The chair of the sixth AHC, Don MacKay of New Zealand, appointed Theresia Degener, a woman with disabilities, a scholar of international human rights law, and a delegate for the Federal Republic of Germany, to effectively draw an agreement in deciding the specific article controversy. He additionally demanded that Degener find a compromise that would adequately reflect the opinions of the IDC women's caucus. Degener in response to this turned to governments and civil society. She listened carefully to the arguments put forward by the women's caucus, which was formed within the IDC. She set out to mediate between countries, led by the European nations, which opposed the specific article of women with disabilities issues and those in favor, such as the Republic of Korea and many other Third World countries.

Countries that favored a specific article for women with disabilities, including the Republic of Korea, emphasized that a specific article would allow each country to clearly and actively solve the problems plaguing women with disabilities. As mentioned above, there are specific articles in other international conventions for women living in rural areas (Article 14, CEDAW) and for children with disabilities (Article 23, CRC), as well as provisions in International Labour Organization conventions. Judging from this, it seemed only logical to have a specific article for women with disabilities. Canada used the twin-track approach, highlighting the need to include a specific mention of women with disabilities in the articles on equality, freedom from violence and abuse, home and family, education, right to health, right to habilitation and rehabilitation, and right to work.

In the midst of heated debate between governments and nongovernmental organizations, among governments, and between and among NGOs as well, people began to propose mediation, where women with disabilities issues would form part of the general principles and the provision on monitoring. Surprisingly, arguments were also flying high among many NGOs and among the women leaders with disabilities throughout the world. Some believed that issues related to women with disabilities should be mainstreamed into all sections within the Convention; others believed that it was extremely important to have a single specific article for women with disabilities. However, NGOs unanimously agreed that, whether it is in the form of "mainstreaming" or a specific article, it was imperative to note all requirements for women with disabilities in the Convention. This stood in dramatic contrast to some governmental delegations, which strongly objected to including issues of women with disabilities in a stand-alone provision.

Ultimately the twin-track approach on gender was supported by representatives of DPOs. However, the women's caucus was determined to include particular issues of women with disabilities to ensure that the issues of women with disabilities would not be overlooked.

At the seventh AHC session the IDC made a proposal for the stand-alone provision to require states parties to (1) "eliminate the multiple and intersectional discriminations of women and girls with disabilities" and "take gender-specific measures" in insuring rights for persons with disabilities, and (2) "implement the obligations set forth in this Convention with a gender perspective in mind." The specific measures discussed in this latter requirement paired the concerns initially outlined in the Korean delegation's proposal with a call for states to develop "national mainstreamed policies and programs" pertaining to women with disabilities.[24]

The women's caucus along with the IDC was particularly opposed to the argument that it would be creating "groups," a notion that hardly applies to more than half of the world's population. The IDC also stressed that the discussion should not refer to "women's issues" but rather include the concept of gender. The national human rights institutions highlighted the need to specifically include women with disabilities in provisions on data and statistics, as well as on monitoring.

Health Services (Article 25)

A discussion of women with disabilities and gender in the AHC would be incomplete without referring to the debate on reproductive rights in the context of the provision on health-care services. The need for access to "sexual and reproductive health services" was a highly contentious issue. Insinuating that an overt reference to sexual and reproductive health services would equate to legalizing abortion in international law, some delegations as well as NGOs vehemently opposed the language. The Holy See, which has observer status at the UN, had particularly objected to any explicit reference to sexual and reproductive health.[25] However, given that persons with disabilities face particular stigma and discrimination in the area of health services, the language was deemed essential.

Indeed, persons with disabilities are frequently denied the rights to reproduce solely on the basis of their disabilities. Women with disabilities, in particular, frequently have no access to basic medical services and support in the course of their pregnancy. This makes Article 25 a particularly important provision. The fact that the right of women with disabilities to reproduce is acknowledged implies more than unhindered access to medical services: it codifies the right to exist as human beings on an equal basis with others, to reproduce, and to bring up children.

Sexual Orientation

There was also a debate over whether to explicitly mention "sexual orientation" as grounds for discrimination. EU delegates repeatedly spoke out in favor of such recognition. However, the debate ran into too much opposition, and ultimately, the grounds of discrimination listed in the CRPD (Preamble, para. (p)) does not include an explicit reference to discrimination on the basis of sexual orientation.

Strategies

A critical factor in the successful campaign for a stand-alone provision on women with disabilities was the support by the Republic of Korea. Its delegation's proposal jump-started the discussion at a high level. Having a member on the delegation who was also a member of the NGO community was instrumental in bridging the discussion between the delegation and civil society, allowing us to coordinate strategies and arguments.

Within the NGO community, the IDC served as the main base; a subgroup, the women's caucus, was created to focus on the issues of gender and particularly women with disabilities in the discussions, also inside the IDC but much more so in the AHC itself. The women's caucus employed a number of strategies: in coordinated and concerted efforts proposals were made and shared with friendly delegations. Through regular meetings, potentially objecting delegations were identified and bilateral meetings were arranged. The IDC's manifold outlets, among them the newsletter of IDC[26] and the IDC Women's Update,[27] were put to good use. Caucus members, for example Disabled People's International, put out background notes as well.[28]

At the end of the sixth AHC it was concluded that it would, in fact, be necessary for the Convention to explicitly include the principle of gender equality, and that the Convention needed to simultaneously address the situation of women with disabilities.[29] To build further and find a solution to the question through a stand-alone provision or mainstreaming,[30] it was helpful to have a facilitator—Theresia Degener—assigned to the issue. Having a facilitated provision meant a certain amount of space was officially allocated to the Article: the facilitator, in addition to holding regular meetings focused on the draft provision, had to regularly report back to the plenary, thus bringing attention to the issue at regular intervals.

The Outcome

In the end, the twin-track approach prevailed. In addition to the stand-alone provision there are various references to women with disabilities and gender-specific needs throughout the text of the Convention. The success has many "mothers," particularly among the hidden sisters: lobbying efforts both inside the AHC and to diplomats in governments all over the world were crucial to achieving this result.

The official term used in the CRPD is "women with disabilities." How, then, do we reflect the perspective of and content of gender (as opposed to sex) throughout the Convention? It was true that the very term that describes women with disabilities is not significantly important. Generally, when we focus on sexual characteristics of women, "gender" has replaced "sex" since the Beijing Conference. In fact, the term "gender perspective" was widely used in order to reflect the advanced feminist perspective and social perspectives of women with disabilities within the major articles related to women with disabilities as a result of the sixth AHC. During the eighth AHC, however, Arabic and African countries mounted strong objections. The use of "gender" in those countries would cause great sociocultural controversy over Islamic family laws and/or religion laws, which forces them to reserve the articles related to women with disabilities. Therefore, the term was completely dropped from Article 6.

The twin-track approach is spelled out in the CRPD as described below.

Preamble

The Convention's Preamble has various references to the issue of women with disabilities. Importantly, it highlights the impact of multiple forms of discrimination (Preamble (p)). The clause acknowledges the pile-up of various grounds of exclusion, which add to the exclusion based on impairment; importantly in conjunction with discrimination based on sex or gender. Previously, the concept of multiple discrimination has only been used in the 1995 Beijing Declaration, which refers to "women and girls who face multiple barriers to their empowerment and advancement because of such factors as their race, age, language, ethnicity, culture, religion, or disability, or because they are indigenous people."[31] This Declaration additionally included the concept of "aggravated" forms of discrimination, which connotes the fact that impairments/disabilities often lead to structural discrimination, which in turn perpetuates a cycle of exclusion, disabling persons with disabilities further and sustaining that cycle rather than breaking it.[32] Given its unique nature in a core human rights treaty, the provision holds particular potential for ensuring human rights well beyond the realm of disabilities.

The Preamble also highlights the increased risk of women and girls with disabilities in exposure to various forms of violence (Preamble (q)). The concept of mainstreaming a gender perspective is additionally reflected as part of efforts to "promote the full enjoyment of human rights and fundamental freedoms by persons with disabilities" (Preamble (s)). The discussion about the role of the family was concluded with a compromise reference to "protection and assistance" for families (Preamble (x)), but that did not include an explicit reference to the role of caretakers.[33]

General Principle (Article 3)

The general principles in Article 3 include "equality between men and women" (Article 3(g)).

Equality (Article 5)

The provision on equality and nondiscrimination, enshrined in Article 5, contains a general nondiscrimination clause recognizing that "all persons are equal before and under the law and are entitled without any discrimination to the equal protection and equal benefit of the law."

Women and Girls with Disabilities (Article 6)

The stand-alone provision on women and girls with disabilities is enshrined in Article 6:

1. States Parties recognize that women and girls with disabilities are subject to multiple discrimination, and in this regard shall take measures to ensure the full and equal enjoyment by them of all human rights and fundamental freedoms.
2. States Parties shall take all appropriate measures to ensure the full development, advancement and empowerment of women, for the purpose of guaranteeing them the exercise and enjoyment of the human rights and fundamental freedoms set out in the present Convention.

The final text is similar to that of Articles 1 and 2 of CEDAW, reflecting the last-minute compromise avoiding any unintended consequences for either this provision or the scope of CEDAW respectively. As in the Preamble, "multiple discrimination" is featured as part of the provision, reflecting the reality of women with disabilities who face multiple forms of exclusion.

Freedom from Exploitation (Article 16)

Article 16 acknowledges the need to protect persons with disabilities from violence and abuse both inside and outside the home and highlights the "gender-based aspects" of such human rights violations (Article 16(1)). Among the measures foreseen to prevent all forms of exploitation, violence, and abuse is also "gender- and age-sensitive assistance," including "information and education on how to avoid, recognize, and report instances of exploitation, violence, and abuse" (Article 16(2)). Also, "gender- and age-specific needs" are to be part of any recovery and rehabilitation measure for victims of violence and abuse. Finally, the provision calls for effective legislation and policies, to include such that are "women- and child-focused" (Article 16(5)).

Health Services (Article 25)

Article 25 pays tribute to what the CEDAW Committee referred to as the "societal factors that are determinative of the health status of women and men and can vary among women themselves, e.g., age, ethnicity, and migration status."[34] It therefore highlights the need for "gender-sensitive health services."

Social Protection (Article 28)

As a result of intersectional discrimination on the grounds of disability and gender, women with disabilities universally occupy the bottom rung of socio-economic status. In response to this sad reality, the CRPD "ensures access by persons with disabilities, in particular women and girls with disabilities and older persons with disabilities, to social protection programs and poverty reduction programs" (Article 28(2)(a)).

International Monitoring Body (Article 34)

Finally, the Convention demands that each state party that nominates a member for the International Monitoring Committee shall take gender balance into account (Article 34(4)). Gender balance derives from the gender perspective, but it is worth asking whether improving the gender balance automatically impacts the self-representation of women with disabilities. When women with disabilities are involved in the process of reporting and evaluating each government in terms of its performance of treaty obligations, they will be more likely to develop appropriate measures to ensure full personal development of women with disabilities. Therefore, the desirable way to advance the human rights of women with disabilities and to ban discrimination based on disability and gender is for women with disabilities to actively participate in the International Monitoring Committee that reviews the issues related to women with disabilities. Their self-representation goes beyond drawing a gender balance.

The Road Ahead

Since women and girls with disabilities are more likely to be exposed to all kinds of dangers such as violence and exploitation, and to be excluded from social or daily life, it is necessary to impose gender-conscious disability policies, programs, and laws to improve the situation and status of persons with disabilities. This effort is well summarized in Article 8 on awareness raising, emphasizing that each government should undertake to adopt immediate, effective, and appropriate measures to combat stereotypes, prejudices, and harmful practices relating to persons with disabilities. Stereotypes, prejudices, and harmful practices relating to women with disabilities are the result of multiple discrimination on grounds of "disabilities" and "gender," suggesting the need for further study about the customs of each society.

The CRPD marks a turning point from vague discussion of the issues of persons with disabilities to the point where the differential treatment between men with disabilities and women with disabilities is clearly recognized, gender equality is acknowledged as essential to human development, a gender perspective is required in all disability-related legal, systemic, and political measurements, the multiple discrimination that women with disabilities suffer is described, and a specific article to correct the mistreatment is included. In this sense, the Convention functions as a stepping stone for the establishment of dignity for women with disabilities, improvement of their human rights, and eradication of discrimination. In terms of sexuality, the Convention also shows the rise of "gender" since the Beijing Conference.

This resulting document is the product of tight networks and the struggle of women with disabilities, who rose above their personal problems to fight against the ill-proclaimed political situation through two big human rights movements: one with disability, the other with gender. The sisterhood of women with disabilities extends beyond borders as women with disabilities converged from every part of the world. However, this is just the beginning. Living in a male-dominated world in which women with disabilities are abhorred and, in many countries, regarded as worthless losers, the day when women with disabilities enjoy their rights and live free from all kinds of discrimination and suppression will surely come only when women with disabilities speak up for themselves to ensure that each government meets its treaty obligations. After all, women with disabilities are, as they have been, important parts of our history with great responsibilities.

CHAPTER 8

Including Deaf Culture
and Linguistic Rights

Liisa Kauppinen and Markku Jokinen

The World Federation of the Deaf is an international, nongovernmental umbrella organization, comprising 133 national associations of deaf people and representing approximately 70 million deaf around the world. The philosophy of the WFD is one of equality, human rights, and respect for all people, with a focus on deaf people who use sign language and their friends and families.[1]

Over the years, the WFD has witnessed discrimination against deaf people in all aspects of their lives. Most disheartening was the banning of sign languages in various countries and institutions and, as a consequence, the great weakening of the communication possibilities of the deaf. Subsequently, the difficulties deaf children and adults have experienced in educational settings and beyond have increased, and the availability of employment opportunities has been significantly reduced. Over 90 percent of deaf children who live in developing countries do not have any chance to receive basic education. Very few deaf children all over the world are able to enjoy a bilingual and bicultural education approach.[2] This has also had the effect that neither linguistic nor human rights have been realized in the lives of the deaf.

It is for this reason that the WFD was among those at the forefront when the process of drafting the Convention on the Rights of Persons with Disabilities began.

WFD Involvement at the United Nations

WFD participated in two important meetings early in the 2002 Convention process: the UN panel of experts and an expert meeting arranged by the Mexican government to consider a proposal for the first Ad Hoc Committee session. In fact, along with government representatives and other UN specialized agencies, the WFD was invited to participate as one of the seven largest disabled people's organizations composing the International Disability Alliance.[3] It was rather disappointing, however, to review the first draft Mexico had prepared, particularly because it had no reference to sign language(s). While perhaps well intended, from the point of view of DPOs it was much weaker than existing instruments. For instance, sign language was mentioned in the 1993 Standard Rules, but not at all in the proposed text. Furthermore, the proposed text was drafted as a social declaration and not a document that resembled any existing international human rights treaties.

A revised draft was, therefore, prepared during the meeting to be further developed at the first AHC session. However, the path for the discussion on this new text, contrary to expectations, was not straightforward. As political power was at stake, Mexico (which viewed itself as the lead state in the discussion on disability rights) again put forward its own draft, prepared for the initial expert meeting rather than the updated text proposal. Following the outcry from DPOs and several government parties, however, the AHC decided to establish a Working Group to develop a working text—a draft that was the basis for negotiations in all subsequent AHC sessions.

This initial experience strengthened the sense that participation of persons with disabilities in the drafting process would be critical if any substantive results were to be achieved. Thus, the WFD remained an active participant through the rest of the process as well.

Nonnegotiable Key Points

While the WFD has been involved in drafting many provisions in the CRPD, the input has been particularly imperative in the promotion of sign language. As the main WDF goal was related to the recognition of deaf people's linguistic rights, the key points were to negotiate explicit recognition for sign language(s) and to ensure its use in communication, access to information, and education throughout life. Furthermore, strong recognition and acceptance of deaf people's linguistic identity, Deaf culture, and the necessity of interpreter services were important.

Indeed, although sign languages were included in all the drafts throughout the process, a careful follow-up was necessary as many attempts were made to remove explicit reference to recognition of sign language(s). The reasons given for these ongoing efforts varied. Many state representatives found it extremely difficult to understand sign languages as natural languages, leading to efforts to omit sign language from the definition of "language" in Article 2 CRPD. The EU, Japan, and some other countries opposed the view that sign languages should be seen as separate, independent, alternative national *languages* with cultural heritage. They suggested instead that they should be viewed merely as "modes of communication."[4]

Such attitudes, however, fail to understand Deaf culture, the concept of sign languages, and how critically important these are to one's social and psychological development. The Deaf community is a tightly knit cultural group with a distinctive shared history, culture, and tradition.[5] It is a conceptual framework of the Deaf world and the Deaf community—one that can be observable and that creates and strengthens one's sense of belonging. The Deaf community should be viewed as a cultural and linguistic minority group whose rights need to be protected. In this regard, then, if equality and nondiscrimination provisions in human rights treaties have any meaning—and all the more so the prohibition of discrimination in the context of the CRPD—it is exactly by ensuring the linguistic and cultural rights of Deaf people. The explicit mentioning of Deaf culture and sign languages thus does not "unjustly" single out particular types of disabilities. Rather, the years of subordination experienced by deaf people and the efforts in some states to eradicate Deaf culture, including the banning of sign language, are evidence of the merit and need for its special protection.

Sign languages have often been misunderstood and subject to prejudice. First, sign languages have a history that precedes spoken language, and they are no different from any other language, save their modality. Sign languages have developed spontaneously among people all across the world who use them for communication, sharing information, discussion about abstract and scientific matters, and telling stories and jokes. Just like spoken languages, sign languages have a structure with grammar rules that allow creation of sentences, signs, and even smaller units. The main difference is in modalities, as sign languages are visual-gesture-(tactual) oriented, consisting of sequences of movements and configurations of the entire body: face, hands, arms, and upper torso. And while there is no single international sign language that would apply to all, the universal features of all sign languages make it possible for people who use different sign languages to communicate with, and to understand, one another. Thus, contrary to suggestions that sign language is pantomime or a simple gesture code that represents the surrounding of spoken languages, sign languages are a visual-gesture-(tactual) (sign) medium that is biologically normal and universal.[6]

Yet another point needs stressing in regard to sign language. When compared to other groups of persons with disabilities, deaf people can potentially be physically present in all situations—home, school, service, and so forth. However, without sign language interpretation they are excluded from the provision of information and education and deprived of social interaction. For deaf children, then, inclusion means growing up with their own language and culture to become bilingual and bicultural members of society.

For this reason the WFD had also taken on itself from early on to promote the "right to be different." The proposal to include it in the CRPD emerged first during the WG (and was debated throughout the AHC sessions). It received support from the leading NGOs and some states, particularly Thailand. The proposal aimed at ensuring two things. First, a positive acclamation/affirmation of differences: not only a passive respect, an abstract value of diversity, but also *acceptance* in abolishing attempts to correct persons with disabilities. Second, the proposal to include an explicit "right to be different" establishes a requirement that states *provide* for the appropriate accommodation of measures for such diversity. The social and cultural aspect of diversity was also stressed as it allows persons with disabilities to carry out their lives without a social requirement to assimilate into the "mainstream" culture; if so, it should be of their own choosing, and thus an integral part of *human dignity*. In the context of deaf people, the proposal meant to ensure an entitlement to recognition and support of our specific culture and linguistic identities. Ultimately, the point was made. While some states expressed concern about what they viewed as creating a "new" or "extended" right, the issue was eventually stated as a fundamental principle of the Convention in a manner that captures both respect and acceptance of disability as part of human diversity and humanity, albeit not as a separate "right to be different."[7]

Another prejudice that required a response was the negative attitudes expressed against the explicit reference to sign languages in the Convention. As discussed above, the importance of sign language and deficiencies created by its absence were largely ignored. Linguistic development and appropriate education are essential to any child's development. They allow personal expression and comprehension of abstract concepts and shape one's relationships, experiences, values, and morals.[8] Studies have also clearly shown that linguistic communication is strongly connected with intelligence and cognitive abilities, as language *of whatever sort* is of extreme importance for development of full intellectual capacities.[9] Thus, language acquisition is considered to be a necessity to personal development and full participation in social life.

In this regard, the debate about the right to education (Article 24) was critical. The discussion arose in a few contexts, particularly on what discrimination against persons with disabilities and deaf people would entail, and with regard to the separate provision on education. There was a general agreement on states' responsibility to abolish discriminatory practices, including obligating them to "reasonably accommodate" persons with disabilities and to adopt special measures (affirmative action) to guarantee full enjoyment of human rights and freedoms (Articles 2, 5(3), 5(4), CRPD). The exact meaning of the concept, however, was controversial among state delegates, in state-NGO discussions, and in the International Disability Caucus itself. From the WFD perspective, the notion of reasonable accommodation, which generally aims at providing persons with disabilities the measures that would place them in line with "nondisabled" persons, must also include two other aspects. It must include an *individualized/personalized* accommodation, that is, adjustments to the type of disability/impairment (for example, accessibility of wheelchairs, availability of documentation in Braille, communication using sign language, computerized programs for deaf-blind); and the accommodation also must include adjustments that are *context specific* (education, workplace, housing, and so on).

With regard to education, disagreements arose as to whether the general education system should be considered preferable to "special education" models. Both states and NGO representatives could be found on either side of the argument. Opponents of special education argued that the child should have a right to choose which educational institutions to attend and that preference for the general education system is in line with the Convention's goal of mainstreaming disability. The toughest opposing parties were found among DPOs, mostly among wheelchair users and organizations for persons with intellectual disabilities, but other good and loyal allies (organizations of blind and deafblind) within IDC supported the efforts of the WFD. State delegates also spoke mostly about the importance of inclusion and inclusive education, but in fact most of them found it hard to understand the diverse needs of different groups of persons with disabilities. Indeed, such a policy does not properly take into account the needs—and rights—of deaf people.

For one thing, one needs to consider the practical ability to provide appropriate "reasonable accommodation" *within* the general educational system.[10] The availability of interpreters, Braille and other modes and means, as well as relevant technological methods of communication is essential to ensure inclusion of children with disabilities—yet these kinds of measures do not guarantee full participation and accessibility for deaf children in all educational situations. If there is one deaf child with a sign language interpreter in a classroom with other children and a teacher who does not know the child's sign language, there will always be several places (corridors, toilets, showers, and so on) and situations (lunch breaks) where there is no communication in sign language. Additionally, free and fluent use of language in direct face-to-face communication is hard to achieve if other children do not use sign language with the deaf student fluently.

Second, greater understanding of the notion of reasonable accommodation in the context of education of deaf people is essential. Specifically, it should be interpreted to include an array of measures that would assist to achieve full inclusion: for example, sign language interpreting service, note-taking services, a chance to study with other deaf students, and bilingual learning materials when deaf students study in mainstream settings. Moreover, for the education system for deaf children to be accessible and constructive, it has to provide a learning environment in which teachers and students know sign language very well (native language level), where sign language is used as a language of instruction in parallel with written language, where students follow bilingual education principles and can use bilingual learning materials, and where they study sign language as a school subject.

Third, it is important to explain to everyone that education of the deaf is not special education but education in one's own language and culture. It is an environment where hearing students can be mainstreamed (reverse mainstream)—notably, the value of sign languages goes beyond deaf people. While it is the first language or mother tongue of about seventy million deaf people around the world, it is also used by many hearing people, such as hearing children of deaf parents and some deafblind who use tactile sign languages. The educational environment envisioned by the WFD is inclusive of both deaf and hearing students. Simultaneously, when deaf students have special education needs, both the bilingual approach and special-education methods have to be used.

Put differently, WFD's goal is societal inclusion, whereby inclusion is not the means but the goal of a society that is open to everyone. Furthermore, as inclusion for deaf children is actualized when they have connection to both spoken and sign languages and cultures, WFD's aim is bilingualism or multilingualism with sign language and Deaf culture.

In light of these reasons, the WFD has put great efforts into including a concept of bilingual and bicultural educational approach in Article 24, and it has drafted, advocated for, and sought to incorporate specific text proposals in this regard into the article on education. During the third AHC session in September 2004, for example, the WFD submitted its comments concerning draft Article 17 (now 24) on education, proposing that the following paragraph would be added:

> Deaf children have the right to receive education in their own groups and to become bilingual in sign-language and their national spoken and written language. They also have the right to learn additional foreign languages, both signed and spoken/written. Each state Party shall take legislative, administrative, political and other measures needed to provide quality education using sign-language, by ensuring the employment of Deaf teachers and also hearing teachers who are fluent in sign-language.[11]

In the fifth AHC session in February 2005, the WFD further proposed additional paragraphs in regard to education stipulating that states parties shall ensure that the educational system aims to "(3a) provide a meaningful and productive education on an equal basis that furthers and fulfils their educational and professional aspirations" and to "(3f) recognize and support individual learning needs of persons with disabilities with provisions of reasonable accommodation and auxiliary aids." The WFD also proposed additions to subparagraph 4, so it would read:

States Parties shall ensure that all girls, boys, young people, women and men with disabilities have full access to inclusive education in their own community *in the language of their own choice in terms of delivery of education information*, including by ensuring the provision of

(g) *Bilingual and/or* multilingual education in sign-language for deaf and deafblind students through deaf and hearing teachers who are *bilingually* fluent in *languages of instruction*, sign-language and *languages of their country*, including the right to choose education in their own groups during primary education, consistent with other provisions in this article.[12]

These proposals did not make it to the final text of the conventions, however, perhaps because our points were not properly understood or because the text proposals were too detailed. Or perhaps the legal language of a treaty required that all the needs of the blind, deaf, and deafblind are stipulated in general phrases. It was indeed the result of Article 24, and ultimately, the WFD had to be satisfied with "compromise sentences," for example, in paragraph 3, which states that "States Parties shall enable persons with disabilities to learn life and social development skills to facilitate their full and equal participation in education and as members of the community," and in subparagraph 3(c), which includes among the "appropriate measures" states are expected to take for this goal, "Ensuring that the education of persons, and in particular children, who are blind, deaf or deafblind, is delivered in the most appropriate languages and modes and means of communication for the individual, and in environments which maximize academic and social development."

Finally, as emphasized earlier, deaf people have a right to preserve their cultural and linguistic identity—a right that is hard to maintain within the general education system without a bilingual educational approach where the language of instruction is a sign language used in parallel with a written language, where everyone uses sign language fluently, and where there are students who have a similar linguistic and cultural identity. Bearing in mind that deaf children have a natural grasp of sign language as an alternative visual-gesture mode of communication,[13] and that other forms of spoken communication may not be possible, it becomes clear why sign language and Deaf culture hold such importance if one seriously thinks about human rights, education, and development for all. Simply stated, one's realization of human rights can only be made through one's own language and culture. For all these reasons, persuading whoever needed persuasion that Deaf culture, sign languages, and educational forums that allow acquisition of both are not a luxury but an urgent need—more than that, a *right*—was a priority of our efforts.

Persuading the Unpersuadable

To overcome the above-mentioned objections and to secure the inclusion of sign languages and Deaf culture in the CRPD, the WFD took a multiple-approach strategy. First, the WFD provided proposals, amendments, and additions to the articles that were discussed whenever it deemed it necessary. "Mainstreaming" the needs—and rights—of deaf people as much as possible throughout the Convention was crucial to ensure that all aspects were addressed both generally, along with the needs of all persons with disabilities, as well as more specifically, along with the particular sensitivities and needs of deaf people. For this purpose, references to all existing international human rights instruments, especially antidiscrimination provisions that prohibit discrimination on the basis of language as well as those promoting everyone's right to his or her own language or culture, were essential. Participation in the meetings of the facilitators of the relevant articles was a key requirement. It provided a forum to raise our concerns in a more intimate environment, which also provided space for a more nuanced discussion during evening receptions and meeting breaks, lunches and dinners, and in multilateral or bilateral meetings.

Second, and relatedly, producing and distributing material on sign languages, Deaf culture, and the effects of banning sign languages was important. As mentioned above, there was a great need in overcoming stigma and prejudice, changing the majority view that sign language is "abnormal"—and all the more important—prevailing over the notion that sign languages are mere modes of communication that can be substituted, changed, and eradicated. Indeed, if one's identity has any meaning, it can only be in relation to one's culture, community, and ways of living; for deaf people (and many others), it inherently means Deaf culture and sign languages.

A third form of engagement that was utilized to advance the key non-negotiable points was arranging a side event on sign languages. This event attracted much attention: the room was full of participants, with many state delegates and some DPOs taking part. Our central points were recognition of sign languages and facilitating their use in national legislations. The representatives from Uganda, Costa Rica, and South Africa presented invaluable examples in this regard. The side event certainly had a positive impact, and it became evident, as after it, the cooperation with state delegates became closer and more active. They helped us to further develop those texts of articles that were important to the WFD.

Fourth, the WFD was fully engaged with ongoing lobbying to states' delegates. This was done in two main forms. One was approaching individual delegates, entering into close negotiations on specific issues with the objecting parties. A particularly nerve-wracking example took place during the eighth and last AHC session. Although there was a sense that the CRPD text was, at that point, almost final, two powerful state delegates, China and Russia, wanted to make last minute changes and eliminate the reference to sign languages from two provisions: Article 2 about the definition of languages (China) and Article 21(e), dealing with the recognition and promotion of the use of sign languages, which Russia proposed to delete. Following immediate and intense conversations the WFD held with delegates' parties, however, both the Chinese and the Russian delegates were persuaded not to insist that the changes were made. With regard to the Russian proposal, it turned out that there was an error in the Russian translation of the draft text. After careful explanation of the meaning of a right formulation in the English version, the Russian delegation was satisfied and withdrew its objection to Article 21(e).

With regard to Article 2, China proposed removing sign language from the definition of languages. Once again, however, in a meeting between the Chinese delegate and the WFD representative, Dr. Liisa Kauppinen, it was possible to both address the concerns of China and clarify the implications of including sign language in the definition. Specifically, because the Chinese parliament uses and translates more than twenty different languages, the Chinese delegate was concerned that including sign languages in the definition of language would require that spoken languages be translated into more than twenty different sign languages, and hence that it would mean a substantial increase in the number of official languages that would be used in their parliament. In response, the delegate was asked how many deaf parliament members were in China. As he replied that they had none, it was possible to clarify that if sometime in the future China had a deaf member of parliament, he or she would need only a few interpreters—certainly not more than twenty different sign language interpreters. Kauppinen also confirmed to the Chinese delegate that not all parliamentary meetings would have to be translated into sign language if the deaf parliament member would not be present. These clarifications relieved the delegate's main concerns, and he subsequently promised to remove the proposal for the change. These meetings and the subsequent understandings reached between WFD representatives and the Chinese and Russian delegates thus paved the way for sign language to remain in the definition of language in Article 2.

Attending and participating in group negotiations with the delegates was a second important line of lobbying. Ultimately, much of this lobbying process was not too burdensome. The negotiations were almost always conducted in good spirit and productive, but frequently lack of sufficient knowledge about Deaf culture and sign languages proved to be the main problem; providing adequate information during the discussions became a frequent pleasure. Furthermore, the approach of the AHC chair Don MacKay was valuable even when the situation felt almost hopeless. He encouraged additional talks and motivated the WFD to continue the discussions with the states' delegates until disagreements were resolved. Indeed, MacKay continuously highlighted that it was the states' delegates, not he, who had the power, and he hence advised holding further discussions with the states' delegates and approaching the facilitators of particular articles.

Personal communication was also crucial in changing attitudes and deconstructing stigma. For many states' delegates, encounters with WFD representatives were the first time they talked to a deaf person. Ultimately, however, they learned—and were impressed—by the fact that it is possible to "conduct business" directly and without effort with a deaf person by using a sign-language interpreter. An important milestone was achieved when one state delegate commented, "I always thought deaf people can't participate, but now I can see that it is entirely possible using sign language and an interpreter."

This was not a unique instance. The use and visibility of sign-language interpreters during the AHC and other meetings and during breaks had a powerful impact on attitudes of state delegations, UN officials, UN staff, and all other people who saw them in their work. This made all people realize that both parties, hearing and deaf, need sign language interpreters to make full communication possible. It was fantastic to note that as people needed their services over time, the interpreters became a natural part of the AHC meetings from beginning to end. After MacKay closed the last

AHC session all people stood up and waved their hands to applaud in the deaf way. This was a truly moving and empowering moment: it meant that all learned this is part of our culture. So, we felt our work had a positive impact with attitudinal change and growing awareness of our lifestyle.

Finally, being part of the IDC and attending its meetings and the steering group also provided forums where it was possible to make a difference. First, having the support of all the other DPOs for securing Deaf culture and sign language in the convention strengthened these interests in the eyes of states' delegates. Considering the respect the IDC received throughout the drafting process, the statements coming out of this body or these organizations were often more readily received. Beyond mere support, and particularly since the third AHC session, creating coalitions and finding appropriate allies became essential. At this point, the number of representatives from DPOs increased to a degree that the Ad Hoc Committee could no longer hear them all. Joint efforts and statements were, therefore, a practical solution as well, and united statements were produced on many issues throughout the drafting process in cases where opinions originally were much divided. Indeed, the support the WFD has had from all the other DPOs and its cooperation with the IDC were invaluable to the success of securing an explicit reference to sign languages in the Convention.

Second, being a part of the IDC was also part of another strategic goal: it meant that the lobbying strategies and the documents produced for state delegates were first tried with the DPOs. To be sure, there was not always consensus among the DPOs and among the NGOs working with the IDC. Persuasion and clarifications of the needs—and rights—of deaf people were often necessary, even in this forum. One striking instance was in the discussions on the relevant definitions that would apply (Article 2). As mentioned earlier, during the beginning of the AHC sessions, there was a dispute regarding whether or not sign language is a "language." The WFD felt it necessary to also propose a definition of language. In cooperation with linguists and their networks a definition was prepared that also included sign languages. The definition stated the following: "*Language* is the *systematic use* of sounds, signs or written *symbols* to represent things, actions, ideas, and states, shared and understood by members of a linguistic community. Following this definition, linguists consider sign language a natural language."[14] The WFD also proposed the definition of "communication":

Communication is the process of exchanging information, usually via a common system of symbols such as but not limited to language. Humans communicate in order to share knowledge and experiences.

Common forms of human communication include speaking, signing, writing, gesturing, and broadcasting.

Means of communication is a synonym for forms of human communication. There are many means of communication, which include Braille, tactile communication methods and augmentative communication methods (e.g., Bliss).

In order to communicate, a person needs a language (whether signed or spoken) and some form of communication (means of communication).

When the definition was presented at the IDC forum, however, the participants felt that the definition was too complicated. The president of the World Blind Union, Kicki Nordström, even exclaimed, "Why should we have a definition that is so difficult that nobody understands it?" Subsequently, the definition was amended and also adopted in the final text to read, simply, "'Language' includes spoken and signed languages and other forms of non-spoken languages" (Article 2, CRPD). While this wording is certainly not perfect—in fact, according to linguists, the precise meaning of the wording "other forms of non-spoken languages" is impossible to understand, the process was nonetheless valuable. Debating the relevance of the proposals and explanations the WFD made and brainstorming on the appropriate wording ensured greater preparedness when the states' delegates were finally approached.

The Next Steps

Ultimately, Deaf culture and sign-languages issues are fairly broadly covered in the CRPD. In Article 2 of the Convention, "Communication" is defined as, inter alia, languages and means and formats of communication, which would inherently contain sign languages according to the included definition of language. Article 3(d) posits as a general principle "Respect for difference and acceptance of persons with disabilities as part of human diversity and humanity." Article 9(2)(e) on accessibility requires states to "provide forms of live assistance and intermediaries, including guides, readers and professional sign-language interpreters, to facilitate accessibility to buildings and other facilities open to the public." The recognition of, and right to, sign languages is further strengthened in Article 21, which requires states to take all appropriate measures to ensure that persons with disabilities can exercise the right to freedom of expression and opinion. In addition to general requirements to provide services and information and accessible and usable formats for persons with disabilities, it includes a few explicit references to sign languages. Article 21(b) requires "accepting and facilitating the use of sign languages . . . and all other accessible means, modes, and formats of communication of their choice by persons with disabilities in official interactions," and 21(e) requires "recognizing and promoting the use of sign languages."

Importantly, sign languages and Deaf culture have received recognition in two other contexts: education and participation in cultural life. Article 24 on education requires states to enable persons with disabilities to learn life and social development skills to facilitate their full and equal participation in education and as members of the community, including by "facilitating the learning of sign language and the promotion of the linguistic identity of the deaf community" and by "ensuring that the education of persons, and in particular children, who are blind, deaf or deafblind, is delivered in the most appropriate languages and modes and means of communication for the individual, and in environments which maximize academic and social development" (Article 24(3)). To ensure the realization of this right, Article 24(4) also requires states to "take appropriate measures to employ teachers, including teachers with disabilities, who are qualified in sign language and/ or Braille, and to train professionals and staff who work at all levels of education." Finally, Article 30 states that "persons with disabilities shall be entitled, on an equal basis with others, to recognition and support of their specific cultural and linguistic identity, including sign languages and deaf culture."

Yet, the wording of the provisions in the CRPD text may still be too limiting, especially as the Convention does not state clearly that implementation of most of the rights stipulated in it requires the use of sign language. For instance, there is no explicit right of a deaf child to learn his or her native language, that is, sign language, although learning a first language would be required with any other child in order to avoid any delays with the child's normal development. Thus, when issues are not fully covered by the treaty, and in order to further entrench the rights of deaf people worldwide, the WFD has used existing human rights instruments and policy guidelines to support its claims. Rule 5 of the Standard Rules on accessibility, for example, stipulates in subparagraph (b.7), "Consideration should be given to the use of sign language in the education of deaf children, in their families and communities. Sign language interpretation services should also be provided to facilitate the communication between deaf persons and others." As no similar provision exists in the Convention, this rule remains an important one for the full realization (and implementation) of the rights of deaf people around the world.

Conclusions

The CRPD is the first ever international treaty that mentions sign language, Deaf culture, Deaf community, and linguistic and cultural identity in a human rights framework. Deaf people have never had such an instrument at the international law level to use as a tool to protect our human rights. It is, therefore, of utmost importance that deaf people learn to use this instrument as much as possible from the individual to the international level. A crucial starting point is that deaf people themselves realize that they are just like anyone else and are an important part of human linguistic, cultural, and all other diversity. This clear awareness relates to awareness that deaf people can influence their quality of life as active citizens, partners, decision makers, legislators, planners, and representatives of their communities.

The CRPD prohibits all kind of discrimination based on deafness and, at the same time, sees deaf people as a linguistic and cultural group. It clearly states that without full linguistic and cultural human rights it is hard for deaf people to enjoy all other human rights. All other people need to understand deeply this very core idea of the CRPD that makes the needs and existence of deaf people and their communities so unique; and simultaneously, the understanding that all are part of global human diversity.

It must be clear from now on, that deaf people all over the world need to learn to use all processes and mechanisms of the CRPD together with other groups of persons with disabilities and all other partners. This is a huge but very rewarding challenge to the WFD and its member organizations—and to all deaf individuals—for many decades to come.

CHAPTER 9

Imagine: To Be a Part of This

Lex Grandia

To be elected to the first committee to draft a text for the Convention on the Rights of Persons with Disabilities was a challenge and an honor for me. At that time I was secretary-general of the World Federation of the Deafblind, a small growing worldwide representative organization of persons with deafblindness. Later I was elected president. That election to the drafting committee happened in the fall of 2003, after the second Ad Hoc Committee session, where UN delegates discussed us, but almost without us. We, the Disabled People's Organizations on the way to form the IDC, were permitted to be in the meetings as observers only from time to time. We observed that delegates clearly did not have any knowledge or experience in the disability field and could not imagine how it is to live with a disability. "Care," "protection," and "vulnerable groups" were often-used words. Disability seemed to be the same as inability.

The negotiations for the Convention eventually came to embrace an unprecedented role for civil society organizations, including DPOs. Making this happen required new partnerships among persons with disabilities—among people who might otherwise have little in common aside from being defined as disabled by their respective societies. We all have our own different life histories, educational backgrounds, cultures we live in, and experience our different disabilities and barriers. We have to make this understood. I was searching for all our different qualities developed and our capacities, to combine them and share them, evolving into a big voice with a lot of contributions to society. In what follows, I reflect on finding the balance between the wants and needs of a specific group—persons with deafblindness—and the larger group of persons with disabilities. Imagine: together we made ourselves heard!

Imagine: The Bottom Lines

Vision and hearing! My body senses best.

—Lex Grandia

We were twelve representatives with a disability in the Working Group, seven from international disability organizations, International Disability Alliance members, and five representatives from different regions. An e-mail list was created to prepare for the face-to-face meeting of the drafting WG, scheduled in January 2004. We were even lucky to be able to have a preparative meeting in Madrid at the end of 2003.[1] There were quite a lot of documents available with proposals for a convention text, produced by different conferences in the past. We needed to decide how we would prepare for this drafting meeting.

We decided to write down the most important bottom lines of what each organization wanted to achieve. I consulted my member organizations in the WFDB and professionals in the field. I looked at resolutions of formal conferences. For the rest, it was necessary to use my imagination with the knowledge I have of persons with deafblindness worldwide. That was not so easy. Persons with deafblindness are very different. Only a few are totally deaf and totally blind. Some are totally deaf and have sign languages as their mother tongue. Most have spoken languages as their mother tongue, being blind or having some hearing or vision left. There are persons with deafblindness with additional physical, intellectual, or psychosocial disabilities. Most persons with deafblindness live isolated in the family or an institution, isolated because of lack of communication, information, and mobility. Lack of education has made it impossible for persons with deafblindness to formulate their rights and needs to participate in society. Most activities with or for persons with deafblindness were related to entertainment, not intended to get deafblind people politically involved. The only clear message from the worldwide community was "get deafblindness recognized and mentioned in a convention as a unique disability."

On 22 November 2003 I formulated the following bottom lines for persons with deafblindness for circulation on our mailing list:

We, persons with deafblindness want to:

- Be considered as persons having a separate and unique disability;
- Be respected as personalities with our own, individual capacities;
- Have a legal status with rights and duties like other citizens;
- Get quality advocacy, in case we are not able to speak for ourselves;
- Develop a communication system, a recognized language to interact with the surroundings, environment and other people;
- Get quality and appropriate interpreters and guide services whenever we need;
- Get quality education and rehabilitation at all ages, based on our capacities;
- Choose our own ways of living, alone or with others;
- Be persons with self-determination and autonomy;
- Be able to read and write, using Braille or large print;
- Get information about society, politics, and all kind, we wish to get according to our personal interest;
- Get access to the information society;
- Be able to live and organize our daily life with accessible tools and technical aids;
- Have access to our own economy: coins, banknotes, money;
- Be able to travel;
- Obtain a qualified and satisfying job according to our capacities;
- Be political and social active;
- Act as artists, authors or other cultural executors;
- Develop and govern our own organization;
- Develop, and be responsible, for our own service programmes.

One wish I could not formulate well was to have the right to do things at our own speed (an action against the speedy society).

I finished the message saying: "and now I am tired, can you understand??"

Imagine: To Reach Consensus

Put your mind into gear, before opening your mouth.
—Old New Zealand sailor after having had a stroke

It is funny to look back at these bottom lines five years after. I did not really use them later during the process, but I must have kept them in mind. Of course, many of them were not specific to persons with deafblindness, but the lines needed to be translated into the situation of persons with deafblindness. It was good to see that, when all of our bottom lines were collected on our mailing list and discussed at Madrid, we had a lot in common. During the whole process one of the big difficulties was to cope with each other's differences within the disability movement. We found out how little we know about the consequences of our different disabilities. During our daily e-mail discussions, every day without any break, during the next three years, we needed to explain ourselves to each other again and again, including which formulations in a proposed convention text would benefit one group or harm another. Mutual respect was needed; the more time pressure we had, the better it worked.

The respect consisted of the acknowledgment of the specific experiences of persons with each different disability. For example, although some deafblind persons in my organization also have psychosocial disabilities, I cannot speak on behalf of persons with psychosocial disabilities. Rather, World Network of Users and Survivors of Psychiatry does. It also required acknowledging that each person is expert in his or her own disability. So each one needed to explain his or her own specific situation and be respected for that. As it became clear, only by listening carefully to each other's histories would it be possible to reach agreement. And we all needed to support these individuals when they explained the same thing in the AHC plenary.

Forms of communication were one such instance. No one else present knew what tactile communication means and how it works. I explained the different means and modes of communication to the IDC. Better still, from time to time there were a few other persons with deafblindness in the AHC sessions, so people could see and/or experience how slowly tactile communication works. The explanation was reiterated in the AHC plenary, with the support of all DPOs. Ultimately, the delegation from Uganda insisted on including tactile communication, and it made its way into the final text. I am not sure why it was Uganda that did this, though it may be because I was at that time very much involved in the founding of a national organization of persons with deafblindness in Uganda. I don't know for sure; I did not ask.

During the process it became important to form alliances in certain areas. Not only did such alliances give a feeling of a stronger voice, but they also offered the possibility to share experiences in advocacy, such as the bad experiences that persons with intellectual and psychosocial disabilities have had living in institutions. They endured forced medication, other ways of forced treatment, and medical experimentation. But these experiences have also happened to persons with deafblindness. I know it even from my own experiences, having lived in an institution for sixteen years. I therefore have to fight against it. And so I have learned from my other colleagues in Inclusion International and the WNUSP how to do that. Similarly, sign languages are important for deaf and deafblind people. So I learned a lot from the advocacy work of the World Federation of the Deaf. Braille, too, is important for blind and deafblind people, so I joined forces with the World Blind Union.

Working with such coalitions required great sensitivity, however. Accessible information and information technology is important for all in many different ways: graphics and pictures or easy-to-read language are acceptable for certain groups, including some persons with deafblindness, but they will not work for Braille users, blind or deafblind. So I needed to support both sides of the issue.

Following the plenary sessions took a lot of energy. It was difficult for me to keep track of all the different issues and the consequences of all the different proposals. During the sessions in New York an enormous number of papers were produced: proposals from delegates, proposals from IDC, daily reactions from IDC to the process, and all the time new lobbying sheets. The papers we in IDC produced every day had influence on the process, and some delegates, including sometimes even AHC chair Don MacKay referred to them. Often, my assistant had to read the papers for me because they were not accessible and I had to think fast.

It was also busy outside the plenary sessions. I was often leading meetings, and I did not have much energy or time to have meetings with individual delegates. At home I was overloaded with e-mails—and reading Braille takes a lot more time than reading print. In that way it was good that I did this work on a voluntary basis. The work was seemingly endless, there were no maximum working hours in any week, any weekend, or any holiday.

I have great respect for Ambassador MacKay, who was chairing the drafting group and the last four AHC sessions. He was able to keep a view from above, yet maintain a feeling for details.

Imagine: Quality of Life

Live while you've got life to live
—Piet Hein, Danish architect and poet, *Memento Vivere*

Many people cannot imagine that persons with deafblindness can have quality of life. There are examples of parents and medical professionals who prefer to abort when they learn that their baby will be deafblind.

When we started to establish working groups in the IDC on certain topics, we created separate mailing lists. I volunteered to coordinate the group on the right to life. My thought at that time was "How can we talk about human rights of persons with deafblindness, when they are not even supposed to live?"

Although the right to life is a shared interest that cuts across types and forms of disabilities, for quite some time no one joined. I could not understand and nobody told me why. After half a year of trying to get my fellows to join the working group, I wrote in March 2005 on the general IDC mailing list, "The working group on the right to life is coordinated by me. Other members are me, me and lonely me. How boring!" That helped. More people joined the group: WNUSP, World Blind Union, Inclusion International, and European Disability Forum. The many communications we had reinforced the sense that we wanted not just a reaffirmation of the right to life, like that found in many other legal documents. Life is more than a biological thing justified by law. It also involves quality of life. Persons with disabilities should have quality of life or have the right to develop it.

In our discussions by e-mail and our information sheets to the AHC plenary, we explained that in too many cases deafblind children are left behind to die. Older persons with disabilities are similarly often considered as having lost quality of life. Persons with disabilities are viewed as suffering, as individuals who are not living and should therefore be released from pain through assisted death. We also knew that compulsory abortion because of a disability had taken place in some states. But who would ever admit that?

My way to convey the message was to start many of the speeches at the AHC with a little poem, showing that I am much more than my deafblindness and barriers. I develop my quality of life by the little hearing I have, but most of all by my fingers, being able to read and write, communicate with other people, being creative in many ways. I had to show, that each person has his or her way of creating quality of life.

About halfway through the drafting process, the IDC submitted a proposal of an article on the right to life (Article 8, later 10). The IDC proposal ("Draft Article 8: Right to Life, Survival and Development") was stated as follows:

1. States Parties recognize and protect the inherent right to life of all persons with disabilities, and shall take all necessary measures to ensure its effective enjoyment by girls and boys, women and men in all stages of life.
2. The right to life also includes the right to survive and to develop on equal basis with others.
3. Disability is not a justification for the termination of life.
4. States Parties shall undertake effective measures to the prohibition of compulsory abortion at the instance of the State based on the prenatal diagnosis of disability.
5. States Parties shall also prohibit all medical, biological and other experiments reducing the quality of life of persons with disabilities, or seeking to remedy a disability against an individual's will.[2]

There were various reasons that we did not get all these points accepted. Many of the reactions I received assumed that we were members of the pro-life movement and therefore against all kinds of abortion. We wanted in contrast to focus only on disability and not on the freedom of women or parents to make their own decisions. Others felt that the key points of the proposal, including the right to development and medical experimentation, were already adequately covered in other articles. Abortion, however, remained a difficult issue to discuss. Thus, although Article 10 on the right to life ultimately requires states to take measures to ensure that persons with disabilities have access to its effective enjoyment, what was left out is that a disability should not be a justification for the termination of life.

I am still not convinced that this is only a question of ethics and morality. I still wonder if it could have been made into legal language somehow.

Yet the result was that the tension surrounding the issue of abortion remained, and our explicit proposal for states to undertake effective measures to prohibit compulsory abortion on the basis of prenatal diagnosis of disability was not included in the final text. But perhaps the reaffirmation in Article 10 of the Convention on the Rights of Persons with Disabilities is nevertheless enough?

Imagine: Supported Decision Making

Be yourself, he said to somebody, but she couldn't, she
was nobody.
—Lex Grandia, after an anonymous Dutch poem

During the process, I began to understand that the CRPD is made for persons who are living with a disability, persons who have the right to be a person before the law. The CRPD is a legal document. I am not a lawyer, so I had to learn this. We had very good lawyers in the IDC, and I began to understand that Article 12 on legal capacity and supported decision making was the most crucial article of the whole CRPD. In this context, we had long discussions about persons not being able to speak for themselves, not being able to understand the consequences of legal capacity—even persons in coma. But it became increasingly clear that legal capacity and legal capacity to act as a person before the law, no matter the type of disability, is the basis and turning point of the CRPD. If we did not recognize this, the whole document would only be a document about nondiscrimination and accessibility, which once again would consign us to be dependent on the goodwill, the care, and the protection of others.

The question, then, was how to make delegates understand the importance of these principles.

During the seventh AHC session in January 2006, Tina Minkowitz and Amita Dhanda (WNUSP lawyers) and I formed a working group to get this message through.

At the beginning, I remember, I started meetings of our little working group with a long explanation about the issue: "We spent the time talking and writing to delegates about our experiences. We now need to realize that we have to change our strategy. Education usually starts where the persons to be educated are and not where we are." So the way to go about it was to challenge their imagination, as if it all happens to them.

On the last day of the seventh session we circulated the following paper to all delegates:

IMAGINE

Imagine if someone else were making decisions for you. They could decide to take you away, lock you up, not listen to you, give you medication, block you from doing your work and living your life with your body and mind the way they are.

WOULD YOU WANT THIS TO HAPPEN TO YOU?

- Wouldn't you have the feeling that you have lost your dignity and want it back?
- Wouldn't you feel your integrity has been violated?
- Wouldn't you want to have support in making decisions without being taken over and to ask for help without being seen any less for it?
- Wouldn't you want to maintain your inherent dignity and be supported to make your own decisions?
- Wouldn't you want to retain your integrity and continue to be you?
- Would you want a Convention that allows forced interventions and does not respect your inherent dignity as a person?

The principles established in this Convention are universal and will apply to all human beings, as much to you as to me.

Let us make a Convention for a world where we can all grow and develop with mutual support.

IMAGINE A CONVENTION FOR ALL[3]

And that, so it seems, was what really made delegates think and paved the way for the adoption of Article 12 on equal recognition before the law.

Imagine: So Many Issues

My tactile world is full of details, small as fingertips,
slowly building my life.

—Lex Grandia

There were a lot of issues important for the WFDB. In fact, the Convention is about all aspects of life, except our funerals. Besides the bottom lines I was carrying with me, one issue of concern was the right to have personal assistance to be able to live at home or as part of the community. That seemed to be a general issue, and it was clearly understood and reflected in Article 19.

The most difficult issue, however, was the article about education. From the beginning it was clear that the majority of delegates would prefer to work on the concept of "inclusive education." From the perspective of the WFDB, though, the fear was that many delegations thought inclusive education meant having all students in the same classroom. It was further worrying that many of my colleagues with other disabilities thought that it is unacceptable to separate or segregate persons with disabilities from the main curriculum and main methods of education.[4] My deafblind friends need to learn different things. They need to learn to use their tactile senses, learn Braille, and learn or develop their own ways of communication—be it sign languages, manual alphabets, computer communication, or whatever is suitable for the person. They need to learn daily life skills using mainly their hands (some with a little bit of hearing and/or a sight that is left) and they need to be able to socialize with their peer students. They cannot see what is on the blackboard or hear what the teacher says. Having a personal interpreter in the classroom can only be used *after* the person with deafblindness has developed all the other necessary skills.

The organizations of the blind, the deaf, and the deafblind were here united in one strong front. In fact we tried to explain to all, that if the school system really has to be inclusive, adapting to the needs of every individual student, it should also have space for blind, deaf, and deafblind students to develop their own skills to participate in society.

Delegates were reluctant to mention specific disabilities in the Convention. But it seems that our presence—and coordinated effort—have made a difference. It took many internal discussions by e-mail, many interventions, and many explanation sheets and proposals on paper. Perhaps more important was that we, the DPOs—and in the context of education, the organizations of the blind, the deaf, and the deafblind—were increasingly considered to be experts in our fields. At the end, negotiations were on an equal basis. So we were as much experts on our area as the delegates were on politics. This issue was painful for all of us and needed an agreement that went much further than just ad hoc politics. But hard work, time pressure, and solidarity did it. Article 24 (3) was included, and it explicitly mentions deafblindness:

> 3. States Parties shall enable persons with disabilities to learn life and social development skills to facilitate their full and equal participation in education and as members of the community. To this end, States Parties shall take appropriate measures, including:
>
> a. Facilitating the learning of Braille, alternative script, augmentative and alternative modes, means and formats of communication and orientation and mobility skills, and facilitating peer support and mentoring;
>
> b. Facilitating the learning of sign language and the promotion of the linguistic identity of the deaf community;
>
> c. Ensuring that the education of persons, and in particular children, who are blind, deaf or deafblind, is delivered in the most appropriate languages and modes and means of communication for the individual, and in environments which maximize academic and social development.

Imagine: It Is Not Over

Waiting hands, how will they ever touch and feel?
—Lex Grandia

Going through the result after the last hectic eighth AHC session, I had the impression I was flying over the globe the last four years, collecting and sorting images of the future. Now the Convention text had landed—and so did I.

Now there is a need to bring this collection of images to my deafblind friends, who still live an isolated life, most of them in poverty. To solve the problems of poverty is very complicated; to break the isolation will take years and years of work. Low expectations need to be changed into images of rights and prosperity. That is what I will try to do now.

CHAPTER 10

Indigenous People with Disabilities: The Missing Link

Huhana Hickey

Since the introduction of the Universal Declaration of Human Rights in 1948, the UN has focused on treaties for groups requiring specific protection. The original Declaration did not address inequality for certain minority groups, including indigenous people and persons with disabilities. This lack of acknowledgment adds to the exclusion and marginalization these groups experience.

The negotiations of the Convention on the Rights of Persons with Disabilities partly overlapped with those concerning the UN Declaration on the Rights of Indigenous Persons. Although concluded simultaneously, UN-DRIP had in fact been in negotiations for approximately sixteen years, while the CRPD had been in negotiations for a relatively short five years. While the CRPD influenced the UNDRIP, which explicitly recognizes that particular attention shall be paid, inter alia, to the rights and special needs of indigenous persons with disabilities, the CRPD barely recognized the UNDRIP. This chapter examines these issues from the perspective of being indigenous persons with disabilities, keen to ensure that the rights of indigenous persons with disabilities be recognized in the Convention. Through the support of the International Disability Caucus, I became a remote IDC member: representing indigenous peoples with disabilities without physically attending the Ad Hoc Committee sessions.

It is my contention that indigenous persons with disabilities were excluded from the Convention's early development because of a dearth of financial resources and their governments' lack of support. An examination of how the Convention was advanced from the perspective of noninclusion of indigenous persons with disabilities additionally highlights the similarities and differences between non-Westernized and Western/industrial state developments in law and policy. While discussions of persons with disabilities commonly depend on the notion of universalism and individual rights, regardless of any cultural-specific identity, the concerns of indigenous persons with disabilities are related to discussions of group rights and cultural relativism that are intertwined with collective identities.

The Marginalized of the Marginalized

In September 2010, James Anaya, special rapporteur on indigenous peoples, presented his annual report to the Human Rights Council in Geneva. His statement to the council on UNDRIP is a powerful summary of the situation of indigenous peoples around the globe:

> The poorest among the poor, indigenous peoples continue to be at the margins of power and, in many cases, disregard of their basic human rights escalates into violence against them. However, they have preserved, generation after generation, an extraordinary wealth of knowledge, culture, and spirituality in the common benefit of humankind, contributing significantly to the world's diversity and environmental sustainability. Still, it is painfully apparent that historical patterns of oppression continue to manifest themselves in ongoing barriers to the full enjoyment of human rights by indigenous peoples. Indigenous peoples continue to see their traditional lands invaded by powerful actors seeking wealth at their expense, thereby depriving them of life-sustaining resources.[1]

Statistics about indigenous persons with disabilities are hard to come by, although, as this quotation demonstrates, the UN recognizes indigenous peoples' status of marginalization. Because of the historically fraught relationship, states are more reluctant to recognize this situation, and therefore it suits them to avoid the issue all together. Indigenous persons with disabilities who have become a minority in their own country through colonization have better documented statistics showing they face greater marginalization as indigenous persons with disabilities than other persons with disabilities and other indigenous peoples who do not experience disability.

In his role as special rapporteur, Anaya identifies in his travels the disparities and multiple marginalization experienced by indigenous people, particularly indigenous persons with disabilities.[2] But this documentation is incomplete. In New Zealand, for instance, indigenous persons with disabilities were not given the opportunity to meet with the special rapporteur despite their request to do so. As indigenous persons with disabilities are often made invisible both by the states and by their own communities, who struggle to understand disability and what it means within their own cultural concept, drawing attention to their living conditions, the lack of opportunities, and the dire state of their rights can only be advanced if such an effort is comprehensively carried out by an international authority such as the special rapporteur whose mandate allows a specific focus.

Two definitional issues in the case of indigenous persons with disabilities have given rise to special difficulties. The first is the complexity of defining indigenous people within the UN system and the related controversy on the meaning of the right to self-determination. This includes the debate regarding the notion of collective (in contrast to individual) rights under international law. Second is the question how disability is or can be defined from an indigenous perspective—a quandary that also reflects some of the debate between a universal versus a cultural relativist notion of human rights. These complexities did not escape the UN negotiations of either the CRPD or UNDRIP. The consequence, however, was that indigenous persons with disabilities were not truly consulted during the development of either document. Ultimately, neither instrument reflects an understanding of disability from an indigenous perspective; neither correctly recognizes indigenous persons with disabilities.

The Challenge of Defining "Indigenous"—Indigeneity Politics and Indigenous Rights at the UN

While indigenous peoples are accorded the same rights as everyone else in the states in which they live, it has long been accepted that they also have certain rights (both customary and treaty-based) to protection and promotion of their rights as indigenous persons. One initial issue for indigenous persons, however, is the difficulty of defining the term "indigenous."

Despite several attempts to precisely define "indigenous," to date, there has been no universally accepted definition. The differential treatments given to the diverse peoples have also created both conceptual and practical problems. While indigenous peoples have moved to identify themselves separately from minorities, differential treatments of both identified groups ensure these disparities continue to exist.

The World Bank has argued that the changing contexts for indigenous peoples mean that their diversity cannot adequately be defined.[3] Therefore, consensus cannot be found by narrowly defining indigenous peoples but only in the recognition of a set of characteristics. Accordingly, the UN Working Group on Indigenous Populations has since defined "indigenous" as follows:

> Indigenous communities, peoples, and nations are those which, having a historical continuity with pre-invasion and pre-colonial societies that developed on their territories, consider themselves distinct from other sectors of societies now prevailing in those territories, or parts of them. They form at present non-dominant sectors of society and are determined to preserve, develop, and transmit to future generations their ancestral territories, and their ethnic identity, as the basis of their continued existence as peoples, in accordance with their own cultural patterns, social institutions, and legal systems.[4]

The preference for identifying specific characteristics of indigenous identity rather than a narrow definition allows for the broader aspects of indigenous identity to be considered. It is also in line with the principle of self-defining one's identity, as set out in the 1989 International Labour Organization Convention Concerning Indigenous and Tribal Peoples in Independent Countries.[5]

The definition of indigenous people has been particularly contentious because of the confusion and (the subsequent ongoing international debate) about the notion of self-determination. Indeed, the issue of self-determination is a challenge for postcolonial governments where the colonized indigenous peoples are the minority and a history of oppression has thwarted a relationship on equal terms. States have been unwilling to endorse self-determination, assuming it would create new political sovereignties. Yet, without self-determination indigenous persons' identity is at risk. For indigenous peoples, the core issue is not the question of citizenship—a concern commonly raised by states and which is clearly outlined for individuals and for groups as a concept in human rights. Rather, it is the issue of being recognized as a distinct collective entity with their own right to self-governance and self-identity, and as a collective people having to bear the same consequences of carrying these rights.[6]

Specifically, the argument of collective rights in regard to indigenous peoples requires two core elements: the right to self-determination and the right to free prior and informed consent, consultation, and participation. These concepts are the precursor to any issues related to the rights to traditional practices, lands, economic negotiations for the group, economic and social regional development, as well as resources. In a sharp contrast from the Westernized individualistic processes implemented in health and disability policy,[7] then, the politics of indigeneity is intrinsically linked to the discussions of citizenship and identity. It is in these debates that the issues of entitlement and equality of rights are often also raised.[8] It is also in this debate where the (lack of) discussion on indigenous persons with disabilities in the UN system has been difficult to tackle.

The Challenge of Defining "Disabilities"

While there have been increasing discussions on the various cultural conceptualizations of disability around the world, the cultural understanding of the notion of disability within indigenous culture is underresearched. Nonetheless, two main observations can be made. One is that the conceptualization of disability is steeped in Westernized concepts of impairment. As a result, attempts to define disability within indigenous peoples' identity have been characterized by resistance to accepting Westernized concepts of impairment and disability. Maori with disabilities, for example, do not relate to the term disability and have coined the phrase *whanau hauaa*, which can be loosely translated to mean Maori who are part of the family and who are uniquely different.

For indigenous peoples, perceptions of disability differ from Western perceptions in language and history and due to the collective approach to their societal framework. Disability was traditionally conceptualized as to whether or not individuals could remain a part of the collective community despite their impairment. Thus, individuals born blind or who acquired blindness throughout life were not necessarily excluded from their community as they could still be contributors, either as healers or by performing some other task making them productive members. If their impairment is, however, a type that would lead to a shortened survival at birth, or of a nature outside the understandings of the time, then that individual would either be killed or removed from the community. This was the case, for example, with a person with a psychosocial condition who is experiencing a psychosis and who may be deemed to be bad for the collective.

The introduction of colonization and the increasing scientific and Western medical and other healing skills brought to the indigenous community have certainly affected indigenous communities. Consequently, in many indigenous communities, exile or killing of individuals with disabilities is no longer practiced. The stigma still exists, however, and indigenous persons with disabilities have to contend with the issue of exclusion and fragmentation culturally, while their social standing in the community further exposes their disparate experiences.

The other difficulty with disability as a Westernized concept is that it is based on a Westernized human rights and disability framework that is often considered individualistic. Indigenous peoples do not easily work as individuals or within individual constructs, however, but embrace a concept of collective or group mentality. That means that while each individual exists as an individual, the individual's decisions and actions are group based. Thus, in order for indigenous peoples to be properly included within the scope of the international human rights framework, particularly the CRPD, this collective framework needs to further develop, and both the indigenous identity and their disability identity need to be endorsed.

Put differently, the situation presents what the UN views as the classic dilemma in international human rights law: how to ensure that indigenous cultural integrity is not compromised, yet also that the claim for cultural relativism is not abused for the suppression of indigenous persons with disabilities. And although the UN has not fully embraced the range of issues around cultural relativism, my answer is that there is a need in an indigenous approach to educate the communities and, furthermore, that such an educational effort has to come from indigenous persons with disabilities themselves. In this regard, work on indigenous concepts of disability is essential. Such knowledge could have informed such issues as what differentiates indigenous thinking from Western concepts of disability and where there may be similarities—even if the way of addressing the issues were different. Importantly, it would also provide the only viable way to clarify and promote *within* indigenous communities the inseparable bond between in- digenous culture and identity and the empowerment of indigenous persons with disabilities. This is particularly so, considering that indigenous persons with disabilities more often than not prefer to remain a part of their indige- nous communities and not be a part of the larger disability community. In- deed, the preference of Maori with disabilities to use *whanau hauaa* rather than "disability" is evidence of their lack of engagement thus far with the mainstream disability community in New Zealand.

Overall, then, a proper discussion on indigenous persons with disabilities would require bridging both the Westernized and the indigenous concept of disability, as well as the collective feature of disablism (that is, discrimination against persons with disabilities) within indigenous culture. Unfortunately, neither of these bridges was constructed throughout the negotiations of the CRPD and UNDRIP.

CRPD and UNDRIP

The CRPD and UNDRIP developed simultaneously—the latter one being completed in June 2006, six months before the adoption of the CRPD. Examining how instruments addressed the particular needs of indigenous persons with disabilities is thus illustrative. While each document presumes to address the issue of indigenous people, neither provides appropriate pro- tection to indigenous persons with disabilities or includes an appropriate recognition of the marginalization and disparities facing them.

The Process of the Draft Declaration on the Rights of Indigenous Peoples (1985–1999)

The process of recognition for indigenous peoples has been ongoing for sev- eral decades. As far back as 1923, such indigenous leaders as T. W. Ratana, a Maori prophet and founder of Ratana, the largest Maori religion in New Zealand, and Deskaheh, an Iroquois tribal chief from Ontario who held a passport from Haudenosaunee, approached the League of Nations to ask for the right to self-govern, live on their own land, and practice their own be- liefs. These requests were denied, but the push for indigenous rights has not abated since.[9] In 1982, the WGIP was established to oversee the promotion and protection of human rights for indigenous peoples. In 1985, it began drafting the Declaration on the Rights of Indigenous Peoples, and after extensive consultation with indigenous groups, the draft was completed by the WGIP and the Subcommission on the Promotion and Protection of Human Rights in 1993. In 1999, the Commission on Human Rights took steps to establish a Permanent Forum on Indigenous Issues, which would review and make recommendations on the proposed draft declaration.[10] In 2002, the Secretariat of the Permanent Forum on Indigenous Issues was established in another General Assembly resolution[11] with the goal to formalize the forum, to create a source of information and coordination for the issues relating to the permanent forum, and to prepare annual reports for the members. One advantage of the appointment of the Secretariat for the Permanent Forum on Indigenous Issues is that indigenous people were subsequently able to participate at in-house meetings at the UN.[12]

Nonetheless, the core of the ongoing international debate continued to be the issue of self-determination from a group/collective-rights perspective, particularly when it was explicitly negotiated by indigenous peoples' representatives. Indeed, governments had originally expected that only government representatives would participate in the WGIP, and when indigenous representatives were appointed, some states refused to work on the draft. Yet, as explained, without self-determination the notion of collective rights and identity of indigenous persons is at risk. Consequently, states that objected to the ratification and acceptance of the draft declaration have often done so on the grounds that the definition of indigenous peoples is too broad. Others have also particularly opposed the inclusion of a reference to the right of indigenous people to self-determination. After much debate and negotiations, however, the reference to the right to self-determination was ultimately adopted in Article 3 of the UNDRIP, stating that, "Indigenous peoples have the right of self-determination. By virtue of that right they freely determine their political status and freely pursue their economic, social and cultural development."

Somewhat surprisingly, UNDRIP did include some provisions for indigenous persons with disabilities. It provides some recognition of their particular needs, stipulating in Article 22 that

1. Particular attention shall be paid to the rights and special needs of indigenous elders, women, youth, children and persons with disabilities in the implementation of this Declaration.

2. States shall take measures, in conjunction with indigenous peoples, to ensure that indigenous women and children enjoy the full protection and guarantees against all forms of violence and discrimination.

Notably, however, inclusion of this article in UNDRIP was done without consultation with the target group. Despite multiple requests for resources to participate in both UNDRIP and CRPD negotiations, none were forthcoming. The work was, therefore, done mostly from home with representatives and with e-mail communications in the hope that they might just listen. This lack of consultation is significant, as ultimately, the article does not require states parties to provide protection tailored to the specific needs of indigenous persons with disabilities. To give only one example, although the article states that particular attention shall be paid to persons with disabilities, it does not ask that special measures be taken to ensure the full protection and guarantees of indigenous persons with disabilities against all forms of violence and discrimination. However, with the high risk of abuse and violence toward indigenous persons with disabilities, there is a need for consultation and participation of this community in both UNDRIP and the CRPD to ensure that they are able to address their disparities, their barriers, and gain a representative voice. Similarly, although women, children, and the elderly indigenous do not face the same discrimination or exclusion from their community because of their identities as women, children, and elderly, they may face greater discrimination if they have impairments. It is therefore imperative that indigenous persons with disabilities are given a voice specifically aimed at addressing their issues. Needless to say, until resources are made available to look into violence, abuse, and the disparities, indigenous persons with disabilities remain an invisible presence within the indigenous and the disability communities. Not only did the CRPD not rectify this omission, but significantly, the lack of protection provided to indigenous persons with disabilities in the CRPD is all the more blatant.

The Drafting of the CRPD

From the outset, indigenous persons with disabilities were not engaged with as a group to be included in the CRPD negotiations. States did not include indigenous persons with disabilities, and there was no focus for this group to have inclusion. A small group of indigenous persons with disabilities who had formed an online network called the International Indigenous Disability Convention Working Group began networking among individuals who attended the AHC sessions. In 2004, the network was invited to join the IDC and two individuals (this author included) were given the role as representatives of indigenous persons with disabilities on that body. While they lacked the funds to attend any of the AHC sessions, with the support of the IDC, as a representative of the International Indigenous Disability Convention Working Group, I managed to attend an IDC meeting in Spain in July 2004. In this meeting, the argument for inclusion of indigenous persons with disabilities in the CRPD was presented, and it was this advocacy that led to Preamble (p), referencing also to indigenous persons with disabilities.

Despite pushing for specific references as well as for a separate article to be included in the CRPD—akin to the articles on women with disabilities and on children with disabilities (Articles 6 and 7)—this goal proved unattainable. The differences in understanding what disability is, the concerns about the indigenous collective (rather than individual) nature of disability, combined with the endorsement of universal concepts of human rights, made these issues unresolvable. The lack of funding further critically hampered the ability to push for such a separate article. Requests made by indigenous persons with disabilities to the state representatives from New Zealand, Australia, and Canada went unheeded. Consequently, at no time were indigenous persons with disabilities able to attend the AHC sessions, nor did they have the resources to talk with state delegates about their desire to be included in the CRPD. Efforts by the International Indigenous Disability Convention Working Group to include proposals that would reflect this position or provide specific reference to indigenous persons with disabilities were thus unsuccessful.

Notably, a few individuals attending the AHC negotiations joined the International Indigenous Disability Convention Working Group and began negotiating on our behalf for an article for indigenous persons with disabilities. This assistance was possible only because these allies represented NGOs and DPOs already attending the sessions, or they were sympathetic UN representatives who were listening to the pleas of indigenous persons with disabilities to be included in the CRPD. Nevertheless, the inclusion of a separate article on indigenous persons with disabilities was refused, and the only success ultimately achieved was Venezuela's last-minute push to include indigenous peoples in paragraph (p) of the treaty's Preamble.

This is a limited achievement. Furthermore, the acknowledgment merely notes a concern for marginalized groups who face multiple or aggravated forms of discrimination, including indigenous persons with disabilities (Preamble (p)).

Disappointingly, then, just as the UN human rights regime has not (so far) properly embraced the range of issues around cultural relativism of indigenous people, it has failed to give appropriate recognition to the diversity of identity as a means to address any issues of disparities and inequities in the CRPD. This is disheartening, particularly considering that the Convention has generally aimed at—and succeeded in—entrenching a social (instead of medical) approach to disability and also a more interdependent notion of human rights. The international community thus missed an opportunity. Rather than create an instrument that reflects and truly accepts human diversity and identities in the twenty-first century, the Convention's final text takes a universalist approach, which, certainly from an indigenous perspective, comes at a high price. As sociologist Ulrich Beck expressed in a 2004 symposium, "Talking Peace with Gods," "Universalism . . . obligates respect for others as a matter of principle, but for that very reason, arouses no curiosity about, or respect for, the otherness of others. . . . [U]niversalism sacrifices the specificity of others to a global equality that denies the historical context of its own emergence and interests."[13]

The implications of these omissions for the implementation of rights and inclusion of indigenous persons with disabilities are tremendous. They have not abated since the adoption, signing ceremony, and entry into force of the CRPD. The practical exclusion of indigenous people from the CRPD since its adoption remains a real concern.

Indigenous Persons with Disabilities and the CRPD:
Do They Have a Place?

The relegation of indigenous persons with disabilities to the Convention's Preamble was certainly not the desired outcome for indigenous persons with disabilities. It implies that the link provided in the CRPD to the UNDRIP is weak.

In an effort to mitigate the disappointing post-adoption results, an agreement was made for indigenous persons with disabilities to remain involved with the International Disability Alliance-CRPD Forum (IDA-CRPD

Forum), formerly the IDC. Two years on, however, this has not occurred. Because indigenous persons with disabilities are not set up as formal NGOs, they are unable to join the IDA-CRPD Forum until they can formalize as an NGO. Indigenous persons with disabilities have also not been to any of the Convention-related conferences since the CRPD's adoption, nor have they been able to attend any meetings related to the CRPD and the UN. Although the reason may be largely attributed to lack of financial resources, the results are disempowering. It has meant that indigenous persons with disabilities are unable to stay abreast of the progress associated with the CRPD and that their voices cannot be included with those of other groups in the implementation and further development of international and national disability law. Until their voices are able to join those of the IDA, they remain unable to ensure their voices join others seeking to see the Convention as a strong instrument for persons with disabilities.

To reduce this disparity, there is a need and a desire to ensure that the cornerstone notion of equal rights and freedoms to *all* human beings is upheld. Originally envisioned in the Universal Declaration of Human Rights, this key value is also stipulated in both the UNDRIP and the CRPD. Indigenous persons with disabilities should thus have the same rights as all others, and their right to recognition and inclusion should be guaranteed at all levels of implementation of the human rights regimes focused on indigenous and disabilities. For this to happen, however, partnerships with other NGOs and states are essential. Hopefully, such alliances can be developed: they are the only route to bring about a real change for indigenous persons with disabilities—one of the most marginalized groups in the world.

Conclusion

The UN has developed two instruments—CRPD and UNDRIP—that grant rights to two groups who have faced marginalization and discrimination directly because of their identities. Persons with disabilities and indigenous peoples have worked hard over many years to ensure that the two instruments are concluded—with the hope of having a voice that has been otherwise ignored. It is, however, still an unfinished piece of work: indigenous persons with disabilities continue to face constant marginalization— certainly, in large part because of the complexities that arise with being both indigenous and living with disabilities. They face not only general exclusion from society as persons with disabilities, but also exclusion from their own indigenous community. It will take time, resources, and commitment from states, NGOs, and individuals to ensure the inclusion of indigenous persons with disabilities at the UN and other relevant international forums as well as at a domestic level.

The UN has not fully embraced the range of issues around cultural relativism. It has failed to place within its instruments, including the CRPD, recognition of diversity of identity so as to address issues of disparities and inequalities. Rather, it upholds a universalist conceptualization of human rights, although it is a form of imperialism that opposes the notion of collectiveness that is common in non-Westernized society.

Underlying the constructs of universalism in human rights and cultural relativism are the right to choose and the freedom to make choices. Through rigidity of practices or beliefs, there is little scope for variants. Culture is not a static concept but is fluid and constantly exposed to change. The ability for cultural identities to diversify, amend, edit, and change their practices according to new knowledge, while still maintaining core cultural and human rights values, will provide a way to achieve a human rights framework acceptable to most societies and communities. When aligning as an indigenous person with disabilities, there is also a strong cultural identity attached to this identity to give a voice within a particular human rights convention, such as the UN disability and indigenous instruments. This is to give recognition to the collective identity of a group and to give indigenous peoples opportunities to comply and meet the needs of a marginalized group within their communities. Indigenous knowledge and beliefs can adapt as has already been shown through the ability to amend and change existing beliefs according to new knowledge gained. It is possible to again adapt and amend when needed to afford inclusion for those often excluded. Indeed, until indigenous persons with disabilities are fully included in the CRPD structure at all levels, they will remain an invisible, unrepresented, voiceless, marginalized, and discriminated-against group; a group that is consequently also at risk of greater disparities as they continue to face their exclusion from the ongoing process of developing international and national disability laws.

CHAPTER 11

At the United Nations . . .
"The South Also Exists"

Pamela Molina Toledo

English translation by Felipe Ramos Barajas

A central element in every democratic agenda in the twenty-first century is
the sharing of power between the state and civil society. This mutual effort
is, by the same token, a central element in the creation of sustainable development that incorporates a sense of respect for the citizens' rights, points of
view, and the principle of shared responsibility.

The active participation of members of civil society with disabilities was
thus particularly important for the first UN convention on human rights in
this century. Not only were we, as persons with disabilities, efficient and professional at discussing issues of critical relevance, but we also offered a profound sense of positive change and creativity to the topics at hand. Unlike
previous interventions in our own countries where participation is still a
grand idea that only exists in the realms of political speech, the efficacy of
this intervention was not only the result of sincere conviction, professional-
ism, and willingness to engage in the issues on the part of the disabled people's organizations (DPOs), but also the sincere enthusiasm from numerous
state delegates and their eagerness to learn about our reality. A reality, that
is, with which few were familiar at this point.

As a member of a small, national DPO based in Chile, I witnessed and
participated in this revolutionary moment of civil society involvement firsthand. This chapter is my attempt to tell the story of how this opening up of the
international political process offers the opportunity to Southern voices to be

salient in the making of international disability rights law. After an introduction to my involvement in the drafting process, I portray the situation of persons with disabilities in Latin American countries and the subsequent work with the International Disability Caucus to address the Southern concerns in an array of provisions. Particular focus is given to the role of Proyecto Sur (the South Project) and its power to utilize international processes so as to ensure that Southern voices of persons with disabilities are being heard.

Thrust into an International Forum . . .

"How did you get here?" Liisa's hands asked me, all the while, her usual sweet and affable countenance transformed into a genuine expression of surprise also shared by Markku, who stood beside her. I smiled. Here I was, in front of the president and former president of the World Federation of the Deaf, standing inside the UN General Assembly Hall in New York, having traveled from Chile, the southernmost country in the world. I was without a Sign-language interpreter. Alone. And yet, filled with joy and willing to learn as much as possible. Even if it meant having to read what other people scribbled down for me, I was ready to affect change in the public policies coming into being at the Convention on the Rights of Persons with Disabilities and willing to ensure that the policies truly guaranteed the rights of persons with disabilities, and especially those of the deaf living in developing countries. I was ready to fight for those whose voice was inaudible, for those who never had the opportunity or means to learn to speak in the dominating language, and for those who had fallen into omission and oblivion.

How did I get there without a cent, without interpreters, without a law degree, without the help of the Chilean government? I had two advantages. First, having become deaf at the age of thirteen, having already learned oral communication, allowed me to acquire verbal skills as any other hearing person would, both written and oral. This in turn permitted me to learn the basics of the grammar and certainly eased the process of learning the basics of the English language as well as my native Spanish. Second, having had lost my sense of hearing at an age when I could both observe *and* become conscious of the changes swirling around me, I was able to comprehend that, despite such changes, I still held the same value as a person. The deaf girl was worth as much as the hearing girl I used to be. It was a great challenge to retain the same dignity while my interpersonal relations, opportunities, and access to resources shrunk as I stopped hearing. I am hugely indebted to the Deaf community in Chile for helping me embrace my *deafhood,* the process of acquiring my deaf identity and my way of living.

Given my curious nature, immersion in visual culture, and frequent use of technology as an alternative tool to access a world focused on the audible, it was not a surprise that I became aware of a Working Group established to address disability rights through the Internet. I was then the president of the Corporation of Real Citizenry of the Deaf in Chile, one of the deaf organizations with the largest youth participation in Chile. CRESOR started in 1997 and focused its advocacy efforts on the defense of our linguistic rights and the right of information and communication access for deaf people. In 2002, CRESOR succeeded in a judicial process, requiring inclusion of interpreters of Chilean Sign Language on television.[1]

After obtaining accreditation, it was necessary to secure funding to afford two weeks in New York. Needless to say, it would be prohibitively expensive to include accommodation and an honorarium for a Sign-language interpreter. As with most Latin American civil society organizations, CRESOR did not benefit from state financial support, nor did its members have the resources to afford such an enterprise. The possibility of Latin American representation thus seemed remote. Nevertheless, a small travel grant from the Ministry of Labour and Social Security of Spain was awarded to me, though it did not include any funds for a Sign-language interpreter. Unable to find anyone willing to work pro bono for two weeks, I offered to cover the airfare costs to a friend on the sole condition that she takes notes during the sessions.

On the third day the notetaker unexpectedly announced she could no longer help me. It was then that I encountered Liisa Kauppinen and Markku Jokinen. Here I was, deaf, female, alone, all the way from the South, without an interpreter or notetaker but with a suitcase full of stories and experiences and hope on materializing and fighting for the human rights of persons with disabilities. There is a lot to say about the state of affairs of the needs of the deaf in our region, Latin America. I was filled with an enormous faith in the collective efforts of persons with disabilities. I knew a systematic, sensible, and enlightening approach to the matter could start to break down the barriers of exclusion, change paradigms and the history of the UN human rights conventions, and with it, those of persons with disabilities of the South.

Despite my enthusiasm, it was tremendously difficult to stay abreast of the events without a notetaker or interpreter, and I took desperate measures to keep informed. One step was to approach a staff member from the Chilean government, requesting she work closely with me. Second, I actively participated in an Internet discussion group that focused on "Human Rights and Disabilities." This discussion group was created and moderated by a Costa Rican journalist, Luis Fernando Astorga, to serve as a capacity-building platform for community leaders throughout Latin America on the issues of the CRPD.

Throughout my time in New York, I used the online discussion forum as a place to both share and gather information. When I was writing my first post, a forty-something-year-old wheelchair-user man and a young blind woman approached me. It turned out to be Luis Fernando Astorga himself, accompanied by Silvia Quan from the Guatemalan Human Rights Commission. They had seen my post in the discussion group and had come to assist me. They explained step-by-step the protocol procedures for participation of individual members of civil society, for joining the International Disability Caucus, as well as practical matters such as the topics being discussed and where to find the transcripts of the day.

Since the IDC sessions were held at the same time as the Committee Plenary Session, there was no official UN translation. Luis Fernando, Silvia, and I were the only Latin American civil society members in the sessions. Silvia used to do simultaneous Spanish-English translation for both of us so that we could participate and bring our South American perspective into the discussions. Soon enough, we began participating as civil society representatives in the meetings of the Group of Latin American and the Caribbean Countries (GRULAC), led by Costa Rican delegate and vice chair of the Ad Hoc Committee Bureau Jorge Ballestero.

Disabilities in the South

According to the World Health Organization, 80 percent of the world's population with disabilities live in developing countries. Latin America and the Caribbean are home to 75 million persons with disabilities. If we add at least four family members for each person with a disability, we have at least 260 million people related in one way or another to a disability. And, as we know, disability is both a cause and a consequence of poverty. The mutually reinforcing relationship between poverty and disability, and thus between disability and exclusion, shows that, besides being particularly vulnerable to social exclusion, persons with disabilities are disproportionally poor. Among poor people, the presence of a disability is disproportionally high.[2] This poverty extends to family members as well.

According to data from UNESCO, WHO, the World Bank, and the International Disability Rights Monitor, more than 80 percent of children with a disability live in the Southern Hemisphere, and only 20 to 30 percent of them attend school.[3] Children with disabilities are frequently excluded from educational systems. In Colombia, only 0.32% of students have a disability. Similar figures are reported for Argentina (.69%) and Mexico (.52%), while slightly higher figures are reported in Uruguay (2.76%) and Nicaragua (3.5%). Lack of public transportation, infrastructure, trained teachers, and teaching materials are the main causes. In Honduras, for example, illiteracy among persons with disabilities is slightly greater than one in two, while that of the general population is one in five.[4] Furthermore, the vast majority—80–90 percent—of persons with disabilities in the Latin American region are unemployed; almost all those who are employed receive significantly lower or no pay at all.

It is moreover estimated that the number of persons with disabilities will rise by 120 percent in the next thirty years in South America, while the rate of growth of persons with disabilities in North America will be only around 40 percent during that same period. Furthermore, some health conditions, such as HIV/AIDS, mental health problems, tuberculosis, malaria, female genital mutilation, and psychological traumas usually found in persons in armed conflict situations, as well as in refugees and migrants, may all be the beginning of an impairment that will eventually result in exclusion and discrimination. Yet while persons with disabilities living in countries in the Northern Hemisphere are more likely to receive extensive medical treatment, thus increasing their life expectancy, in the Southern Hemisphere, those same people would surely become yet another statistic in the death rate.[5] The vast majority of persons with disabilities in the Latin American region do not have access to health services in general, and most certainly not to disability-friendly hospitals. Moreover, persons with disabilities are frequently rejected by insurance companies.[6] Clearly, then, the topic of disability in Latin America and the Caribbean is directly related to that of exclusion and poverty.

Despite the disproportionately high number of persons with disabilities in Latin America, most civil society organizations at the UN were from Europe and the United States. The overrepresentation of Northern Hemisphere leaders was an inceptional problem of the IDC. The South, particularly Latin America, had almost no representation. This was in part due to the high costs of airfare and lodging in New York. There was also a language barrier: all the IDC official meetings, advocacy meetings, trainings, lectures, and events, as well as the informal sessions, were held in English, and no translation was offered in formats other than audible ones.

In view of this situation, in 2006, the Inter-American Institute on Disability and Inclusive Development, then chaired by Luis Fernando Astorga, joined with Handicap International to create Proyecto Sur. Proyecto Sur was an initiative focused on supporting leaders with disabilities from developing countries so that they could participate and affect positive change in the different processes of the UN. Proyecto Sur's focus was not only on leaders from Latin America but rather on leaders from all over the world, especially those countries that had been traditionally excluded from participating in the elaboration of previous conventions.

It was only fair and necessary to increase the representation of Southern leaders in the decision-making processes in the first human rights convention of the twenty-first century. After all, the CRPD was the first convention to implement an effective process for co-responsibility and concerted participation between states and members of civil society. However, this also required training such leaders on the methodology used in such events, on UN procedures and protocols, and also to familiarize them with a large amount of information, especially in regard to previous documents that were generated by the Working Group.

It also necessitated promoting effective lobbying and advocacy efforts on the part of Southern leaders, as well as focus on future efforts centered on the ratification and implementation of the Convention in their respective countries. And so, the first group of Proyecto Sur delegates arrived in New York in 2006, in time for the AHC seventh session. All of them belonged to DPOs.

The Proyecto Sur team, guided by Astorga, immediately joined efforts with IDC and with GRULAC, where we had the possibility of voicing our opinions. Under the leadership of Jorge Ballestero, our demands and points of view were channeled toward the larger discussions. GRULAC's weight during this crucial stage was greatly augmented by Mexico's leadership as a proponent of the Convention and the first AHC chair, Luis Gallegos of Ecuador. This combination allowed Proyecto Sur to directly affect change and thus to become an influential factor in the writing of the CRPD.

With regard to the IDC, the goal was to enrich the collective efforts while also bringing our own vision, priorities, and needs, thus reflecting the reality of the South. The IDC demonstrated a large degree of flexibility and willingness to incorporate our Southern leaders in the decision-making process. Soon, we integrated thematic working commissions dealing with women, infants, legal capacity, disability definition, employment, and health issues among others, as well as teams focused on specific chapters. For the IDC, our participation meant increased legitimacy as the true spokespersons for the global movement of persons with disabilities.

To work with IDC required more than enthusiasm. We needed leaders fluent in English and Spanish. Such interpreters were found among our Southern civil society colleagues, removing the language barrier. With the interpreters, it was possible for Proyecto Sur to participate equally in all the meetings.

During the eighth session, we took a more proactive role. As most of the leaders from the seventh session returned, there was a sense of familiarity. We also felt more at ease with the procedures and hence more empowered. "Southern" spokespersons were chosen to participate, among others, in the IDC Board of Directors, the meetings regarding the definition of disability, GRULAC meetings, and the groups that addressed the issues of legal capacity and international cooperation. The capacity to respond rapidly and the close teamwork gave our Southern leaders (thirty-five in the seventh session; more than forty in the eighth) great political clout within IDC, GRULAC, and the AHC, as well as in the general work of the CRPD.

The establishment of Proyecto Sur was significant. It provided renewed enthusiasm, which increased the efficacy in the advocacy work. Everyone united: Latin America, the Caribbean, and the countries of the Global South ensured the visibility of the millions of persons with disabilities who had previously been excluded from the development and, thus, effectively impacted the decision-making process. Indeed, it was reflected in the IDC's structure. With the increasing number of domestic, regional, and international NGOs, most of them DPOs, attending the eighth session, full inclusion in the formulation of the Convention was finally achieved. They remained faithful to their motto "Nothing about us without *all* of us."

Gaining Respect and Trust of Government Representatives

It is rather common to see governments dismiss, a priori, propositions made by civil society representatives while designing, defining, and implementing public policies and laws, especially when these refer to human rights and social and economic development. Governments tend to assume that such suggestions are futile, disorganized, and that they lack a political and legal basis for their practical approach. Thus, for instance, our request that Chilean Sign Language be recognized as a language was dismissed on the Chilean government's assumption that it lacks grammar and structure, and, overall, proper definition—although clearly, deaf people from the inception of the nation have used it. In the same vein, public servants often reach out to civil society for purposes of personal gain. They do this not in an effort to listen to them but rather to use them to legitimize the choices and decisions they have already made.

Eradicating this kind of perspective from the Convention negotiations was particularly difficult—as a Chilean proverb says, "it was an ant's work." It required patience and a systematic approach. Often, discussions with the delegations came about over a cup of coffee or in an exchange of ideas during breaks. This bonding was significant in the removal of otherwise seemingly indestructible barriers, which would have made it very difficult to achieve our goals. However, a few elements significantly contributed to the process of generating trust in the validity and efficacy of our efforts as civil society.

First, the development of a disciplined, cohesive, democratic, and representative internal organization of IDC and Proyecto Sur was critical to making our case. The experience and diligence shown by all leaders with disabilities who were well versed in the issues of human rights and in the processes of the UN demonstrated both the justness of our cause and legitimated our presence at the negotiating table. This became an ethical imperative that bonded everyone in guaranteeing the rights of all persons with disabilities and suggested the capability to impose this imperative on any other personal or particular effort.

As the process developed, our relationships with large, international networks, including NGOs and government entities, became more important. Many leaders with disabilities participated in the process, named by their governments as official governmental delegates for the AHC, furthering the perspective needed to affect change. An IDC Internet discussion group, in both English and Spanish, facilitated the inclusion of the viewpoints of far-flung individuals. This e-list, still active today, will be a useful tool as we move into the post-Convention environment, aiming to increase the number of ratifications, to accompany the work of implementation and monitoring, to harmonize and reform existing laws that do not abide by the

Convention's guidelines, as well as to articulate new dispositions in the other treaties of human rights and their monitoring committees.

Finally, it was critical that CSOs learned practical means to work together smoothly and efficiently. CSO's reactions to the draft texts were always pertinent, prompt, technical, and proactive. Proposals were produced both onsite, working in teams, and via the Internet, giving constant feedback to those who represented us in the informal sessions. Our lobbying efforts were insistent and systematic. Our statements included personal testimony as well as diligent research provided by IDC and Proyecto Sur about social reality and domestic and international legal frames. Persons with disabilities who were at the UN showed just how capable we are to exercise, defend, and even teach our rights.

A Human Rights Convention with Southern Taste

Julio Fretes, a blind Paraguayan lawyer and a key participant in the cause of human rights in the South, observed in 2006, "This convention already has a Southern taste!" The work done by Southern leaders with disabilities had a profound impact in the Convention's final text. The Southern taste significantly impacted not only the articles discussed below, but also Articles 6 and 7 dealing with women and children with disabilities respectively, Article 17 addressing forced treatment, and Article 25 regarding sexual and reproductive health.

Everyone Means Everyone: The Definition of Disability

IDC and Proyecto Sur clearly stated at the beginning that a convention would be acceptable if and only if the human rights of all persons with disabilities, in all their diversity and heterogeneity, were properly protected. There are invisible disabilities and groups of persons with disabilities that are more excluded than others. That is the case of intellectual and psychosocial disabilities; persons with short stature (dwarfism), and others. For Proyecto Sur, addressing environmental, economic, and cultural barriers as causes of disability was also important, given that, in our countries, these barriers make it difficult to fully develop and be part of society.

For this reason, we emphasized and defended an extensive definition of disability starting from the concept of a person with disability. It was also

fundamental for Proyecto Sur leaders that the focus of the final text emphasizes the social paradigm of disability, centered upon the environmental
and attitudinal barriers, more than in the functional or corporal "deficiency." It required more than the Standard Rules on the Equalization of
Opportunities for Persons with Disabilities, possibly more than the definition of disability in the Inter-American Convention Against All Forms of
Discrimination against Persons with Disabilities (the Guatemala Convention).[7] Thus, when the informal sessions did not yield a consensus, and the
IDC compromised on following the Standard Rules without definition in
the Convention, Proyecto Sur could not support this position. For Proyecto
Sur, reverting to the Standard Rules was not an option.

Our work in this regard was almost solely done through the Group of
Latin American and Caribbean Countries. GRULAC, particularly the Bra-
zilian and Argentinean delegates, took our position as theirs and played a
major role by pushing the need for a social definition of disability. At times
it felt like swimming against the current; at other times, it felt like the consensus was lost. During a break in one of the last informal meetings about the
definition, I approached IDC representative Kicki Nordström, Swedish
leader from the World Blind Union, and asked her to support GRULAC in
defending the social paradigm of disabilities. In return, she asked that GRU-
LAC work toward achieving a consensus in regard to psychosocial disabilities. It was a difficult task: Brazil's internal legal frame did not allow the
delegation to accept the inclusion of psychosocial disability in the definition.
We nonetheless tried. Upon this agreement, the IDC publicly pronounced its
support for the inclusion of social and environmental barriers as causes of
disability. As Nordström proclaimed in the plenary, "GRULAC is no longer
alone. It is now IDC and GRULAC together, against China and Russia."

Finally, after a series of informal hallway conversations, and one day
before the end of the eighth session, we reached an agreement that it is
important that the Convention contain provisions addressing disability
concepts as tools for change. It was important for this move to separate the
concepts of intellectual disability from mental disability. This in turn allowed ample conceptual room for the eventual incorporation of psychosocial
disability in national laws. Working together, IDC and GRULAC managed to
persuade the EU members to accept the social paradigm of disability, thus
consecrating the idea in the Preamble and Article 1 (on purpose) of "persons
with disabilities." The Convention was thus established with a strong emphasis on social development and an evolving concept of disability. It assumes

that removing societal barriers and providing accommodation to persons with disabilities is the appropriate way to ensure our full inclusion and participation in society on an equal basis with others, rather than forcing persons with disabilities to conform to societal concepts of "normalcy."

The definition was a true compromise. It was not entirely what we would have wished, and everyone had to give up something in order to secure a greater objective. Nonetheless, we secured the minimum guarantees and legal tools to ensure that the North and South would allow persons with disabilities to enjoy the protection of the law and the respect and basic equality that we deserve. The CRPD adopts a broad, cross-disability approach and does not restrict the ability of states to recognize additional groups of people as being covered by the treaty.

Indigenous Persons with Disabilities

From the beginning, the IDC proposed that the Convention contain a specific reference to such minority groups with disabilities who face multiple forms of discrimination and exclusion as indigenous persons with disabilities and ethnical, sexual, and racial minorities, as well as persons with disabilities who live in rural zones. For Proyecto Sur, this point was central, as a significant percentage of people under this category reside in Southern countries.

Nevertheless, this proposal was never incorporated in the document until the eighth session. In this last AHC's session, Proyecto Sur agreed that Lenin Molina from the Latin American Network of Non-Governmental Organizations of Persons with Disabilities and Their Families, who was also appointed as a Venezuelan governmental delegate, would include a proposal to reference the issue in the Preamble. There was no written version that could be subjected to voting or consensus, however, and when the text treaty was brought for a vote on 25 August 2006, no mention of indigenous persons with disabilities was included. When this was brought to Molina's attention, he spoke at the plenary and asked to include his proposal on indigenous persons with disabilities in the final text. After much confusion, AHC chair MacKay called for a recess to allow the delegates to reach an agreement. On the realization that Molina and Venezuela were not alone, the Costa Rican and the Cuban delegations, along with Proyecto Sur met to quickly draft a proposal. It was voted upon in the plenary session and subsequently included in paragraph (p) of the Preamble. Ultimately, the indigenous persons with disabilities and other minorities were included in the Convention.[8]

At-Risk Communities and Humanitarian Emergencies (Article 11)

The existence of a specific article focused on the protection of the integrity of persons with disabilities in situations of risk, such as humanitarian emergencies, armed conflicts, foreign occupation, and natural disasters, was precarious until the end of the AHC's eighth session. Mentioning such situations was of fundamental importance, especially for developing countries and the Middle East, where persons with disabilities are constantly exposed to such natural disasters and armed conflicts. However, proposals to do so received strong opposition from the United States, along with Canada and Australia. In an effort to compromise, "foreign occupation" was removed from the article and cited, instead, in the Preamble. The U.S. and its allies' opposition remained nonetheless, and their delegates continually strove to eliminate the article.

Since there was no consensus, Chairperson MacKay proposed that the article be voted on, leading the IDC, along with Proyecto Sur, to carry out a significant lobbying campaign. This was a case in which informal conversations proved very useful; ultimately, the provision remained in the Convention. Given that the opposing party was very powerful, it was heartening to see the large number of countries who voted to keep Article 11. Despite poverty, powerlessness, and U.S. might, Southern countries were supported by many other countries. Social justice and humanitarian protection prevailed. This was a historic moment for many of us, crowned by a warm round of applause. The voting pad was full of green lights, the color of hope.

Access to Justice (Article 13)

Exercising and defending human rights requires equal access to the judicial system, in all its instances. For some persons with disabilities, especially from most Northern countries, the issue of access to justice would not be as necessary and urgent as in the South.[9] It is a right taken for granted. For

Southern countries, conversely, the issue is of fundamental importance, especially for those who live in rural areas and speak indigenous languages. A few examples will suffice to illustrate the ignorance in the current legal system of our countries. A deaf person who faces prosecution and shows up at the hearings/trial handcuffed is being barred from exercising the right to legitimate defense, since he or she is not given the opportunity to use his or her hands to communicate. In other cases, deaf people were not given a professional sign-language interpreter, with the task assigned to a family member, limiting the possibilities of fairness. Finally, there have also been cases where blind lawyers have been denied licenses to serve as judges, because of their disability.

The Convention's text from the first session had no reference to basic topics of access to justice, taking them for granted. However, a proposal for what is now Article 13 was submitted during the fifth AHC by a Chilean human rights lawyer and disability expert, María Soledad Cisternas. Being the founder of the first law program on disability in Chile and a blind person herself, she was excluded from participation, because she was "just a civil society representative." Through the Chilean delegation, she fought and created the necessary space for fairness in our participation at the plenary. Her contribution on access to justice was supported unanimously by all of the delegations, and, ultimately, a separate comprehensive article on the issue was adopted.

International Cooperation

The idea of a specific article on international cooperation stemmed from the Working Group. Luis Fernando Astorga proposed it, and later on the IDC joined this proposal when GRULAC and other entities requested its support. When Proyecto Sur came about, we started working proactively and joined efforts with IDC to achieve a separate article on a multidirectional cooperation effort that included not only North-South cooperation but also North-North, South-South, and South-North cooperation. The main goal was to have an integral, inclusive development perspective, that is, a process in which all the stakeholders can participate, without discrimination, in the exchange of good practices so as to allow economic, social, cultural, and political development and in offering innovative solutions to the problems we face. Also, an "inclusive development perspective" takes disability as a transversal topic to be included in all actions to overcome poverty. During this process there was a great measure of cooperation between the IDC and Proyecto Sur.

The inclusion of this article was a long, difficult process, mainly due to the opposition of the EU, United States, and Australia. However, a large amount of lobbying took place throughout this time. Hallways and cafeterias became our battleground. Without a doubt, the issue of multidirectional cooperation played a significant role during the discussions, showing that international cooperation means not just providing financial resources to the South, but exchanging resources, experiences, technologies, and innovations for our daily life. Ultimately, our proposals and lobbying, with support of a few delegates—predominantly the representative of Liechtenstein and the Mexican facilitator of the informal sessions—international cooperation was enshrined in Article 32. It is an innovative provision in a human rights treaty and a new beginning for the understanding and development of international cooperation.

Monitoring the CRPD: From Words to Actions

The position of IDC and Proyecto Sur in regard to monitoring was very clear: a strong, independent expert body is needed to strengthen and monitor the effective implementation of the Convention. We strongly opposed another toothless convention whose efficacy and practical implementation could never be completed.

To achieve the desired goal, the intervention of DPOs throughout the discussion on monitoring, both domestic and internationally, was indispensable. During the informal sessions, civil society delegates from Proyecto Sur played a crucial role in lobbying and, significantly, also worked closely with Jorge Ballestero. In fact, the latter responded to our request and helped to obtain a time extension of the last informal session that allowed us to reach an agreement about the incorporation of the term "experts with disability" as members of the International Monitoring Committee, and about the need for a clause in the article establishing balanced gender and geographic representation. Indeed, today, a large number of experts with disabilities are members of the International Monitoring Committee. The IDA-CRPD Forum constantly monitors these experts, checking both on expertise as well as their commitment to advancing disability rights and working with DPOs. Once again, we were able to exercise our right to have "Nothing about us without us!"[10]

Absence of Legal Capacity Equals Civil Death

If a person with disabilities is divested of his or her legal capacity, he or she will be unable to enjoy any other rights. The social and human rights paradigms require that the person be given the opportunity to communicate and express what he or she really wants. A custodianship, or an interdiction, is most certainly not the answer to the problem. Support in the decision-making process, which is different from a replacement of the person in the process, is an inalienable right in the exercise of a person's legal capacity with or without disabilities.

The World Network of Users and Survivors of Psychiatry played a fundamental role during the discussion of this topic. In the last AHC session, Proyecto Sur worked closely with WNUSP as well as Inclusion International and the IDC to ensure that an alternate model of support in decision-making was considered (and, indeed, ultimately adopted) as a viable alternative for persons with disabilities. As has been discussed elsewhere in this volume, this was a controversial issue, made more so by the insertion of a footnote to the proposed provision on legal capacity toward the end of the negotiations. The presence of this footnote ignited feverish cooperation between the various players on civil society's side. Proyecto Sur members from Arab countries strongly and actively supported our effort with their governments. Expert translations of the term "legal capacity" in Chinese, Russian, and Arabic, and expert opinions collected from both North and the South were also used, along with strategic alliances struck with delegates from different countries and particularly with GRULAC's president.

Proyecto Sur also worked assiduously, sending letters to all diplomatic delegations. We obtained positive responses from some of them. Moreover, owing to Article 12, the systematic and coordinated work between Northern and Southern CSOs increased dramatically, subsequently advancing North-South equality. By translating messages from English to our Spanish-language discussion list, the online discussion became a full-fledged "Legal Capacity Task Force," a virtual discussion group focused on the issues of legal capacity.

Inside Proyecto Sur, Julio Fretes, president of the National Coordinating Committee for the Promotion of the Rights of People with Disabilities in Paraguay, was our spokesperson on legal capacity—and a strong advocate. His contributions to lunchtime informal meetings organized by the IDC were invaluable. It is truly sad that his early death prevented him from seeing his work materialize.

Article 24: Inclusive Education for All

Finally, Proyecto Sur and the IDC were strong advocates for defending the rights of every child and adult to inclusive education. Proyecto Sur, along with the IDC, carried out awareness campaigns with the delegates, so they could see the need to transform the educational system to have actual educational inclusion. This inclusion needed to be effective so that all persons with disabilities could enjoy the benefits of education. This point was especially important given Southern countries' lack of human, technical, and technological access to overcome the educational divide that separates children and adults with disabilities.

Opinion was not unanimous in this matter, with disagreements about the status of sign language and references, in the text, to age limits. In the case of deaf and deafblind persons, inclusive education requires learning in our natural linguistic and cultural environment to allow children to develop a consistent and affirmative identity.[11]

Many countries strongly opposed the idea that sign language and other alternative means of communication are inherent to one's identity and critical as pedagogic tools to enable learning life, social, and cultural development skills. Yet, the intensive work of the World Federation of the Deaf, its Latin American allies, and the World Blind Union, as well as the World Federation of the Deafblind, UNESCO, and UNICEF prevailed. The regional linkages in Latin America were put to good use, also on behalf of the World Federation of the Deaf, to ensure increased awareness and finally support for the recognition of sign language by GRULAC diplomats. No other legal treaty had thus far expressed so clearly the inescapable link between education and development of the linguistic and cultural identity of human beings on the premise of diversity.

Conclusions

Many stories can be told about how Southern CSOs actively influenced the construction of a new history of human rights, from the astonishment of "how did you get here?" in 2004, to being honored with the opportunity to serve as the IDC spokesperson for the South during the press conference in which CRPD approval by the UN General Assembly was announced. The people from the South stopped being an exception and became necessary representatives of a collective and public opinion. We became the voice of all persons with disabilities in developing countries. We are now present either physically or technologically in the process of implementation of the Convention. We are those who live, work, and build our world in the language of those feelings that are usually hidden behind the heard word.

Are you willing to let us share our power with mainstream society? The question warrants a strong positive answer. This is what we, who have been excluded from the possibility of a country, of a Latin America, of a South that is part of an equitable world built by all of us, ask of you. Only a convention validated by the global community of persons with disabilities, without exclusions, will have the authority and the support to achieve success and to significantly change the lives of the persons with disabilities around the world. Indeed, changing history is possible only when states and civil society work concurrently. With our advocacy, expertise, patience, hopes, and solidarity we can achieve an inclusive, diverse, and better world.

This is why Southern DPOs must be present in all instances and all stages of CRPD implementation in each of our countries. This is the new mission of continuity of the Latin American Network of Non-Governmental Organizations of Persons with Disabilities and Their Families—successor of Proyecto Sur—and the International Disability Alliance–CRPD Forum.

Certainly, many challenges still need to be addressed. First, improving the composition of the CRPD International Monitoring Committee is needed. Providing, as part of the joint IDA-Monitoring Committee program, training sessions oriented toward civil society submission of shadow reports and advocacy of legal reforms is critically important in this regard. Second, generating opportunities for active involvement of and participatory dialogue with persons with disabilities in all monitoring, planning, programming, and decision-making processes is needed. DPOs must also consider the importance of promoting and generating Latin American federations, having a decentralized administration and leaders aware of the regional realities. Simultaneously, these leaders still belong to global movements. This combination would assure the efficacy of our actions, which will in turn benefit the persons with disabilities of the region. Third, promoting and maintaining the UN Voluntary Fund on Disability to guarantee the participation and representation of Southern CSOs in international monitoring committee meetings and in other relevant conferences is essential. Finally, the fight for full exercise of legal capacity is ongoing all around the world. Pseudo-solutions are not the answer, as they perpetuate structures of exclusion and block the ability to exercise and fully enjoy human rights for all persons with disabilities, whether those disabilities are intellectual, psychosocial, or physical. All forms of structures of exclusion, such as interdiction, curatorship, declaration of "absolute incapacity," and forced institutional confinement, still in use in the laws of our countries, cannot be accepted under any circumstance and need to be revoked.

The CRPD is a historic and fundamental step forward in the struggle that still goes on. It is an international tool, a fruit of social and political willingness of a collective effort that aims to build new and more diverse and inclusive utopias. As the poet Alfred Tennyson concluded in "Ulysses,"

Tho' much is taken, much abides; and tho'
We are not now that strength which in old days
Moved earth and heaven, that which we are, we are;
One equal temper of heroic hearts,
Made weak by time and fate, but strong in will
To strive, to seek, to find, and not to yield.

CHAPTER 12

Voices Down Under:
An Australian Perspective

Heidi Forrest and Phillip French

The negotiation of the Convention on the Rights of Persons with Disabilities and its Optional Protocol is a monumental achievement of intergenerational significance. In the course of the negotiation process, the social relations of disability fundamentally changed, not only at the international level, but also within individual nations, including Australia. Indeed, at least for a time, the centrifugal power relations that scatter the needs and concerns of persons with disabilities to the periphery of their societies and of international relations were reversed. In their place, the UN system and many governments adopted a new and democratizing ethic of partnership and collaboration with persons with disabilities by placing them at its center. This ethic was as empowering of persons with disabilities as it was civilizing of international lawmaking. Persons with disabilities were invested with the opportunity to describe their lived experience in their own voices, to imagine a world in which they were not degraded and oppressed, and to be agents in the creation of a new legal paradigm that would attempt to capture those imaginings.

In this chapter we provide an Australian perspective on the CRPD negotiation process. During the period of the CRPD development we were president (Heidi Forrest) and executive director (Phillip French) of People with Disability Australia (PWD-Australia). With a number of colleagues, it was our great privilege to participate in the CRPD consultation and negotiation processes at the national, regional, and international levels on behalf of persons with disabilities. Apart from our organizational roles, we both also have direct personal and family experience of impairment and disability. Our participation in the process was, therefore, experienced on a deeply intimate as well as on a public representational level. For this reason, we approach the task of recounting our CRPD adventure with some trepidation. In an important sense, it is simply not possible to reduce our public and private encounters to a single linear narrative. Yet encounters such as ours must be recorded, however incompletely, because the role civil society played in the development of the CRPD is now central to our collective identity as a disability rights movement.

People with Disability Australia

PWD-Australia is a national cross-disability rights and advocacy organization. It is a disabled people's organization, and its active membership consists exclusively of persons with disabilities and organizations of persons with disabilities. PWD-Australia was founded initially in 1980, in the lead-up to the International Year of Disabled Persons in 1981, and ultimately as the result of a resolution carried at the conclusion of the First Handicapped Persons Conference held in Australia. It was founded to provide persons with disabilities with a direct "voice of our own," adopting words that would become the motto of Disabled People's International, which was established in the same year. Originally PWD-Australia was established at the state level in New South Wales; it later federated with other state and territory bodies to form Disabled Peoples International (Australia) (DPI(A)). However, DPI(A) collapsed in 1995 and for a period of seven years Australia lacked a national cross-disability coordinating mechanism and representative voice. To fill this lacuna, and following extensive consultations with members and colleagues, PWD-Australia amended its constitution in 2002 to resituate as an organization that operates at both the national and New South Wales levels.

PWD-Australia's work has always been framed in terms of human rights, and it has a very distinctive, activist, rights-based culture. Perhaps because of this, PWD-Australia was more acutely aware of the need for, and the potential of, an international treaty on disability rights. It meant that we were instantly alert to movements within the UN system toward such a treaty, and that we were predisposed to engagement in its development.

Working with the Australian Government

The CRPD was developed during a period of ultraconservative Australian government, during which there was a significant retraction from previous commitments to human rights and disengagement from international human rights dialogue and institutions. In fact, during this period the Australian government positioned itself in the UN system as the leading critic of multilateral human rights institutions and oversight arrangements, openly questioning their legitimacy, integrity, and efficiency. Consistent with this position, the government was initially opposed to the development of an international instrument that would deal with the dignity and rights of persons with disabilities. However, when pressed it did not oppose the consensus, saving Australia from a humiliating legacy.

This was also an era in which our government was ruthlessly critical and destructive of NGOs involved in international human rights oversight, openly challenging their legitimacy and the degree of influence they were perceived to have over UN human rights treaty bodies and independent experts. This influence was prosecuted as a threat to the sovereignty of states, and as a primary reason for what it constructed as the inefficiency and failure of the UN human rights system. Domestically, public funding was withdrawn from many NGOs for disadvantaged population groups. Public funding for the remaining organizations was made conditional on acceptance of gag clauses in funding contracts. The government attitude to the UN human rights system, and the participation of NGOs in human rights advocacy, particularly at the international level, presented substantial risks for any organization that sought to participate in international human rights processes, particularly if this involved criticism of the Australian government.

Notwithstanding the apparent groundswell of support for an international human rights convention that would deal with the human rights of persons with disabilities, the Australian government was initially very active among a small number of nations that attempted to maneuver the Ad Hoc Committee away from what many thought was its clearly expressed mandate. During the first AHC session, the Australian delegation argued strongly, both on the record and in informal negotiations with other states, that Resolution 58/168[1] did not authorize the AHC to develop an international instrument on the rights of persons with disabilities, nor, in particular, did it mandate the development of a particular type of instrument. Instead, it argued, the resolution merely authorized the AHC to "consider proposals" for an international convention, and the use of the term "convention" (with a small "c" in the resolution) was not to be understood as limiting the types of instrument that might be considered. In this second respect, the Australian delegation expressed a view on the record that a protocol or annex to an existing human rights treaty might be preferable to the development of a "stand-alone" human rights convention. Off the record, in informal negotiations, the delegation pressed hard for an optional protocol or annex to the International Covenant on Civil and Political Rights.

While this position may have been the result of Australia's general antagonism to the international human rights system, it did not necessarily stem from an insincere concern that the development of a new international human rights convention might simply duplicate existing human rights rather than resolve the reasons why existing instruments had not effectively protected the human rights of persons with disabilities. Also, the delegation raised concern over a new treaty potentially eroding human rights protection. Consequently, the Australian delegation initially argued that the real task of the AHC was to "clarify the extent to which the rights and dignity of persons with disabilities are promoted and protected in existing instruments and to seek to close those gaps."[2]

This negotiating position, which was broadly equivalent to that by other key constituencies, such as the European Union, in the initial stages, had the effect of hijacking most of the first session to discuss the AHC mandate rather than matters of substance. During this time, there was only limited awareness among Australians with disabilities of the events that were taking place in New York. The government had not consulted with persons with disabilities on the process. Very few Australians with disabilities knew that the possibility of an international treaty that would deal with the rights of persons with disabilities was even being debated. Nevertheless, PWD-Australia and some other organizations were closely monitoring these developments and became very alarmed at the positions being advanced by the Australian delegation in these sessions. This alarm was intensified by reports from international colleagues who had directly observed the sessions, alerting us to the negative role the Australian delegation was playing not only on the record but, perhaps more significantly, in the informal negotiations.

In an effort to bring critical attention to the issue within Australia, following the first session, PWD-Australia collaborated with the (Australian) Disability Studies and Research Institute to conduct a one-day seminar in Sydney on the proposed development of the Convention. The seminar attempted to raise consciousness about convention negotiations and initiate a dialogue between the Australian government and key Australian DPOs about Australia's position. The Australian Human Rights and Equal Opportunity Commission (as it then was known) and some leading Australian disability studies and human rights academics also participated in the seminar.

While our objectives for the seminar were achieved in part, overall it proved difficult to persuade many of the national representative groups that this issue deserved priority attention. Very few chose to participate in the seminar. Most asserted the view that domestic issues were a more important focus of attention and that a treaty of this nature would be unlikely to have much impact in the Australian context. Additionally, most expressed the view that development of a convention on the rights of persons with disabilities would take many years, if it could be achieved at all. These views had the unfortunate effect of reinforcing the Australian government view that the convention negotiations were of little interest or concern to Australians with disabilities. Certainly, it would have appeared to government delegates at the seminar that there was little domestic political risk associated with the position it was agitating in New York.

As disappointing as these views were, they did not erode the belief of persons with disabilities in the significance of the effort to develop an international convention on the rights of persons with disabilities, or in the potential for such a convention to stimulate fundamental positive change in their lives at the Australian domestic level. However, quite apart from these issues, the seminar galvanized in us a sense of responsibility for Australia's unproductive conduct to date in the convention negotiation process. It strengthened our resolve to influence the Australian government to take a more positive (or at least a less negative) role in the negotiations, not only for the sake of Australians with disability, but also to ensure that Australia did not thwart the potential for a human rights instrument that would benefit persons with disabilities around the globe. We thus began to agitate for Australia to reposition itself as a good international citizen and expert contributor to the negotiations.

Throughout the CRPD negotiation process, even when the Australian government's contribution was at its most positive, the proposition that any international instruments should not result in changes in the scale or scope of Australia's international obligations constituted a glass ceiling through which our advocacy could not penetrate. The Australian delegation could not, and would not, advance or agree to an obligation that it did not believe was already accommodated by Australian law or programs, nor would it advance or agree to an obligation that it did not believe to be a direct application of existing international law. This approach to the interpretation of the CRPD still has the potential to limit the implementation of the Convention within Australia, notwithstanding that there has now been a change of government, and a very active and positive reengagement with the UN human rights system.

A more immediate strategic outcome of the seminar, however, was PWD-Australia's decision to seek accreditation with the AHC so it could participate in the negotiations. We concluded that this step was necessary to ensure that Australians with disabilities had a direct voice in the negotiations, one that could be distinguished, if necessary, from our government's position. It had become clear to us that, whatever our own limitations, no other DPO was, at that time, better positioned or motivated to perform this role. Not very many weeks later our application for accreditation had been submitted, and we were on a plane headed for New York to participate in the second AHC session.

The Framework for Participation

The adoption of GA Resolution A/RES/57/229,[3] encouraging states to involve persons with disabilities, representatives of DPOs, and experts in the preparatory processes to contribute to the AHC work, and to include them in their delegations, had an immediate and surprising impact on the Australian government's strategic approach to the negotiations, given its recent position. Consequently, the government consulted with national DPOs (and some other groups) prior to the second session. However, this consultation was limited to letters seeking views on the matters in the draft agenda for the meeting, with very little time for response. Nor did the description of the issues properly disclose the position being argued by the Australian delegation.

This approach to consultation attracted very significant criticism for its superficiality and inaccessibility to most Australians with disabilities (there was virtually no opportunity even for the national organizations that were asked to contribute their views to consult their membership and constituency about the issues). The disability sector's reaction to this consultation method was to stimulate a fundamental and positive change in the trajectory of the Australian government's approach to consulting with the sector following the second session. In our view, a second and equally powerful stimulus for this change was our ability to participate in the second session and publicly state disability-sector views that were contrary to those of the Australian government. By these means, Resolution 57/229 had an immensely civilizing effect on the Australian government's approach to involving Australians with disabilities in the formulation of its contributions to the AHC.

Also somewhat unexpectedly, in the lead-up to the second session, the Australian government embraced the imperative to include persons with disabilities in its official delegation to the AHC. The representative was selected from the Australian government's then official advisory body, the National Disability Advisory Council of Australia (NDAC). Members of this body (and its successor) are appointed by the government in a personal capacity and have no responsibility either to represent the views of the disability sector or to report back to the sector for their activities. Additionally, prior to the second session, NDAC had not engaged in any consultative or policy-development process related to the Convention that could have provided a proper basis for a "representative" contribution to the delegation. Nonetheless, ultimately, the representative selected was a person of considerable talent and integrity who made an important contribution to reshaping the delegation's approach to the AHC mandate.

Following the second session, a wider range of groups, including PWD-Australia, were invited to nominate individuals for selection as the "disability-sector representative" on the delegation. However, PWD-Australia took the view that this role would be too compromising of our independence, that it was preferable that we retain the ability to express views opposing the government position, if circumstances called for it. The disability-sector representative selected to participate in the Australian delegation from the third session forward was, however, a person with whom we had a close working relationship. Within the constraints of her role, she was able to very effectively work with us and other Australian and international nongovernment participants in the AHC to ensure that our views were considered and supported wherever possible.

Apart from the disability-sector representative, the Australian government delegation to the AHC comprised a representative from the Human Rights Branch of the Australian Attorney-General's Department, a representative of the Disability Policy Unit of the Australian Department of Families, Community Services and Indigenous Affairs (as it then was), and a representative of the Australian Human Rights and Equal Opportunity Commission. Although the delegation was to work under a limited and negative brief for most of the second session, the individuals in the delegation were personally very responsive and accessible to us and respectful of our views, even when we vigorously opposed their "minimalist" position in the open plenary sessions. This was as unexpected as it was welcome. We were initially very concerned about the potential for political attacks upon us by the Australian government, both during AHC sessions and at home, given its general antagonism to the participation of NGOs within the UN system. However, we experienced nothing of this nature.

Of course, in part, our success in working with the Australian delegation was built on a carefully constructed diplomatic framework. A key element was a self-imposed "no surprise rule," which simply meant that we always briefed the Australian delegation on our views, and provided them with the text of our interventions in the debate, prior to any public statement. Over time, this diplomacy came to be reciprocated by the delegation. We also always attempted to argue a positive alternative to a position adopted by the Australian delegation with which we did not agree, rather than by attacking the delegation. Another key element of our approach was to recognize that the individuals participating in the Australian delegation had to work subject to constraints within their brief. We accepted that there would be some "no-fly" zones where it would be futile to attempt to persuade the delegation. Where these no-fly zones existed, we instead focused our lobbying on delegations that had scope to consider our views.

Over time, we developed a nearly seamless relationship with the Australian delegation based on an increasingly constructive give-and-take at informal as well as formal levels aimed at securing a desirable text. At times this meant that members of the Australian delegation would participate in meetings we convened with representatives of other civil society organizations, and on other occasions we were invited to participate in sensitive meetings between the Australian delegation and other delegations. It is still surprising to us that this could have been achieved in such a negative domestic human rights policy environment. Although the Australian government had not wanted or endorsed the creation of a new human rights instrument for persons with disabilities, it eventually decided to embrace this agenda and played an increasingly positive and activist role in the negotiations from the third session forward.

Our National Consultations

In Australia, the disability-representative sector is a hotly contested space, as indeed it is in many other countries and at the international level, with many organizations competing for recognition and legitimacy. Several "generations" of DPOs coexist in this space, not altogether peacefully. They include first-generation organizations structured according to particular impairments or conditions, second-generation organizations structured on a cross-disability and cross-population group basis, and third-generation organizations structured according to a particular population group (e.g., women, indigenous persons, and persons from culturally and linguistically diverse backgrounds). Additionally, various types of organizations claim representative legitimacy. They include DPOs, disability-rights and advocacy organizations, peer-led service providers for persons with disabilities, parent- and family-based organizations, industry groups for disability service providers, and professional associations. Nor are these organizations distributed equally across state and territorial lines. These dynamics, coupled with Australia's geography and low population density, make it very difficult for DPOs to caucus, achieve consensus, and work in strategic alignment on issues of common concern. One very negative consequence of this is that disability public policy in Australia is dominated by a parent-carer and service-provider agenda.

During the early period of the CRPD's development, and until PWD-Australia repositioned nationally, Australia did not have a national cross-disability, cross-population group peak representative body for persons with disabilities. When the conservative government was first elected to office in 1996, it attempted to use federal funding mechanisms to "rationalize" its relationship with existing impairment-specific and population-group-specific national representative organizations. They were compelled to participate in a process that would ultimately see the establishment of a supervening body, now known as the Australian Federation of Disability Organizations, which finally became operational in 2003, after several years of bitter fighting. The Australian Federation of Disability Organizations is now regarded by the Australian government, and it describes itself, as "the" national representative voice for persons with disabilities, but in reality it is still struggling to achieve legitimacy among the wider community of persons with disabilities and their organizations in Australia. Suspicion and resentment of the Federation, which was perceived as created by government, was particularly acute during the CRPD negotiation process. Yet as the negotiation process progressed, it was positioned by the Australian government as the principal coordination mechanism and ultimate representative body for channeling the sector's views.

It was in the context of these very challenging dynamics that PWD-Australia chose to engage at the national, regional, and international levels as an Australian nongovernment contributor to the negotiation process, and that we undertook national consultations with persons with disabilities on the CRPD draft text. These dynamics help to explain why we adopted such a hyperdemocratic and decentralized consultation process within Australia, and why we so strongly adhered to positions negotiated within Australia in our international representation.

When the Working Group draft proposal for the Convention was released in early 2004, the Australian government provided PWD-Australia with a substantial grant to undertake a national consultation process with Australians with disabilities on its behalf. We did so in collaboration with the Australian Federation of Disability Organizations, which by that time had been established but was not yet operational, and the National Association of Community Legal Centres, which included in its membership Australia's disability-discrimination legal centers. Until that time PWD-Australia and the National Association of Community Legal Centres had been the principal Australian participants in the CRPD negotiation process, so together we were apparently viewed by the Australian government as most capable of undertaking this work.

Australia's population concentrates on the vast coastal fringes, raising distinct issues for the rural and remote community, which also includes the indigenous populations. In order to effectively consult Australians with disabilities about the CRPD text we had to devise a methodology that was capable of responding, as far as possible, to our geographic and population group diversity. We opted for a multimodal strategy that made maximum possible use of technology, as well as providing for plenary and targeted face-to-face encounters. Our technology-based consultation processes included a national toll-free number, a designated consultation e-mail address, and a web-based blog to support discussion and debate. We also created a website that provided a static repository of information about the negotiation process, and web links to other relevant sources of information (the e-mail and blog were also accessible from this website). These modalities were supported by an active online consultation strategy, which involved the daily dispatch of e-bulletins through listservs throughout the sector. These modalities had virtually unlimited potential to reach persons with disabilities across Australia, provided they could use some form of technology.

For those who could not or would not avail themselves of technologies we conducted public meetings in each capital city in Australia. These public meetings were used to raise awareness about the development of the CRPD and to seek the views of participants on key issues. To facilitate this, each meeting used a range of consultation techniques, including plenary brainstorming, small group discussion, and an "open mike" component that provided the opportunity for longer statements. These public meetings were undertaken on a partnership basis with major cross-disability, cross-population group representative, or rights and advocacy organizations in each state and territory (except Norfolk Island). We viewed this power-sharing approach as fundamental to democratizing the consultation process, building the capacity of our sector overall to engage in the CRPD negotiation process, achieving a grass roots-based consensus on issues, and avoiding the potential for destructive rivalries and jealousies. This would not have been possible if one or a few organizations were viewed as dominating all others. Incidental to their primary purpose, the meetings also provided a good opportunity for the partner organizations to increase their profile and engagement with their local constituencies, and this helped build social capital in the disability rights movement in Australia.

We also undertook a number of specifically targeted events to capture the views of particular constituencies. A daylong workshop seminar was conducted for national leading representative organizations. These organizations and their representatives are distributed across the country, so we provided them with the necessary funds to meet in one place. Prior to the event, we developed and circulated a detailed background and issues paper that helped to ensure that the day's deliberations were well informed and that key issues could be considered in detail. We also conducted a number of focus groups targeted to particular population groups, including persons with intellectual disability, children and young people, women, persons from rural and remote communities, indigenous persons, and persons from culturally and linguistically diverse backgrounds. In most cases, these focus groups were conducted in partnership with a relevant representative group for that constituency. Some of these focus groups were conducted face-to-face, while others were conducted by teleconference or online conferencing, in light of the above-mentioned challenges. Of course, all our consultation modalities incorporated any impairment- and disability-related adjustments required by participants.

The outcome of this consultation process was a major report to the Australian government, which outlined in great detail the views of Australians with disabilities not only about the WG draft text but also on a wide range of other relevant issues. Although we never had access to the Australian delegation's brief for the third (or any other) session, it was clear from the positions adopted by the Australian delegation in these meetings that this submission was very influential. Indeed, in many areas it appeared that the Australian government had adopted this advice in full. A second major benefit of this consultation process was that it provided Australian NGOs that were participating in the AHC with a detailed foundation for their lobbying activities. It was apparent to our own government, and to the many other delegations we briefed on our policy positions, that our views were well researched and considered and that they had genuine representative legitimacy.

After the sixth AHC session, once a revised text proposal for the Convention was in hand, we conducted much more specific and targeted consultations with major national and state representative groups about the key issues remaining in contention at the AHC level. These included such issues as an approach to legal capacity, compulsory assistance, inclusive education and sensory impairment, definition of disability, and, most importantly, in relation to the proposed implementation and monitoring framework. We used the funding available to fly representatives of these organizations in to attend a series of "roundtables" held in three capital cities. At the conclusion of these consultations, we again produced a detailed report to the Australian government, which became apparent was very influential in the drafting of the Australian delegation's brief for the seventh and eighth sessions.

Working in the Asia Pacific Region

GA Resolution 57/229 also "invited" the UN regional commissions to make available to the AHC suggestions and possible elements to be considered in proposals for a convention. The UN Economic and Social Council for Asia and the Pacific (UNESCAP) held two very important regional meetings in 2003. The first of these produced the so-called Bangkok Recommendations, which had a significant influence on key aspects of the debate in the second session.

Even more important, the second meeting produced the so-called "Bangkok Draft" text for the Convention—possibly the most significant of the many contributions made to the WG, heavily influencing the scope, structure, and content of the WG draft. Indeed, its influence extended beyond the WG draft, to the ultimate text of the CRPD itself, particularly in relation to such issues as the social model of disability, inclusive education, and international cooperation. These regional meetings placed major emphasis on the participation of DPOs and independent experts, many of which were funded to attend, as well as governments. Quite brilliantly, UNESCAP framed these meetings as those of an "expert working group" in which each of the participants had equal status. The outputs therefore reflected the views of participants and did not require formal support from the region's governments.

Both regional meetings played a critical role in building awareness of, and support for, the Convention in the Asia and Pacific regions. They were also crucial in ensuring that the views of DPOs from developing and transitional economies in the region received equitable attention in the development of the Convention. Although a number of DPOs from Asia and the Pacific did, in fact, participate in the AHC, the costs of attending two- and three-week AHC sessions in New York twice a year were simply prohibitive for most of these organizations. The UN Regional Headquarters in Bangkok was an infinitely more accessible venue for these groups.

Our regional processes did have one significant limitation. They were very heavily dominated by Asian interests, often at the expense of Pacific interests. Asian diplomatic dominance is perhaps unsurprising given the vast differences in the size and composition of the regions, but even so, participation and representation sometimes lacked any proportionality. Perhaps most seriously, of the seven regional representatives selected for participation in the WG, not a single one came from a Pacific country. Paradoxically, although Australia is geographically situated in the Pacific, in the UN system our government is part of the "Western Europe and Others Group." This is also the case with New Zealand, which was selected to participate in the WG. Of course, these groupings do not apply to NGOs. Consequently, we invested a great deal of effort in attempting to achieve some proportionality in representation for the Pacific region by pursuing the nomination of a representative of a Pacific DPO as the nongovernment regional representative. However, these efforts were ultimately unsuccessful and all regional WG members were drawn from Asia.

The Australian government alignment with the Western Europe and Others Group also led to some asymmetries between our work in Australia, Bangkok, and New York. Although the Australian government could have done so, notwithstanding its other diplomatic alignment, it did not participate in the UNESCAP Expert Working Group meetings. In the lead-up to the WG meeting and the third session we attempted to persuade the Australian government to commit, at least in principle, to support for the terms of the Bangkok Draft, and to engage more actively with Pacific governments in the Convention negotiation process, but we did not have any particular success. This was a source of acute frustration to Asian and Pacific DPOs, and indeed, to a number of government delegations from the region. In New York, we often closely caucused with (the few) participating CSOs and governments from the Pacific region; however, the Australian delegation had no formal caucus with these governments, and it was therefore difficult to persuade it to take up issues of particular regional significance (e.g., the aggravated disadvantage of persons with disabilities living in small island nations and communities). The lack of participation of Pacific nation governments in the AHC exacerbated the invisibility of Pacific Islanders with disabilities in the negotiation process.

We had slightly more success from our direct efforts to kindle engagement and support from Pacific governments in the convention negotiation process. Following the second session we wrote to all parliamentary heads of Pacific nations, urging them to take an active role in the Convention negotiations and also to support participation of their national representative DPOs in the process. A number of Pacific governments responded very positively and sent delegations to some sessions of the AHC. The government of

Vanuatu even went so far as to appoint a representative of its national representative DPO to represent it in the AHC negotiations. We were able to work very closely with that delegation for the remainder of the negotiations in efforts to bring a Pacific Island perspective to the issues in debate. However, in the final analysis, the results of all these efforts are disappointing. The CRPD does not contain any explicit element that acknowledges or responds to the specific disadvantages faced by persons with disabilities in island communities.

A much more positive by-product of these and other efforts has been broader recognition of the need to build the capacity of Pacific governments and national DPOs in the region. With our colleagues in the Pacific we were able to influence the establishment of a focal point on disability in the Pacific Island Forum Secretariat in 2006. We also have invested significantly over a number of years in the development and establishment of the Pacific Disability Forum, a coordination mechanism for the region's DPOs, which was finally established in 2004. Over time, these initiatives have the potential to ensure that the Pacific region is more visible in international disability policy processes.

Working with the International Disability Caucus

Only a very small number of CSOs participated in the first AHC session. Our entry to the negotiation process in New York therefore coincided with that of many other groups and preceded the establishment of what was to become the International Disability Caucus. With many others we were, therefore, faced with the challenge not only of finding ways to work with the government delegations, but also of finding ways to work with each other.

No one can doubt the significance of the IDC impact on the course of negotiations. It was, overwhelmingly, a potent positive influence on the AHC deliberations, and, for the most part, its policy positions reflected the needs and aspirations of persons with disabilities around the world. However, the IDC was far from monolithic, nor was it particularly democratic or inclusive. There were many tensions and gulfs between groups. The lack of accessibility of the UN headquarters, language and communication barriers, "North/South" perspectives, and the very limited time we had to caucus with each other accentuated these problems. The initial view of the organizations that constituted the International Disability Alliance that they were the only legitimate spokespersons in that forum was a major obstacle. The outward expression of this dynamic changed over the course of negotiations, but it persisted to the end nevertheless. In the later stages it sought to manifest in what might be conceptualized as a "veto" power that particular members of the IDA sought to impose on policy positions others thought preferable. On a number of key issues, we felt this did not serve the broader disability rights movement well and that IDC functioning was too often characterized by suppression of viewpoints that were inconsistent with those of particular dominant actors.

In part for these reasons, our relationship with what was to become the IDC changed over the course of negotiations. In the early stages, particularly during the second session, we invested enormous energy in efforts to establish a democratic and participatory civil society caucus. Later, when it became clear that some of the most negative dynamics in the caucus would not be overcome, we were more selective of our alliances in the group and our investment of time in its processes. We worked much more along a horizontal dimension with likeminded groups within the caucus to elaborate and embolden the policy issues that were of concern to us, and increasingly left it to others to argue these positions vertically within the caucus. In a way, this could be considered a selfish way of working, but it was the most economic use of our limited resources, and it allowed us to maintain a primary focus on our persuasive efforts with the government delegations. We observed that many of our colleagues, in effect, were doing the same. At the same time we remained grateful for those colleagues who persisted with the effort to influence the IDC.

One of the greatest difficulties we had with the IDC politics was the expectation of some dominant members that we would, in effect, surrender any policy position they disagreed with. Given the extensive background work we had undertaken with grassroots organizations in Australia, we took the view that while we should maintain a flexible approach to achieving our policy objectives, we were not at liberty to make fundamental changes to those objectives without first consulting the constituency we represented in the negotiations and articulating these changes to our government. This led to outright conflict with some IDC members on issues such as inclusive education and inclusive employment (which were, from our point of view, generally favorably resolved), and legal capacity and compulsory assistance (which were not resolved). At one point, particular members of the IDC purported to "expel" us from the IDC because we would not accept their veto of our policy position on legal capacity and compulsory assistance: a gesture we, and most of our colleagues, simply chose to ignore. Privately, we received a great deal of support and encouragement for our positions on these and other issues from colleagues within the IDC.

Our Wins and Losses

The CRPD is, overall and fundamentally, a remarkably positive text, but it is not a perfect text. From our point of view, there were wins and losses in the negotiations, some of which may not ultimately matter much, others of which may end up mattering a great deal. We only have the capacity to reflect on a few of them here.

From the outset we took the view that the Convention ought to recognize the multiple and aggravated forms of discrimination and disadvantage experienced by particular population groups, and that it ought to impose a specific state obligation to address this disadvantage. At the beginning of the negotiations this position was not supported by dominant IDC members or by many government delegations, including the Australian delegation. However, that changed over the course of the negotiations. The ultimate inclusion of articles (and other specific text) in relation to women and children with disabilities is, therefore, a remarkable achievement by activists in civil society (of which we were just one) and within the government delegations. Conversely, the failure of the CRPD to refer, in a substantive article, to other minority groups, including indigenous persons, other cultural and racial minorities, and persons with high support needs is disappointing, as it potentially entrenches the invisibility of these groups within human rights discourse and, even more seriously, also in implementation efforts.

The CRPD recognition of the central importance of reasonable accommodation to nondiscrimination in the area of disability is a very important achievement. Perhaps more than any other element of the text, reasonable accommodation will ensure the CRPD's traction against the most persistent human rights violations persons with disabilities experience. Nevertheless, this achievement is, in our view, potentially very seriously undermined by the ill-considered phrasing of the definition of "reasonable accommodation" in Article 2, which refers to "adjustments not imposing a disproportionate or undue burden." The double-barreled test, especially if directly incorporated into domestic legislation, sets the threshold of obligation far too low in our view (and each element of the test has the potential to pull down the other). We would have preferred a different formulation that would require adjustments to be made up to the point where they become an "unjustifiable hardship."[4] Ultimately, we will have to trust that the treaty body will interpret the test as unitary and strict, in spite of its weasel words. We are also very disappointed by the use of the word "burden" in the definition of reasonable accommodation, which very directly perpetuates one of the most destructive stereotypes to which persons with disabilities are subject.

The CRPD is underpinned by a social model of disability, in which disability is understood as the result of the interaction of persons with impairment with environmental barriers. This conceptualization of disability means that the whole thrust of the CRPD is on the removal of these barriers to equality, participation, and inclusion, rather than on the prevention and treatment of impairment, and that is a very good thing indeed. Nevertheless, there are serious problems in the CRPD that arise from the radical, social constructionist version of the social model that was championed by some elements of civil society in the negotiations. The most serious of these include the attempt, at several places in the text, to distinguish between "disability" and conduct. For example, in Article 14 we read that "the existence of a disability shall in no case justify a deprivation of liberty" and in Article 23 we read that "in no case shall a child be separated from parents on the basis of a disability of either the child or one or both of the parents." Essentially, the first thing such formulations do is to appear to confuse impairment with disability. What they probably mean is that a person's impairment (say, intellectual or psychosocial impairment) should never itself justify deprivation of liberty or the separation of parents from a child. This would not prevent the state from intervening where that person's conduct (e.g., the threat of harm to self or others) justified such an intervention. However, in many situations a person's conduct will be a characteristic of impairment, for instance, when a person with acute mental illness causes harm to another person because in a state of psychosis he or she has developed false belief about that person, or lacks inhibition about causing harm to another person. In other cases, a person's conduct will be a product of his or her disability (properly understood). For example, persons with autism or who are deafblind may cause harm to themselves or others as a result of the frustration they experience in being unable to effectively communicate with others.

It is simply not possible or appropriate to separate conduct from impairment and disability. Consequently, this formulation may prove very difficult to effectively apply. It not only may miss its target, but it may also lead to a serious erosion of the protection the CRPD ought to extend to particular individuals with disability.

We have already noted that in key respects we held a different view from some other members of the IDC on the issues of legal capacity and compulsory treatment. The point of departure was on "ultimate" issues, and we were on common ground on all other points. Very briefly, it was and remains our view that there are specific circumstances where it is both ethically defensible and affirmatively required, from a human rights perspective, for legal capacity to be exercised on behalf of another person, where that person lacks the instrumental capacity to do so personally, due to the level of his or her impairment or disability. Similarly, we hold the same view regarding the need to provide persons with compulsory assistance, where their impairment or disability presents a serious risk of harm to themselves or others.

What nobody appeared to disagree with in this debate was the long history of, and continuing potential for, abuse of such arrangements. Nor, if we understood correctly, did anybody seriously imagine that such arrangements could be eradicated, even if this was desirable. No comprehensive alternative to them was, or could be, presented in the debate. Therefore, from our point of view, even if the protagonists could not agree on the ultimate desirability of these measures, they should have been able to agree that such measures ought to be subject to strict safeguards against abuse, and that these ought to be legislated in the CRPD. We viewed this as particularly necessary to ensure reform in state regimes with abusive practices in these areas.

Ultimately, Article 12 more or less successfully achieves this with respect to substitute decision making, but Article 17 fails miserably to do so in relation to compulsory assistance. It essentially reposes no explicit rights in persons with disabilities, and imposes no explicit obligations on states, in relation to compulsory assistance. In our view, that is a matter for very great regret.

Conclusion

In marked contrast to the position the Australian government started from in the negotiations, it was among the first governments to sign the CRPD when it opened for signature on 30 March 2007, and it did so while Australia was still governed by an ultraconservative government that remained antagonistic to international human rights oversight. Australia was also among the first nations to ratify the CRPD and did so on 17 July 2008. By this time more than a decade of conservative government had been swept aside and Australia had begun to energetically reposition itself as a leader in international human rights. It is interesting to speculate the reasons why Australia committed to the CRPD at a time of retreat from international human rights. There were no doubt a number of factors at play. However, we believe that PWD-Australia's strategy of persistent, diplomatic, positive engagement with our government played no small part in achieving this.

Australia also acceded to the Optional Protocol in August 2009. Of course, even with this development, our Australian journey is still at its beginning. Our focus has now moved to CRPD implementation, and we face an immense challenge to persuade Australian governments that the CRPD speaks to them as directly as it does to nations with less evolved disability policy and programs. Indeed, one of the ironic legacies of our success in positively engaging the Australian government in the negotiation process is the need now to dismantle its firm belief in its own perfection! Since ratification Australia has introduced the National Disability Strategy 2010–2020. The National Disability Insurance Scheme (NDIS) will hopefully, among other things, embody our initial efforts at CRPD domestic implementation. It was endorsed by the federal government in 2011 and is a ten-year commitment from all levels of government aimed at focusing on inclusion and the participation of people with disability on an equal basis with other Australians. Currently in Australia we are in the process of implementing the NDIS. The NDIS is a funding, support and governance mechanism that commits to providing people with a disability the opportunity to live fulfilling and active lives. It has the potential to make the convention real and meaningful in the lives of Australians with disability. The CRPD negotiation process entailed many complexities, challenges, frustrations, and disappointments both within Australia and internationally. Nevertheless, for us it was overwhelmingly a positive and productive experience. When we read the text of the CRPD, we see very many concepts, and even words, that can be traced back to our own interventions in the debate, and to the awareness-raising, drafting, and lobbying efforts we undertook with colleagues in the IDC, with other Australian NGOs, with the Australian delegation, and, indeed, at our own initiative. Like so many other persons with disabilities who participated in the negotiation process, whether in New York or in their local community, we feel a deep personal connection and pride in the CRPD, in spite of its deficiencies. Although it may be formally the product and possession of governments, in a very genuine and substantial way, the CRPD is our own collective composition: a synthesis of the diverse experiences and aspirations of persons with disabilities around the world; a fabric in which our past lives and future hopes are interwoven with those of others. Yet, even more than this, at a personal level, the quality of our experience of the CRPD negotiation process is measured not only by its political and legal outcome, but also in terms of our own life journeys. We have encountered new ideas, learned new skills, developed new insights, and forged new friendships. The process not only transformed international law, it also transformed the lives of many of those who participated, ourselves among them.

CHAPTER 13

Monitoring the Convention's Implementation

Marianne Schulze

The negotiations on the Convention on the Rights of Persons with Disabilities coincided with a vibrant debate over the need for an overhaul of the reporting system to the so-called treaty bodies[1] and therewith the framework for monitoring the national implementation of international human rights obligations. Moreover, the Convention was set to be the first human rights treaty negotiated following the 1993 Vienna Declaration and Programme of Action, which not only sought to increase the national application of human rights dramatically but also emphasized the importance of establishing national human rights institutions. Additionally, the question of monitoring— not only at the international but decisively also at the national level—was one to which all stakeholders, including disabled people's organizations and the UN entities, particularly the Office of the High Commissioner for Human Rights, attached great importance. Monitoring was, finally, also one of the few discussions to which international human rights organizations, such as Amnesty International, which otherwise largely confined themselves to observing the negotiations, contributed actively.

Thus, the negotiations of the monitoring provision (Article 33 of the CRPD) were distinct from many of the other provisions: the first-time participation of NHRIs in the negotiations of a human rights treaty[2] was of particular significance to the monitoring provision. The abundance of civil society organizations was enlarged due to the active support of international human rights groups. With deliberations underway on reforming the reporting mechanisms for existing human rights treaties to increase the impact at the national level, there was also a structural undercurrent in the debate, which was not at play in negotiating the other provisions.

As a result, the CRPD not only breaks new ground by framing human rights through an accessible and inclusive prism,[3] but also sets a new standard with regard to monitoring implementation at the national level. The obligation to provide for a national monitoring mechanism, with the active participation of civil society, has significant potential to raise the bar for monitoring at the national level generally.

This chapter provides an overview of the growing importance of monitoring at the national level and the reflection of this fact in the negotiations of the CRPD. Furthermore, the two provisions on monitoring that are standard for core human rights treaties, the international committee and the Optional Protocol, and their negotiation are summarized.

The Starting Point

The negotiations of the CRPD started against the backdrop of seven core human rights treaties, each with its own international reporting process.[4] While firmly grounded in the notion that the Convention was not to create any new rights[5]—and therewith mechanisms—it was understood that the reporting and monitoring scheme of the Convention was to follow established systems. Then again, there was a clear understanding that this established system was faulty and needed to be developed further. Also, the sense that something needed to be done to increase the interplay between the national and international levels—that is, the monitoring at the UN level and the implementation on the ground—needed to be strengthened.

Increased Importance of National Monitoring

The backdrop to the discussion of creating a mechanism to oversee the implementation of the CRPD at the national level can be sketched as follows: human rights are frequently bemoaned as being ineffective because the implementation mechanisms lack "teeth," namely, accountability and monitoring processes.

The monitoring system for the core human rights treaties of the UN focuses on member states having to submit regular reports to an expert committee established by the UN. In addition to written contributions, the expert committees also invite the member state to a dialogue session to discuss the report's contents by posing questions and looking into ways to improve the situation on the ground. Some of these "dialogues" could be perceived as shams, given that a large number of states tended—and some continue—to view the reporting process and subsequent discussion as a public-relations stunt. What is more, it has become increasingly clear that without a third opinion from within the country under scrutiny, it was almost impossible to develop an accurate account of the implementation gaps and challenges. The increasing role of civil society as a provider of additional— frequently critical—information on a state's human rights record is now manifest in the unwritten but well-practiced expectation that a decent ex- amination of a member state's human rights record will include at least one report by a civil society organization of said country.

The dependence of international experts on national experience high- lights the need for a mechanism to bridge the international with the na- tional realm: How can the experts find reliable sources at the national level? How can one ensure that the national institutions—state as well as civil society—are aware of the process and will provide information in time? What happens if the state does not report in time? Even more important, though, what happens with the recommendations the experts issue at the end of the dialogue? Who will make sure that there is follow-up?

Particularly the last concern is where human rights standards seemed to be eroded frequently. State delegations diligently engage with the independent ex- perts in a sincere dialogue, accept criticism with varying degrees of humbleness, and agree naturally to recommendations made far away from home. Frequently the buck stopped right there: little to no information was shared back at home, with rarely a public discussion as a follow-up to the dialogue held at the UN.

What is more, much of the human rights discourse of states was directed toward the outside rather than the inside: the addressees of "urgent ap- peals to uphold human rights standards" were far more often found in international forums and other countries than the domestic realm. By and large, the Cold War era was a time when human rights—and therewith their application—were discussed as applying to "the others," that is, a country in the opposite ideological spectrum rather than on home ground.

Human rights as part of the foreign policy public relations machinery officially came to an end as early as 1993. A World Conference on Human Rights was held in Vienna, close to the border of the now physically removed

iron curtain. The discussions there saw the first shift toward increased engagement between the UN—that is, the member states respectively—and
civil society. NGOs made a strong showing and influenced the debate as well
as the outcome.

The Vienna Declaration proclaims, among others things,

> the solemn commitment of all States to fulfil their obligations to
> promote universal respect for, and observance and protection of, all
> human rights and fundamental freedoms for all in accordance with
> the Charter of the UN, other instruments relating to human rights,
> and international law. . . . Human rights and fundamental freedoms
> are the birthright of all human beings; their protection and promo-
> tion is the first responsibility of Governments. . . . [I]t is the duty of
> States, regardless of their political, economic, and cultural systems,
> to promote and protect all human rights and fundamental freedoms.

The Debate over Treaty Body Reform

The steadily increasing ratification of core human rights treaties is a most
welcome sign of states' commitment to human rights standards, particularly their implementation. An increase of states parties also means an
increase in the number of reports that need to be written—at the states'
end—and assessed—at the treaty bodies' end. A rapidly growing backlog of
reports for most treaty bodies and an overburden of reporting requirements—
sometimes of overlapping nature—have led to a debate over reforming the
reporting system and therewith the treaty bodies.

The Principality of Liechtenstein, after becoming a UN member state
and ratifying the core human rights treaties, was overwhelmed with reporting requests, also due to its rather small administration. Subsequently, Liechtenstein spearheaded the discussion over treaty body reform. A 2002 report
by the UN secretary-general stressed the need for a more coordinated approach by the human rights treaty bodies, including a standardization of
the reporting requirements, and suggested that the overlapping of reporting
requirements be addressed through a single report.[6] As the negotiations of
the CRPD neared conclusion, efforts to harmonize reporting guidelines and
establish a common core document to cover the overlapping aspects of core
treaty reporting were getting under way.[7]

Philip Alston, former chair of the UN Committee on Economic, Social and Cultural Rights, entered the debate on treaty body reform in the context of the negotiations of the fifth Ad Hoc Committee. In a panel discussion organized by the OHCHR, Alston observed that the monitoring part of the core human rights treaties had never been planned or thought through thoroughly.[8] Alston urged the adoption of new ways. One suggestion he had received was to hold videoconferences with government officials in charge rather than poorly briefed bureaucrats.

"What do we want to get out of these bodies?" Alston asked. His answer included a list of key elements, such as focused priorities, national-level links, provision of funding and resources, expert input, and efforts to build constituencies, include private actors, and involve UN agencies in a meaningful way. Subsequently, the AHC followed up with a side event and growing discussion. In its report to the General Assembly following its sixth session, the AHC held that innovation was necessary in relation to monitoring bodies by providing for "both national and international monitoring."[9]

At that point, the OHCHR provided an expert paper to the AHC that outlined the status quo of the discussion and highlighted the main purposes of monitoring. This document highlighted five themes: (1) a proper diagnosis of the human rights situation; (2) effective evaluation and setting of priorities; (3) creation of partnerships between states and rights-holders; (4) creation of opportunities for capacity building and awareness raising; and (5) protection of the victims of human rights violations.[10]

National Monitoring

Reflecting the increasing importance of a national basis for overseeing implementation, the need for a provision on national monitoring took hold. It was raised not only in the context of a general monitoring scheme but also in the specific context of protection against violence and torture.

Drafting the Provision on National Monitoring

Experts, CSOs, and NHRIs supported a provision on national monitoring early on in the process. After the first round of negotiations, during a regional meeting in Ecuador, the Declaration of Quito was adopted, reflecting a regional commitment to the negotiations and calling for the "best mechanisms" to ensure accessibility for, and inclusion of, persons with disabilities in all spheres of life.[11] Soon after, in October 2003, a regional meeting in Thailand developed elements to be included in the draft convention. The "Bangkok Draft" proposed a stand-alone provision on a national implementation framework to "monitor, promote and enforce compliance" with the Convention; and that the framework should "operate in accordance with the Paris Principles."[12]

The Principles Relating to the Status of National Institutions,[13] commonly referred to as the Paris Principles, stipulate the framework for the independent work of NHRIs. Furthermore, the Bangkok Draft suggested that such a national implementation framework be established in consultation with persons with disabilities and their representative organizations (Article 34(b)). This involvement should also pertain to the institution's policies and processes (Article 34(c)). The idea of a focal point—as a primary coordinator and center of expertise within the administration—was also among the suggested elements, which made it into the subsequent provision (Article 34(2)). Finally, a subparagraph foresaw a procedure ensuring the evaluation of legislation, policies, and programs in the drafting stages to ensure accessibility for and inclusion of persons with disabilities (Article 34(2)).

The Working Group,[14] which produced the foundational draft of the CRPD, took on the idea of national monitoring. NHRIs were present in this round of consultation and—supported by various NGOs—emphasized the importance of mechanisms for national implementation. Governments responded favorably, some requesting that civil society develop the idea further.[15] The WG agreed on a brief text, which reflected many of the elements of the Bangkok Draft, under the title of "national implementation framework." It stipulated: "States Parties shall, in accordance with their legal and administrative system, maintain, strengthen, designate or establish at the national level a framework to promote, protect and monitor implementation of the rights recognized in the present Convention."[16] The idea of a focal point (see above) was also included.

For a while, it appeared that the issue of monitoring might be lost to ongoing debates concerning treaty reform within the UN. Finally, the sixth AHC saw substantial amendments to the draft text on national monitoring. Importantly, the NHRIs prepared a comprehensive proposal on monitoring, linking the national and international levels, foreseeing a complaints procedure and a global disability rights advocate.[17] Their proposal included an article on the "Establishment of a National Monitoring Body." It reflected the Bangkok Draft, adding a one-year deadline for establishment following entry into force. The powers of the body were specified—at a minimum— as monitoring of national compliance with the Convention, proposals on existing and draft legislation, initiation and support of complaints at the national level, making recommendations to authorities, involvement in awareness raising, and serving as a liaison to organizations representing persons with disabilities as well as international stakeholders.[18] An explicit reference to the Paris Principles and references to the various aspects of independence were also featured. A proposal by the delegation of Israel expanded and specified the powers and functions of the "National Human Rights Institution" even farther.[19]

Importantly, Amnesty International, as a well-established human rights NGO, entered the negotiations at the sixth AHC. In a paper titled "Strengthening Implementation at the National Level,"[20] Amnesty International outlined its criticism of the general status quo on monitoring as well as specific flaws in the AHC's draft on monitoring. Amnesty International stressed the important features ensuring the independence of national monitoring bodies, highlighting, among other things, the need to bring cases on behalf of persons with disabilities in domestic courts or to pertinent international bodies respectively. The importance of national action plans, as well as the explicit mention of adopting and implementing national strategies, was also underscored by Amnesty International. Specifically, the development of benchmarks and indicators for such strategies and plans was suggested as an explicit reference.

Amnesty International also had specific suggestions to make in clarifying the role of a governmental focal point. It described several interrelated tasks. First, it should facilitate coordination across different ministerial departments as well as local, regional, or federal authorities as applicable, including the collection of data and statistics as required for effective policy programming and evaluation of implementation. Second, this focal point should cooperate both with civil society and organizations representing persons with disabilities as well as national and international institutions. Finally, it should undertake or coordinate government activities in the area of awareness raising, educating the general public, training, and capacity building. [21]

The OHCHR submitted an expert paper[22] to the seventh AHC that recommended the inclusion of a provision that builds on Article 17 of the Optional Protocol to the Convention Against Torture, which foresees the establishment of national preventive mechanisms, independent bodies in charge of monitoring anti-torture policy. The expert paper also recommended the "express mention being included of a requirement to strive for the representation of persons with disabilities in the mechanism."[23] The experts also recommended "express reference to the Paris Principles" so as to "underline that effective monitoring depends on the independence of the national mechanism." After further negotiations, the following text was agreed as Article 33 CRPD:

> 1. States Parties, in accordance with their system of organization, shall designate one or more focal points within government for matters relating to the implementation of the present Convention, and shall give due consideration to the establishment or designation of a coordination mechanism within government to facilitate related action in different sectors and at different levels.
> 2. States Parties shall, in accordance with their legal and administrative systems, maintain, strengthen, designate or establish within the State Party, a framework, including one or more independent mechanisms, as appropriate, to promote, protect and monitor implementation of the present Convention. When designating or establishing such a mechanism, States Parties shall take into account the principles relating to the status and functioning of national institutions for protection and promotion of human rights.
> 3. Civil society, in particular persons with disabilities and their representative organizations, shall be involved and participate fully in the monitoring process.

Various elements of the Bangkok Draft made it into the final text, including the focal point and a mechanism to coordinate governmental implementation efforts, enshrined in paragraph 1. The frequently floated idea of a global ombudsperson or disability advocate was not included.[24]

The second paragraph focuses on monitoring outside the framework of government, providing for one—or more—independent mechanisms. A direct reference to the Paris Principles is included. That said, compared to Article 17 Optional Protocol to the Convention Against Torture the language is weaker in that the Paris Principles are to be "taken into account." Note also that there is no specification of a time frame—whereas the Optional Protocol to the Convention Against Torture foresees one year. Based on the reporting requirements under the CRPD, the time frame could be interpreted as being two years following entry into force for the state party, that is, the deadline for the first country report (Article 35(1) CRPD).

The effective and meaningful inclusion of persons with disabilities and their representative organizations was an early feature of the provision. In line with the overall spirit of the negotiation process, the necessity of non-governmental representation matured into an acceptable fact. Note that the requirement of civil society involvement (Article 33(3)) is supported by the general obligation to "closely consult" and "actively involve" persons with disabilities and their representative organizations in the development and implementation of legislation, policies, and other decision-making processes (Article 4(3) CRPD).

In a subsequent thematic study,[25] following a request by the Human Rights Council,[26] the OHCHR underscored the fact that the CRPD makes a distinction between the implementation aspects of the Convention and the need for protection, promotion, and monitoring. Accordingly, the OHCHR recommended that the functions be kept strictly separated, stressing that persons with disabilities and DPOs be involved in protection, promotion, and monitoring, in line with the Paris Principles.[27]

The Hidden Monitoring Provision

The Convention also foresees monitoring as part of safeguarding freedom from exploitation, violence, and abuse. Article 16(3) states:

> In order to prevent the occurrence of all forms of exploitation, violence and abuse, States Parties shall ensure that all facilities and programmes designed to serve persons with disabilities are effectively monitored by independent authorities.

The provision, hidden in the Convention's catalog of rights, is part of the comprehensive protection of integrity, which includes freedom from torture or cruel, inhuman, or degrading treatment or punishment, freedom from exploitation, violence, and abuse, and protection of integrity (Articles 15–17 CRPD).

Safeguards for protection from violence through monitoring can be traced to the Principles for the Protection of Persons with Mental Illness and the Improvement of Mental Health Care,[28] which include a provision on monitoring, providing for inspection of mental health facilities, to investigate and resolve complaints as well as ensure appropriate judicial proceedings for professional misconduct.[29] The WG reflected this aspect in its discussion of Freedom from Violence and Abuse—then Article 12.[30] The consolidated drafts by the facilitator show strong support for the provision from governments as well as civil society, particularly DPOs.[31]

The obligation to ensure effective monitoring in this context is not linked to the independent mechanism in Article 33(2). Article 16(3) leaves open all possibilities, including establishment of a link to the national preventive mechanism foreseen in Article 17 of the Optional Protocol to the Convention Against Torture, for countries that ratify the protocol.[32] The inclusion of persons with disabilities and their representative organizations in the monitoring activities of the independent authorities is guaranteed by way of Article 4(3) stipulating states' general obligations and through the general principle of participation and inclusion set out in Article 3.

Article 34—International Monitoring

International monitoring, the establishment of a treaty body, is part and parcel of every UN core human rights treaty.[33] Certainly the discussion of treaty body reform referred to earlier surfaced and resurfaced throughout the negotiations, and wishful thinking of overcoming the shortcomings of the established monitoring mechanisms peaked through the considerations. In the end, though, pragmatism prevailed.

First, it was clear that the discussions over treaty body reform were not going to be concluded at a substantial level any time soon.[34] Thus, there were too many "ifs" to leave this issue completely open, and it was too soon to inject elements of potential changes[35] that may—or not—reflect the outcome of treaty body reform. In that seven years after the conclusion of the CRPD treaty body reform has still to be concluded, this train of thought has been proven correct. Second, the unwritten understanding that the CRPD was not to create any new rights also meant that it would not be established at a standard less than that of the previous core treaties. The provision for international monitoring in other treaties therefore equaled the establishment of such a body for the CRPD. Even if some delegations pointed to the potential cost of an additional body as well as the added burden of another reporting system, in the end there was a certain sense of morality in all this: if the debate over treaty body reform could not be concluded, then at least the monitoring of the rights of persons with disabilities should not fall short of established standards.

The fact that international monitoring equates to a (in)direct financial contribution by member states, in order to support the operation of the body, as well as the fact that potential international scrutiny always has a distinctly political aspect, meant that delegations took a vital interest in the discussion. This in turn implied that the draft provision and its discussion were a given rather than requiring the push that was certainly necessary for other provisions.[36] As a consequence, the role of both civil society and NHRIs was focused on utilizing the possibility of advancing the status quo, making the most of the "necessary innovation."[37]

One example of such efforts was the IDC and NHRI proposal to have a global disability rights advocate,[38] that is, an enhanced and refined role for the special rapporteur on disability.[39] The advocate was to provide knowledge and support to increase awareness about the need for accessibly and inclusive human rights in line with the Convention.[40] The idea did not enter into the final provision, and the special rapporteur on disability remains the only international advocate who is appointed by the Commission for Social Development, whereas the other special rapporteurs and advisers are mostly appointed by the Human Rights Council.

The innovation that the CRPD does include, as per the urging of the IDC and NHRIs, is the consideration of persons with disabilities as members of the CRPD Committee. Reflecting both the impact that persons with disabilities had on the negotiations as well as their key role throughout the Convention,[41] it seems self-evident that persons with disabilities should explicitly be given a role in the international monitoring body. However, thus far treaty bodies have only stipulated that states shall give due consideration to "gender balance" as well as "equal geographic distribution." [42] The Convention thus breaks new ground in establishing the requirement of "participation of experts with disabilities" (Article 34(4)), carrying the motto "Nothing about us without us" to new—international—levels. This is the first time that "an instrument promotes participation in its treaty body by the particular cluster of persons whose rights it sets out to protect." [43]

The IDC and NHRIs did not stop there. Their vision of full and equal participation included a seat at the table discussing the nominations: the idea that DPOs—alternatively OHCHR—should be involved in the creation

of shortlists for potential candidates for the CRPD Committee, did not suc-
ceed.[44] Given the broader implications of such a precedent well beyond the
core treaty bodies, it was not surprising that states did not find the proposal
acceptable.

Optional Protocol

The International Covenant on Economic, Social and Cultural Rights, adopted in 1966, was fitted with an optional protocol in 2008, two years after
the CRPD was adopted and some forty-two years after it was concluded.
Optional protocols to core UN human rights treaties by and large provide
a mechanism that allows individuals, after having exhausted all available
national remedies, to petition the international monitoring body.[45] As the
example of economic, social, and cultural rights highlights, they usually
come well after the core treaty is adopted and in force, even if the International Covenant on Economic, Social and Cultural Rights may be an extreme example.[46] The Optional Protocol to the International Covenant on
Civil and Political Rights is the only one to have been adopted simultaneously with the core treaty.[47]

The Optional Protocol to the CRPD came about very fast and mainly on
states' initiative. The discussions of a possibility of an optional protocol did
not turn serious until a closed-door negotiation during the seventh AHC,
which led the representative of the Principality of Liechtenstein to volunteer
to draft a proposal by the next meeting, held a few days later. Subsequently,
the draft was put together with the support of the OHCHR and serious discussions commenced immediately. The speed of events implies that nonstate
entities, including DPOs and NHRIs, were largely excluded from the drafting process of the Optional Protocol. That said, it clearly garnered the support of civil society, no less because it adds an important element to the
monitoring tools of the Convention.

Conclusion

The CRPD provision on national monitoring brings home the pledge of the
Vienna Declaration. It builds a bridge between the national and international levels by providing for a strengthened national monitoring regime.

It also reemphasizes the great and growing importance of civil society involvement, not least in explicitly foreseeing the participation of persons with disabilities and their representative organizations.

The positive impact of the Vienna Declaration on the process and the final result needs to be stressed. In particular, the continued involvement of NHRIs in human rights processes can only be encouraged. Equally, the selective but very effective intervention of established human rights NGOs such as Amnesty International should not be underestimated. Their moral and political weight undoubtedly helped propel the discussion to a level that made innovation possible at a time of great but largely unresolved debates over improving monitoring mechanisms. While the target at the international level was clearly missed in the grand scheme of things—not wanting to minimize the importance of the advances that were clearly made—the discussion yielded a clear improvement for human rights implementation at the level where it is most urgently needed: at the national level. The challenge in the bigger picture is to broaden it to the benefit of human rights implementation more generally.

In the context of the CRPD there are a multitude of challenges in bringing the national monitoring provision to life. The effects of marginalization and exclusion have left a mark on persons with disabilities and the capacity of their representative organizations. Additionally, too few have broad human rights knowledge and can thus fully utilize the manifold treasures the Convention undoubtedly holds, including obligatory effective national monitoring. The training about human rights generally, as well as the principles of inclusion and accessibility in light of the CRPD, are essential requirements in assisting efforts toward effective and meaningful monitoring at the national level.

CHAPTER 14

The Role of National Human Rights Institutions

Andrew Byrnes

The negotiation of the Convention on the Rights of Persons with Disabilities was a remarkable process. The extent of civil society participation—above all by persons with disabilities and Disabled People's Organizations—and their insights and perspectives affected in fundamental ways both the style and structure of the negotiations and the form and content of its outcome, the CRPD and the Optional Protocol to the Convention.[1]

The development of the Convention was notable also for the involvement of another group of actors—national human rights institutions and national disability institutions. This was the first time that these institutions had played a coordinated and significant role in the negotiation of an international human rights treaty. The CRPD is also the first UN human rights treaty in which specific reference is made to national mechanisms of this sort as part of the formal machinery for monitoring the implementation of a treaty.[2] National human rights commissions and equality commissions or mechanisms, active in working with governments and NGOs during regional and international negotiations, put forward many substantive proposals relating to the content of the draft convention (including proposing a central role for NHRIs in its implementation and monitoring) and worked with their national governments and disability communities to influence the content of the draft convention. In addition to the independent presence and activities of NHRIs, a number of government delegations also included representatives of national human rights commissions, so, as with NGOs, the points of influence of NHRIs in the process were multiple but not always completely visible.

This chapter provides an overview of the role NHRIs played in the development of the Convention, in particular through their representation at regional and international meetings, and during the negotiations in the Ad Hoc Committee of the UN General Assembly that led to the adoption of the Convention in 2006. NHRIs made a major impact on the form and content of the Convention, and they will continue to do so through stimulating the further engagement of NHRIs in the implementation and monitoring of the human rights of persons with disabilities.

National Human Rights Institutions and National Disability Institutions

At its first session in 2002, the AHC decided to include both "national human rights institutions" and "national disability institutions" in its call for contributions to the deliberations on a new convention.[3] These two categories of institution are different. The first—NHRIs—are bodies established under national constitutions or other laws with a responsibility for promoting and monitoring the implementation of a variety of human rights, sometimes including disability rights. The other category comprises institutions established at the national level, in some cases within the executive government, in other cases independent of the government, with responsibility for promoting and implementing the rights of persons with disabilities or developing policy on disability issues. Many countries have both types of institution, sometimes with overlapping mandates. In India, for example, the National Human Rights Commission of India (an independent institution) and the Office of the Chief Commissioner for Persons with Disabilities (located within the government) both carry out a variety of functions in relation to the advancement of the rights of persons with disabilities. While both NHRIs and national disability institutions were involved in the development of the CRPD, the focus of this chapter is on the role that NHRIs played in relation to the CRPD.

The last twenty years have seen a proliferation of NHRIs. Spurred on by the support for such institutions at the Vienna World Conference on Human Rights in 1993 and a concerted campaign by the UN and other bodies to promote the establishment of these institutions, states in all regions of the world have established NHRIs, whether for political expediency, to appear as a good international citizen, or through a genuine commitment to enhancing national protection of human rights. NHRIs have been seen as a bridge between international standards and national law and practice, as well as an effective means for implementing the human rights guaranteed in national law. Their location as part of the domestic political context means that they are closer to and understand the local political, social, and cultural context and are not easily dismissed by domestic audiences as officious or culturally imperialist outsiders.

National institutions for the protection of human rights have taken a variety of legal and institutional forms. A major concern of those who urged countries to establish NHRIs was to avoid a situation in which countries established Potemkin-village-like NHRIs, which had no real capacity to evaluate and critique the human rights performance of the state or to advance the protection of human rights at the national level. Accordingly, in 1991 at a workshop in Paris,[4] a group of NHRI representatives drew up the Paris Principles. Intended to set out the minimum formal criteria necessary for a national human rights institution, the Paris Principles were endorsed by the UN Commission on Human Rights in 1992[5] and subsequently by the UN General Assembly in 1993.[6] While not without their limitations, they have become the established framework for assessing the status and functioning of NHRIs. The extent to which an NHRI complies with the Paris Principles is the basis on which various groupings of NHRIs determine whether individual NHRIs should be admitted to their number (and recognized by the UN and other bodies as entitled to exercise particular privileges, including the right to participate in international meetings).[7] Compliance with the Principles is also one of the criteria by which civil society groups and others assess the human rights performance of individual states and NHRIs.

The Paris Principles require a national institution to have "a clearly defined, broad-based human rights mandate, incorporated in legislation or (preferably) constitutionally entrenched; independence from government; membership that broadly reflects the composition of society; appropriate cooperation with civil society, including NGOs; and adequate resources."[8] In addition, the principles require that NHRIs should (1) monitor any violations of human rights and be permitted access to groups or individuals with knowledge of existing or threatened violations; (2) advise the government, the parliament, and any other competent body on specific violations on issues related to legislation and compliance with international human rights standards; (3) encourage the government to ratify human rights instruments and contribute to state reports to regional and international institutions or committees; (4) educate and inform in the field of human rights and formulate and implement educational human rights programs; and (5) prepare and publicize reports on any human rights matter and utilize the media.[9]

As individual states began to establish NHRIs, those institutions started to organize themselves, in order to coordinate their activities and to share their experiences. This has taken the form of an international coordination body—the International Coordinating Committee of National Human Rights Institutions[10]—and four regional associations of NHRIs.[11]

The ICC-NHRI was established by NHRIs in 1993 and has played the role of principal representative of NHRIs at the UN level. The ICC-NHRI was originally a loose global association of NHRIs comprising sixteen members (four from each region);[12] it became an incorporated nonprofit entity under Swiss law in 2008.[13] Morten Kjærum, a former director of the Danish Institute for Human Rights and former chair of the ICC-NHRI, has identified the three major functions of the ICC-NHRI as "(1) liaison among institutions at the global level and with the UN; (2) accreditation of national institutions that comply with the Paris Principles; and (3) organization of the international conference every second year."[14] The ICC-NHRI, on behalf of and in consultation with its members, also develops positions on substantive issues, and the negotiation of the CRPD is an example where the ICC-NHRI not only was concerned about the procedural rights of accredited NHRIs in the process but also developed policy positions on the form and content of the draft treaty.

Of the regional NHRI groupings, the Asia Pacific Forum of National Human Rights Institutions, established in 1996 and incorporated as a separate entity in 2002, has been the most active, both in its region and in terms of international engagement.[15] Until recently, it had been the only regional association to have a permanent secretariat. Together with the European Group of NHRIs, it was the most active grouping of NHRIs during the CRPD negotiations, working with and through the ICC-NHRI during that process.

NHRIs have had to work hard to have their particular special status recognized within the UN. Long used to dealing with states and NGOs, those involved in organizing meetings under UN auspices have had some difficulty in working out where NHRIs fit into those established patterns of contestation and engagement. NHRIs are institutions of the state, but intended not to be institutions of the government—their actions frequently differ from the states' diplomatic goals and activities. Nor are they NGOs, although they may share many of the same goals and also play an important role in holding government to account in relation to states' human rights obligations. But confusion about NHRIs' status has led to confusion about how they take part in meetings. Sometimes they are placed with NGOs, at other times with international agencies, and sometimes they are simply overlooked.

The emergence of NHRIs and their desire to play an international role independent of governments has posed challenges for NHRIs themselves, their home states, and others involved in international forums. The ambiguous status of NHRIs has given rise to the question of whether NHRI representatives should be members of government delegations appearing before UN human rights treaty bodies or other bodies reviewing the human rights record of the state. Previously, NHRIs had only that option, or the option of gaining accreditation as or through an NGO, to make an international appearance. However, with the support of the Office of the High Commissioner for Human Rights, the position became accepted before the UN Commission on Human Rights (and has carried over into the Human Rights Council, following lobbying on this issue) that NHRIs that have been accredited with "A" status by the ICC-NHRI, as well as regional organizations of NHRIs, may participate in Human Rights Council proceedings. This formal recognition has not automatically been translated into all other UN forums (NHRIs are, for example, currently lobbying for similar recognition before the Commission on the Status of Women), though the distinctive role of NHRIs is gradually being recognized in different parts of the UN human rights system.

Notwithstanding the continuing battle for formal recognition of their distinctive status and consequential procedural rights, NHRIs have made significant progress, moving from being viewed as participants expected to have a view primarily on the topic of NHRIs to actors entitled and expected to express views on a range of issues. As Richard Carver has noted, the participation of NHRIs in UN human rights bodies has moved "to a qualitatively new level."[16]

National Human Rights Institutions and Their Participation in the Convention

NHRIs were not formally invited in their own right to the first meeting of the AHC, 29 July to 7 August 2002.[17] The omission of an explicit reference to NHRIs led to advocacy by the OHCHR and a number of NHRIs to ensure that they were afforded an appropriate place in the work of the AHC from that time on. The then High Commissioner for Human Rights, Mary Robinson, made the point in April 2002, and her Special Adviser on National Institutions, Brian Burdekin, addressed the Committee at its first session in July 2002. He referred to the High Commissioner's views that it was "of utmost importance that not only states but also NHRIs and NGOs are able to contribute their experience to the elaboration of the new Convention."[18]

Consequently, the AHC at its first session in 2002 explicitly invited NHRIs and national disability institutions to contribute to the Committee's proceedings,[19] and included these bodies in the draft resolution submitted to,[20] and approved, by the General Assembly.[21] There was, however, still no specific reference to the full participation by NHRIs in the work of the Committee. NHRIs and their advocates believed that they had valuable contributions to make, considering their legal and political location at the domestic level and their experience in the field of disability.

The second AHC meeting featured a vigorous discussion about the potential makeup and operation of a working group that would formulate the text of the eventual Convention. Amid the vigorous discussion among states and NGOs on the balance, origin, and representativeness of potential members of the proposed WG, NHRIs received little attention. However, NHRIs present at the session[22] made several statements in which they noted that NHRIs, along with NGOs, had been invited to participate in the AHC's deliberations.[23] NHRIs pointed out that they brought expertise in the protection of human rights to the discussions, that they had a "specific commitment to the issue of disability in the context of human rights," and that their absence from the proposed WG would weaken it.[24] The NHRIs underlined that it was not their purpose to reduce the NGOs' representation on the WG, but unless NHRIs were added, "NHRIs will be the only participants present at the AHC Meeting not to be represented on the WG." Thailand, Morocco, and other states supported the inclusion of NHRIs. The decision ultimately adopted provided that the WG would consist of twenty-seven state representatives, twelve NGOs, and one NHRI.[25] The ICC-NHRI representative, Charlotte McLain of the South African Human Rights Commission, attended the WG on behalf of NHRIs.

Collaboration and Input into the Negotiations

NHRIs took various steps to ensure that their views were taken into account during the negotiations. This included the action taken by the ICC-NHRI and the regional NHRI associations to alert their members to the process, to elicit substantive input, and to facilitate participation by NHRIs in the actual negotiations, to coordinate NHRI positions, and to liaise with relevant NGOs and governments.

NHRI activity took place not just at the meetings of the AHC but also at regional meetings. At its seventh annual meeting in November 2002, for example, the APF considered the role that Asia Pacific NHRIs might play in the negotiations and discussed a number of substantive issues relating to the adoption of a new convention.[26] The paper presented to that meeting noted that in light of the roles that were foreseen for NHRIs under the Paris Principles, NHRI members might take a variety of actions in response to the international developments on disability. These could include reviewing the situation in their own countries, advocating the value of a new convention to their governments, contributing to national and international discussions on a convention, and ensuring that NGOs were aware of the developments and were able to participate in national discussion of the issue.[27] It suggested that there were two major issues for APF to consider: supporting its members' participation in the drafting process and reviewing the merits of the proposals that might be put forward.[28] The meeting agreed "to respond positively to the invitation of the UN AHC to participate independently in the development of the possible new convention"[29] and endorsed a number of recommendations. Of particular relevance to the international engagement of the APF and its member institutions were the recommendations that the APF secretariat provide support "for the activities of its member institutions in responding to the AHC recommendations" and "in cooperation with its member institutions, develop and advocate proposals for a possible new convention for the consideration of the AHC."[30] The APF subsequently convened a small working group of some of its members to do this.[31]

Prior to the second AHC session in late July 2003, there were a number of regional meetings of NHRIs or meetings at which they were present, the conclusions of which were forwarded to the Committee.[32] In March 2003 members of the Network of National Institutions for the Promotion and Protection of Human Rights of the Americas met in Costa Rica to consider disability issues. They agreed, inter alia, "To urge the governments of the respective countries to evaluate the possibility of supporting the drafting and, if applicable, the approval of an international convention on disability, as well as the participation of national institutions and NGOs in the AHC established for that purpose."[33]

In April 2003 an important workshop was organized in New Delhi by the APF in conjunction with the Commonwealth Secretariat and the British Council, hosted by the National Human Rights Council of India.[34] That meeting welcomed the international developments and the invitation to NHRIs to participate, and set out a number of elements that NHRIs considered should be embodied in any new convention.[35]

A number of African NHRIs, together with government representatives and NGOs, met in Uganda in June 2003 and adopted a declaration setting out desirable elements for inclusion in a new convention, including a recommendation that a convention should include a requirement to establish "effective national monitoring mechanisms with due respect to the . . . Paris Principles." [36] European National Institutions also formulated a joint position on the proposed convention that was submitted to the second AHC session in June 2003.[37]

Another significant regional meeting was held in June 2003 at the UN Economic and Social Commission for Asia and the Pacific. This meeting brought together government representatives, NGOs, NHRI representatives, and other experts[38] and adopted a series of substantive recommendations on the possible content of a convention that were presented to the second AHC session.[39] A further regional workshop organized by the UN Economic and Social Commission for Asia and the Pacific in October 2003[40] produced a draft convention[41] that was presented to the AHC, one of the documents considered by the WG at its January 2004 session.[42]

Participation in the AHC and Related Meetings

NHRIs participated actively in all AHC sessions, appearing under the designation "NHRI." The ICC-NHRI nominated a representative, initially Charlotte McClain from the South African Human Rights Commission, and then Anuradha Mohit, special rapporteur on disability of the National Human Rights Commission of India, to attend the sessions and to coordinate NHRI interventions and lobbying. The APF had a presence at the sessions, and individual NHRIs attended as well, some regularly.[43] There were also a number of NHRI representatives on national delegations (for example, Australia and New Zealand).

NHRIs circulated discussion papers, draft articles, and proposed amendments, and made oral interventions during the debates in the Committee.

The APF in particular devoted considerable resources to development of detailed position papers on the content of a new convention.[44]

Some Issues of Particular Concern to NHRIs

NHRIs were committed to achieving a strong convention that was rights-based, embodied a social model of disability and a substantive concept of equality, and reflected the lived experiences of persons with disabilities. NHRIs were also concerned to ensure that there were effective mechanisms at the national and international level to facilitate and monitor the implementation of the Convention, and that remedies were available to those whose rights were violated. NHRIs made written and oral interventions and engaged with delegations on almost every article of the draft convention, reflecting the extensive experience of many NHRIs in protecting rights of persons with disabilities. This section selects three issues of particular importance to NHRIs, and explores the development of proposals with regard to those issues.

General Obligations and the Importance of Economic, Social, and Cultural Rights

The Convention includes civil and political rights, and economic, social, and cultural rights, as well as a number of rights, such as the right to accessibility, that might be characterized as "hybrid rights."[45] The inclusion of economic, social, and cultural rights for persons with disabilities was critical. NHRIs and NGOs wanted to ensure that these guarantees were capable of bringing benefits for persons with disabilities, and also to ensure that the analysis and practice relating to economic, social, and cultural rights in the four decades since the drafting of the ICESCR—in particular the immediate applicability of many aspects of economic, social, and cultural rights[46]—was reflected in the new convention.

The initial signs were not particularly promising. Although there were proposals put before the WG of the AHC that included express treatment of obligations with regard to economic, social, and cultural rights, the draft adopted by the WG, which otherwise drew on these proposals, contained no reference to these obligations.[47]

NHRIs took up this issue. In its written submission to the third AHC session,[48] the APF pointed to this omission from the WG's draft and urged the Committee to include a provision along the lines of the Chair's draft so that the Convention "does not simply reflect the thinking of fifty years ago without regard to the significant advances in the understanding of the nature of economic, social and cultural rights in the last decades."[49] The point was reiterated in the oral intervention made by APF on behalf of the NHRIs present at the session;[50] others expressed similar views.

The upshot was the inclusion by the Chair in October 2005 of the following draft Article 4(2):[51]

> With regard to economic, social and cultural rights, each State Party undertakes to take measures to the maximum of its available resources and, where needed, within the framework of international cooperation, with a view to achieving progressively the full realization of these rights, except where achieving progressively the full realization of these rights would result in discrimination on the basis of disability. The chair explained that the provision was intended to avoid the need to include language relating to progressive realization in many articles of the Convention, as it would be "repetitive and often difficult to include such language in individual articles, since many of them contain a hybrid of civil and political, and economic, social and cultural rights, including nondiscrimination."[52]

He noted that the Committee had accepted that the obligation of nondiscrimination was immediately realizable—hence the explicit provision to that effect.

Notwithstanding this effort to address the issues of economic, social, and cultural rights, this draft was not satisfactory to some states, to NHRIs, or to a number of NGOs, including the International Disability Caucus. NHRIs argued[53] for an amendment along the lines of the Bangkok Draft (also largely reflected in the IDC text).[54]

The European Union, reflecting these concerns, had proposed the replacement of the words "except where achieving progressively the full realization of these rights would result in discrimination on the basis of disability" with "without prejudice to the immediately applicable obligations emanating from international human rights law."[55] This amendment was included in the version of Article 4(2) that was adopted in the final text of the Convention.

This is an illustration of one important matter on which NHRIs had a significant input and, together with like-minded states and NGOs, were able to improve the text of the Convention on an issue of theoretical and practical importance. While the lobbying and advocacy did not achieve the wording that NHRIs would have preferred, the final text goes a long way toward underlining the immediate realizable nature of many obligations under the Convention.

Provision for Remedies

Another issue of concern to NHRIs was the need to include in the Convention a requirement that states parties ensure that an effective remedy be available to a person whose rights under the Convention were violated. Once again, proposals put before the WG included such provisions,[56] and there was support for such a provision from some states, NGOs, and NHRIs at the WG deliberations.[57] However, the issue was contentious,[58] and the WG draft included no explicit provision on remedies. Its report noted:[59]

> Both the Bangkok draft and the Chair's draft included in this section a paragraph on remedies. Some members of the Working Group noted that while the International Covenant on Civil and Political Rights includes such a provision, the International Covenant on Economic, Social and Cultural Rights did not. It may be difficult, therefore, to include such an article in a convention that elaborates the rights contained in both Covenants. The AHC may wish to consider this issue further.

As they had with the question of economic, social, and cultural rights, NHRIs also took up this issue. In its written submission to the third AHC session,[60] the APF noted the omission of a provision on remedies from the WG's draft and urged the Committee to include such a provision in the Convention.[61] The point was reiterated in the oral intervention made by APF on behalf of the NHRIs present at the session;[62] others expressed similar views.[63]

Opinion on the issue was still divided at the fourth AHC session, when Article 4 of the WG's draft was discussed once again. A number of states, NHRIs, and NGOs were strongly supportive of a provision on remedies,[64] while other states considered that it was not appropriate to provide for remedies where both civil and political rights and economic, social, and cultural rights were being addressed in the same article, given the lack of international consensus on remedies in relation to economic, social, and cultural rights and the absence of a remedies provision in the ICESCR.

The issue returned to the AHC in 2006 in the form of a consolidated text prepared by the chair that built on earlier discussions and the work of facilitators of individual articles. The text of draft Article 4 contained no reference to remedies. The chair's cover letter made no reference to the issue of remedies in its discussion of the revised draft Article 4.[65] The failure to include such a provision was once again criticized by NHRIs and others.[66]

Even as late as the eighth session in August 2006 (the final full substantive session of the Committee), a number of states continued their efforts to have a provision on remedies included.[67] However, there was still insufficient support for such a provision and the final text of the Convention makes no specific reference to states parties' obligations to ensure that there are effective remedies for violation of the rights guaranteed in the treaty.[68]

Monitoring Procedures at the National Level

The question of what international and national monitoring and implementation procedures should be included in the Convention possibly produced more proposals than any other area covered by the treaty. Although a welter of both imaginative and more traditional suggestions about possible monitoring mechanisms were put forward, it was only relatively late in the process that serious consideration of the issue took place. Notwithstanding the creativity and innovation involved in many of the proposals put forward,[69] regrettably, the final outcome was a series of monitoring procedures that hewed very closely to existing models, though with some improvements.

NHRIs were understandably interested in the implementation and monitoring procedures. Given their role as domestic institutions with a mandate to promote and protect human rights at the national level, they were concerned to ensure that provisions dealing with national implementation took account of their existing functions and experience in the area of disability, while not losing the opportunity to strengthen implementation and monitoring at the national level in other ways. They also saw the establishment of an effective international monitoring procedure as important. Consistent with the expectations of the Paris Principles that NHRIs will engage with the international human rights system, they were concerned to ensure that consideration was given to how NHRIs might contribute to the work of any international monitoring body and how their work might be supported by such procedures.

NHRIs were active, individually and collectively, in advancing proposals on both national and international level monitoring; many of their ideas contributed to the discussion and formulation of proposals by states and NGOs. Conversely, NHRIs themselves drew on ideas put forward by states and a number of NGOs and individual experts. This was one of the many areas in which there was extensive cross-fertilization between the different actors in the negotiations of the Convention. Although NHRIs were closely involved with the proposals relating to international monitoring, this section focuses on national level monitoring—an area of particular concern to NHRIs and in which they are given an explicit role for the first time in the text of a UN human rights treaty.

At the first AHC session in 2002 there were already suggestions as to the appropriate form of monitoring procedure.[70] Further proposals followed for the second session in June 2003, some emanating from regional meetings in Latin America, Asia Pacific, and Africa.[71] Following the second session, a meeting convened by the UN Economic and Social Commission for Asia and the Pacific in October 2003 adopted a draft convention containing national and international monitoring procedures.[72] A number of proposals for monitoring and implementation mechanisms were laid before the WG,[73] the most extensive of which was the Chair's Draft, which drew on the Bangkok and other drafts and added some further options.[74] The proposals as to international procedures included the establishment of a new human rights treaty body with a range of powers and of an international disability ombudsperson.

Proposals as to national monitoring procedures ranged from the very general to quite detailed proposals. Mexico, for example, had suggested in its original draft convention the inclusion of an article that provided "In accordance with their legal systems, States Parties shall promote the establishment and strengthening of national institutions responsible for safeguarding the rights and dignity of persons with disabilities."[75] By contrast, the chair's proposal was much more ambitious and detailed, and would have stipulated that states parties designate an independent national institution to "monitor, promote and enforce compliance" with the Convention; the institution would have had to comply with the Paris Principles and to have been established in consultation with and ensure the continuing involvement in its work of persons with disabilities and DPOs.[76] The draft article went on to identify a range of functions and powers the national institution should possess based on the Paris Principles. The chair's proposal included a further procedure for regular domestic reporting under the Convention, for which a designated institution would be responsible.[77] This was doubtless an ambitious proposal, especially for those states that did not have NHRIs, or NHRIs with the required independence and competence.

The WG considered only the question of national monitoring and did not have time to consider the question of an international monitoring mechanism for the Convention.[78] Even that discussion was characterized by considerable disagreement.[79] Indeed, the footnotes to the draft article on national monitoring in the report of the WG were longer than the draft article itself.[80] The modest WG proposal on monitoring[81] provided that states parties should "designate a focal point" within government to facilitate implementation of the Convention and "give due consideration to the establishment or designation of a coordination mechanism" (draft Article 25(1)); it also provided that states should "maintain, strengthen, designate, or establish at the national level a framework to promote, protect, and monitor implementation of the rights recognized in the present Convention" (draft Article 25(2)).

This draft article identified two distinct components: the implementation of the obligations under the Convention—primarily a responsibility of the executive government—and a monitoring and enforcement role that could be played by an institution independent of the executive government, such as an NHRI.

NHRIs and others were not content with this text, which was discussed at the fourth AHC session. In its submission to the fourth AHC session, the APF stated that it was "a very weak provision that fails to reflect the potentially important role that national institutions could play in monitoring the implementation of the convention and thereby promoting its full implementation" and that[82]

the provision also fails to reflect that many states have established national human rights institutions—many of which comply with the Paris Principles—which perform important functions in the promotion and protection of human rights at the national level. A number of these institutions already exercise functions in relation to disability. The new convention should build on these developments and encourage states to encourage independent national institutions to monitor the implementation of the convention at the domestic level—a process, which can only enhance the implementation of the convention.

The APF suggested that the WG revert to the type of provision proposed in the Chair's Draft.

Despite some discussion of monitoring at the fourth session, most states wished to defer serious consideration of the issue until the substantive content of the Convention was more or less established. This preparedness to delay the discussion was also motivated in part by a desire not to preempt the results of the ongoing review of the UN human rights treaty body system then under way and/or to establish a mechanism that would not fit within any reform of that system.[83] For some states, this was a genuine reason for delay, for others merely a convenient pretext.

By the time monitoring came back onto the agenda of the AHC in 2005, both NHRIs and NGOs had refined their earlier proposals. At the sixth AHC session in August 2005, NHRIs circulated a proposal on monitoring,[84] which drew on a number of sources,[85] and had many commonalities with the IDC proposals. The NHRI proposal provided for the submission of a baseline report, the development and implementation of a national action plan on implementation of the Convention, and the designation of a national institution that complied with the Paris Principles and had wide range of powers to monitor implementation of the Convention and for the promotion and protection of the rights of persons with disabilities. It also provided for the establishment of a new human rights treaty body (with the power to entertain individual and collective complaints, to initiate inquiries, and to conduct thematic studies), and specifically provided for formal links between domestic human rights institutions and NGOs and that committee. The proposal further suggested the establishment of a global disability rights advocate, and for a review conference of all states parties five years after entry into force of the Convention.[86]

The issue was not resolved at the sixth session but was taken up by the Committee at its seventh session in early 2006, at which the Committee considered a Chair's draft text that did not make any changes to the 2004 WG draft of Article 24.[87] NHRIs, NGOs, and states were active once again around the monitoring procedures.[88] After further discussions, the chair circulated a draft that included a reference to the Paris Principles.[89] This Chair's Draft also included a further paragraph ensuring the involvement of persons with disabilities and their representative organizations in the monitoring process.[90]

However, this was not yet the final form of the article, as states wished to allow for flexibility to reflect their constitutional arrangements (including the fact that in some states, including federal states such as Canada, responsibility in relation to matters covered by the Convention was shared between different levels of government.) Accordingly, in draft Article 24(1) the words "in accordance with their system of organization" were added, while in draft Article 24(2), the reference to "an independent mechanism" was replaced by a reference to "a framework, including one or more independent mechanisms, as appropriate."

Conclusion

The discussion above has shown that NHRIs were actively engaged in the negotiations on the CRPD and contributed significantly to the discussion of policy and content of the new convention. The three issues examined in this chapter are just some of the issues on which NHRIs contributed to the debate and negotiations, but they are ones of particular importance to the institutional position of NHRIs and to the improvement of the lives of persons with disabilities. While there is little doubt that NHRIs were a voice in the debate, they were but one among many, and the voices of persons with disabilities were many more; accordingly the impact of NHRI contribution should not be overrated.

Where NHRIs were pursuing common goals with the NGO community and had significant support among states, the goals staked out by NHRIs were more likely to be achieved. The inclusion of a role for NHRIs (and the reference to the Paris Principles) in the national monitoring of the Convention is an important advance that resulted from a productive alignment of interests and advocacy. The recognition of the fact in Article 4(2) of the Convention that economic, social, and cultural rights are not subject only to progressive realization, but have elements that can be directly enforced, also reflected not just a push by NHRIs on this theme, but an initiative that succeeded because of the support from NGOs, and a number of influential states. Conversely, the failure of the efforts to obtain a specific right to a remedy in the Convention (though it may be implicit) reflected the fact that, despite common cause being formed between NHRIs, NGOs, and some states, there was opposition from a large number of states (including Western states).

Quite apart from the substantive guarantees contained in the Convention, NHRI involvement in the process was important in other respects. It provided the occasion for regional groupings of NHRIs to use their networks to elicit information and suggestions for input into the negotiations, ensuring that the expertise of NHRIs in the field of disability was taken into account in the development of the treaty. It also provided an opportunity for NHRIs to link across regions, though this was primarily across the Asia Pacific and European groupings of NHRIs, with lesser participation from African and Latin American NHRIs. Equally important, it provided a stimulus for NHRIs and their networks to identify gaps in their work on disability issues and to take steps to remedy those gaps. It also primed NHRIs through their networks for the next stage in the development of the Convention—the ratification and implementation of the treaty—and to play the role assigned to NHRIs by the treaty itself.

Article 33 on national implementation and monitoring of the Convention will prove to be a significant advance in human rights law and in the advancement of the rights of persons with disabilities. Although less clear and prescriptive than NHRIs may have wished, the clarification of the content of the provision, especially with regard to NHRI involvement in the process of implementation and monitoring, has begun,[91] as has the work of NHRIs in taking up the mandate assigned to them by the Convention.

CHAPTER 15

The New Diplomacy

Maya Sabatello

This chapter summarizes the main observations and examines some of the theoretical aspects behind the work of civil society organizations at the United Nations, based on the work of such groups during the drafting process for the Convention on the Rights of Persons with Disabilities. By doing so, it aims to address the questions posed in the introduction: What were the forces that enabled the drafting process to take place in such a speedy and comprehensive manner? How did the interaction between state delegates, nongovernmental organizations, national human rights institutions, and other experts in disability rights play out? What role did cooperation among NGOs play in this process, and what can account for the successes and failures? Which voices were heard throughout the negotiations, and why? Finally, how did the CRPD negotiations compare to previous similar international law processes? The experience of the CRPD can only be understood in comparison to previous international processes at the UN. While other international treaties in the human rights realm were also characterized by NGOs' participation, the International Campaign to Ban Landmines and the Coalition on the International Criminal Court are particularly important points of comparison because they marked the first times CSOs initiated and greatly affect the process. In much the same way as the Ad Hoc Committee included the perspectives of persons with disabilities and disabled people's organizations, the process for the ICBL and the CICC included perspectives of leading CSOs. Indeed, the ICBL network and its founding coordinator, Jody Williams, were jointly rewarded with the 1997 Nobel Peace Prize for their achievement; and the term "new diplomacy" was coined in the aftermath of these two international processes to acknowledge the considerable coordination and engagement of civil society in international processes.[1] Yet there were important differences, as the legal background and expertise of the participants in earlier international law-making process was well established. While a comprehensive examination of this latter issue is beyond the scope of this chapter, highlighting some of the most striking similarities and differences is helpful in the overall assessment of what lessons can be learned from the disability rights movement to further advance human rights more generally.

One note of caution is in place. By the last, the eighth, AHC session, over one hundred DPOs were accredited to take part in the negotiations, in addition to other NGOs that enjoyed consultative status with the UN Economic and Social Council. The number of representatives for each organization differed—having anywhere between one and a few dozen representatives.[2] Thus, the book clearly cannot claim to provide complete coverage of all the voices raised during the negotiations. The perspectives brought in this volume nonetheless reflect the diversity of disabilities and the organizations presented at the AHC in terms of their geographic and regional distribution, size, and purpose, as well as their previous experience—or lack thereof—in participating in legal advocacy initiatives in an international forum. The overall collage of views presented here therefore not only sheds light on these questions but also provides authentic firsthand testimonies of human rights actors in the twenty-first century.

The Disability Rights Movement at the UN

When Mexico initiated the drafting of the CRPD in December 2001, the disability rights community was not set up in any particularly powerful form. Furthermore, there was a need to unite the community's historically diverse, pluralist, and contrasting points of views. However, once the initiative to draft the CRPD was under way, the involvement of the disability rights movement accelerated in a way and manner that no doubt is unprecedented in the drafting of an international human rights treaty.

The success achieved as a result of disability rights activism is also undisputed. As the authors in this book have discussed, the final text of the Convention reflects much input from disability rights activists. Although the Convention was not intended to create new rights, in reality the rights enshrined in it certainly have innovative features. The CRPD unconditionally recognizes persons with disabilities as subjects and as rights-holders. It emphasizes social barriers as a main cause of exclusion of persons with disabilities and requires not only the removal of physical barriers but also, significantly, the elimination of negative attitudes, stereotypes, and prejudices that play a role in the discrimination and exclusion of persons with disabilities. Among the CRPD's general principles is the notion of "respect for difference" and inclusion, issues that were strongly advocated by a few of the authors of this volume, while awareness raising and accessibility are elaborated on in separate provisions (Articles 8 and 9). The Convention thus clearly marks a shift from the medical and charity model of disability and emphasizes the social dimensions of impairment and disabilities respectively.

Other important articles are stand-alone provisions on data and statistics, international cooperation, situations of risk, and monitoring, including a conference of states parties to consider the implementation matters (Articles 31, 32, 11, 40). As discussed in Chapters 6 and 7, the "twin-track" approach with regard to children and women was also successful, and both groups have a separate provision along with mainstreaming their rights. The provision on women and girls with disabilities further provides for the recognition of multiple discrimination (Article 6). Finally, Article 12 explicitly recognizes the crucial right to legal capacity.

Beyond specific provisions, the treaty is also innovative in its transcendence of conventional boundaries in international human rights law. As Frédéric Mégret points out, the Convention features a shift from a state-centric approach to a more participatory model of treaty making (and of developing international law), an emphasis not only on negative rights but also on positive ones, and a blur of traditional dichotomies, such as public/private, state/individual, individual/community, vertical/horizontal, domestic/international, and others.[3]

The Culture of Negotiations

As the authors in this volume have described, throughout the process, NGOs, DPOs, and NHRIs contributed their perspectives and set their priorities, informed the process, shaped the agenda, and articulated future expectations. As in other social movements, they turned to a variety of techniques and forms of engagement to make the case for disability rights. Significantly, a few methods were of particular importance.

Proposed Amendments to the Draft

An important way for NGOs to contribute to the negotiations was ongoing, hands-on involvement in the drafting of the various provisions. As NGOs could not submit text proposals by themselves, collaboration with states' delegates was critical: only proposals that were endorsed by state delegates and presented at the AHC as their own were immediately incorporated into the draft text. This limitation often required approaching states' delegates directly and persuading them of the rightfulness of a proposed amendment to garner their support. Flyers, statements, and other fact-sheets were also distributed throughout the sessions. Additionally, amendments to the draft were possible subsequent to the AHC chair's appointment of facilitators to smooth disagreements about specific articles. As a few of the authors discuss, these latter openings provided an important opportunity for CSOs to contribute to the process—indeed, at times, leading to a change of heart.

The "blurred" distinction between civil society representatives and states' delegates created other important opportunities to bring influential experts' opinions to bolster proposals from *within* the AHC. As discussed in Chapter 7, the collaboration between Mi Yeon Kim, a civil society representative with a formal hat as Korea's delegate, and facilitator Theresia Degener, the German delegate and a world-known expert in women's disability rights, paved the way to adoption of the twin-track approach with regard to the rights of women with disabilities.

As the authors in this book make clear, their power of persuasion was built on two things. First, disability rights activists continually referenced existing international instruments as a primary source—a strategy that, in return, achieved a number of things. For one, as in other social movements, references to existing laws enabled the activists to leverage the power of law as the source that defines and legitimizes the relationships between states, individuals, and other groups and, accordingly, to claim what they are already entitled to.[4] And in distinction from other social movements, this strategy assisted in dismantling the historical "ability barrier." It vividly demonstrated the fallacy of viewing persons with disabilities merely in terms of their *inabilities* and showed that their legal expertise and abilities clearly exist.

Second, the legal discussion opened the space for renegotiation of the meaning of human rights provisions. Showing the limitations of existing interpretations and their inapplicability to persons with disabilities enabled activists to recreate and redefine the content of rights, ensuring that they will have the impact—and be relevant—in the disability context. It was particularly useful to draw on day-to-day examples and practical experience learned from projects that succeeded (or not) on the national level. Indeed, the advocacy line that focused on nondiscrimination in the context of legal capacity and the inclusion of separate provisions on access to justice, on an explicit *right* to live in the community, on education in the most appropriate languages and modes and means of communication, and on international cooperation in the final text of the treaty are evidence of the success of this strategy: the gaps opened enabled rethinking of the rights involved.

CSOs also pressed their arguments on nonlegal grounds. In previous international-law processes, particularly the CICC,[5] the major human rights organizations (such as Amnesty International, Human Rights Watch), who are well known for their legal expertise in international forums, were lead actors. Consequently, their form of engagement during the negotiations was overwhelmingly based on legal mechanisms. As should be clear from the accounts in this book, however, not all DPO representatives at the UN had a legal background. Many relied on their vast expertise of disability and the experience that the laws in place are simply not enough. For many others, the UN negotiations were their first encounter with advocacy on the international level. In some aspects, this may have been a disadvantage. Getting familiar with the international system, its procedures, and its legal terminology, particularly when the forms of communication are inaccessible, were time consuming. But it also had a benefit: fewer ties to traditional legal thinking and ability to think creatively "beyond the legal box." As Lex Grandia put it, since it was impossible to transfer the message in abstract legal terminology, the nonlegal alternative was "to challenge their imagination, as if it all happens to them"—which indeed yielded the desired response as ultimately incorporated in Article 12 of the CRPD.

Experts' Impact

Legal discourse without new evidence or persuasive explanation is not, however, likely to yield a significant change. To bolster the proposed amendments, activists thus resorted to experts to raise a voice on critical issues. Expert panels were particularly critical at the earlier stages of the drafting process when the trust in the disability rights activists was still young, and it was still essential to persuade parties of the need for the CRPD.[6] In other instances, as the experience of Save the Children shows (Chapter 6), enlisting the support of UN-associated experts was particularly valuable.

The *"Brown v. Board of Education* Effect"

Activists and DPOs (e.g., Inclusion International and Save the Children) used another technique to transfer the messages behind the proposed amendments to the draft: providing firsthand testimonies of persons with disabilities who experienced discrimination and who could point to what should have been done differently.

Certainly, the ability to bring additional representatives and speakers to the UN varied, as, generally, the organizations struggled with limited financial and other resources. However, the leaders of DPOs often utilized this method, sharing their personal experiences (e.g., Chapter 9). While the goal of this strategy was clearly to create a change in a legal document, it also aimed to change the course of the debate. First, such testimony provided authoritative knowledge and firsthand information that were not otherwise available. Unlike the ICBL process, where figures about the number of landmine victims, associated costs, and the increasing number of mines were readily available,[7] or the CICC where women's vulnerability to abuse in conflicts was evident in view of the experience of former Yugoslavia (hence enabled the inclusion of gender-specific crimes in the treaty),[8] comparable comprehensive statistics were not existent during the drafting of the CRPD. Personal testimonies were thus crucial to at least partially substitute for this lack of information. Second, personal testimonies also created an almost unavoidable emotional impact. In much the same way that the seminal U.S. Supreme Court case *Brown v. Board of Education*[9] cited social scientific evidence of the negative psychological and social impacts of segregation policy, appeals to personal justice were a reminder that segregation is inexcusable and has social effects far beyond those who are discriminated against. Inclusion is important not only for persons with disabilities but also for the type of society that we aim to live in.

Side Events

Another way NGOs and DPOs bolstered support for specific text proposals was through the organization of an array of "side events." The events commonly attracted between a few and dozens of people, including state delegates, UN officials, and civil society representatives. Side events generally took place during lunch breaks, and every day a few side events were held simultaneously. Overall, more than one hundred side events took place throughout the AHC sessions, covering ostensibly all pertinent issues to the Convention.[10] Some side events were also allocated specifically to briefings to and by state missions, for example, the European Union and the World Bank. And while the events had an educative aspect, importantly, they also boosted the quality of the relationship with state delegates. By providing examples and practical demonstrations (as discussed, e.g., in Chapter 8), these events enabled clarifications and elaborations on the proposed amendments and hence facilitated the negotiations.

Special social events organized during the AHC sessions also made a difference. One particularly memorable event was an evening organized by the Landmine Survivors Network during the third AHC, featuring a live-music concert by the internationally recognized band Blind Boys of Alabama. Another was a screening of the film *39 Pounds of Love*. The film is an inspirational documentary featuring thirty-four-year-old Ami Ankilewitz's trip to the United States to meet the doctor who diagnosed him at age one as having spinal muscular atrophy, with a prognosis that he would not live beyond age six. Building on their personal contacts, civil society representatives from Disabled People's International, the World Union for Progressive Judaism, and Ability Awareness recruited highly active state actors, including the UN missions of Canada, Israel, and Mexico, to cosponsor both the event and a reception afterward.

Hundreds of delegates, UN officials, and civil society representatives attended the events, and their impact was immense: they showed capabilities when one doubts they exist and they offered "time off" from intense negotiations, assisting in breaking deadlocks when negotiations seemed to reach an impasse. These events offered something different from late-night meetings: a time to interact and to discover individuals beyond their formal role and their perceived ability or disability. Ami's story, in particular, offered attendees an opportunity to relate to his experiences as a person with disabilities, to reflect on the discrimination he endured, but also realize his power, liveliness, sense of humor, love of life, and options when the social barriers are removed. As the Costa Rican delegate expressed, "It's one of those films that make you realize that what we do here does make a difference."[11] Thus, such events created solidarity among all attendees, a sense that things *can* be different.

"Naming and Shaming"

Whereas the aforementioned side events may have been "carrots," the old method of "shaming and blaming" was the "stick." The combination of the methods discussed above can certainly account for this technique's success. State delegates' positions about the various proposals were as public as the disability rights community's praise or criticism. Responses to state positions were available in formal recorded statements by disability organizations in the sessions' daily summaries but, importantly, also in the daily bulletin, flyers, and fact-sheets CSOs distributed every morning. As evidence grew that an alternative to the exclusion of persons with disabilities exists—indeed, that it is merely a matter of political will—refusing to follow suit would have caused embarrassment. Thus, despite much criticism raised in recent years about the limitations of "naming and shaming" as an advocacy technique,[12] its impact throughout the drafting process was significant. With hundreds of persons with disabilities in the UN corridors, in the negotiating room, in the various meetings, and in the cafeteria—all with watchful eyes on "resistant delegates"—it became impossible to avoid a dialogue.

Advocating for Consensus—the International Disability Caucus

The unique role of the IDC in negotiating the Convention was justified by common assumptions that relatively large-scale coalitions of "like-minded" organizations are essential to advance a particular human rights agenda, and that advocating in one voice is preferable because it reflects—and subsequently entrenches—a "normative consensus."[13] It also aimed to avoid the politicization of the process,[14] which would have jeopardized the potential for success. Furthermore, this method was assumed to be an inherent part in the development of a collective identity—an aspect of human rights activism that scholars studying social movements often see as vital.[15]

Over time, the IDC turned out to be a well-respected and highly appreciated actor at the negotiations. Furthermore, as the IDC represented a variety of disability needs, it enjoyed a greater sense of legitimacy in the eyes of state actors. Proposals for amendments of the draft were thus often taken more seriously when delivered by the IDC (rather than by individual organizations), and the IDC had a priority in making statements at the plenary.

Challenges to the bonds between CSOs within the disability rights movement existed, however. Not all organizations were part of the IDC or felt they had influential power in it, even if they were formally members. As Chapters 5, 10, and 12 illustrate, it was not always easy for CSO representatives to balance between the interests of being part of the powerful coalition and remaining faithful to their constituencies. Some found the IDC's sense of collective identity not only foreign, but also alienating. Being part of this coalition was therefore not a given but an individual and organizational decision undertaken according to the goals and identity they wanted to uphold.

This subsequently raises the question of whether being a coalition member was indeed critical for advancing specific interests in the treaty. How well did non-IDC members do in advancing their goals?

The answer is not clear-cut. It seems to depend on various external factors that played a role in the negotiations. Disability Rights International's extensive experience in human rights advocacy before supranational policymaking forums and connection with relevant UN bodies prior to the negotiations leveraged the organization's credibility when its views diverged from those of the IDC (Chapter 5). PWD-Australia (Chapter 12) explicitly found its horizontal collaborations with member states to be more fruitful than the one offered by the IDC and scored success due to its close relationship with the Australian mission. Conversely, its failure to incorporate a provision on cultural and racial minority groups cannot be attributed, in light of the experience of indigenous persons with disabilities, to its work independent of the IDC. Also achievements gained by Proyecto Sur (Chapter 11) can be greatly attributed to the organization's close partnership with the Latin American and Caribbean countries. The disproportionately high number of persons with disabilities in this region, and the echo of the historical exclusion of the South from human rights developments, facilitated IDC acknowledgment (and subsequent incorporation) of their voices. Southern DPO representatives were thus positioned more strongly to strike deals with IDC members.

In contrast, although indigenous persons with disabilities were IDC members, they had only very limited success in getting their message across, and the few sympathetic voices from within the IDC were insufficient to achieve full inclusion of indigenous persons with disabilities in the Convention text (Chapter 10). The UN's unresolved politicized attitude toward indigenous peoples, particularly among powerful states (e.g., New Zealand, Canada, and Australia), arguably prevented consideration of their proposed article at the plenary. Simultaneously, the content offered, which differed significantly from the mainstream human rights regime, was too much for the "conventional" disability rights activists to endorse.

Overall, while undoubtedly a powerful actor at the negotiations, the IDC was not the only route for DPOs to achieve success. The IDC was characterized by both internal and external conflicts and cooperation,[16] as well as by a political dynamic of its own. While in principle it was inclusive and did have some extensive internal deliberations, not all disagreements were alleviated. Openess to "other" different cultural backgrounds was limited from within. Arguably, then, the IDC, with the IDA's leadership, had followed what large human rights movements as well as previous international law processes have previously done: establishing itself through inclusion and exclusion, yet in a way that would ensure that it would not have competition.[17] Indeed, this explains the diverging views about the IDC among the participants and authors in this volume. For some, it was a flexible and representative body that allowed for much collaboration; others viewed it as exclusive and nondemocratic. The voting for IDC's decisions reflects this tension: while consensus was the goal, DPOs, particularly IDA members (in contrast to other NGOs), had the final say.

Technology and Internet Communication

The use of technology and Internet communication was central to the successful facilitation of civil society's work and exceeded that in previous comparable international forums. First, from within, the disability rights online listserv, including separate "groups" for controversial articles, played a vital role in ensuring that everyone within the disability community was abreast of the discussion—and, importantly, in facilitating disagreements.

This was crucial, as much of the work was done behind the scenes and in the intervals between AHC sessions; furthermore, the intensity and multiplicity of the meetings during the sessions made it impossible for one to attend all of them. Moreover, the Internet forum enabled people from all around the world to take part in the negotiations. While the UN Voluntary Fund on Disability enabled CSOs from the least economically developed states to attend the sessions,[18] many others could not—for financial, physical, and other constraints. Their voices were nonetheless heard through the listserv: indeed, the additional online group established for Proyecto Sur members well exemplifies this point (Chapter 11). Conversely, Internet communication may have created what Barbara K. Woodward termed "communicative capitalism":[19] those who did not have access to the Internet or were not successful in explaning their position through this route of communication were left out. Thus, although Internet communication was key in highlighting important omissions from and additions to the draft text, distortions in the desired content as adopted and missed opportunities—possibly, as in the case of indigenous persons with disabilities and Pacific Islands communities (Chapters 10, 12)—may have occurred.

Second, the Internet also enabled speedy communication with state delegates and UN officials, including the UN Secretariat. Dissemination of text proposals, statements, and explanations was easy, requiring merely the pressing of the "send" button. In much the same way that it was invaluable in facilitating the resolution of disagreements from within, it also mitigated disagreements between NGOs/DPOs and official delegates and UN officials once face-to-face meetings took place at the plenary (see, e.g., Chapter 4).

Third, Internet communication solidified the sense of identity. It created familiarity and a sense of association with people who never physically attended the AHC sessions, creating links between DPO and NGO representatives, state delegates, and UN officials who were informed and partners throughout the process. It shed the "status shields" that often exist in international forums, creating a global community of advocates for disability rights. Importantly, it also led to greater openness and willingness to listen, coupled with a sense of responsibility to properly respond.

Finally, the use of technology was instrumental in the overall participation of persons with disabilities throughout the process. Because the audibility and vision of the participants varied significantly, conventional communication formats provided only a limited solution. Made aware of this limitation, the AHC continuously requested that efforts be made to facilitate accessibility to UN premises, technology, and documents.[20] In practice, the improvements were never complete or sufficient. Individual representatives and organizations had to resort to their own technologies and assistants to remain informed (see, e.g., Pamela Molina Toledo's account, Chapter 11). Certainly, much collegiality and ad hoc voluntary solutions were required from the disability community in this context. However, it also meant that negotiations were not always as optimal as one would have hoped—yet another testimony to the critical importance of accessibility to ensure the full inclusion of persons with disabilities in society.

Communicating the Broader Picture

International legal reform would not have taken place without the hard work of the many organizations and individual experts who participated in the Convention negotiations, either at the AHC sessions or from afar. But other broader factors played a role in the successes and failures as well, without which the story would not be complete.

First is the matter of disability rights. Regardless of the various conceptualizations of disability, disability is an integral part of common human experience. Today, one in four people has a person with disabilities in his or her immediate circle of friends and relatives,[21] and it is estimated that most people will experience some sort of an impairment at some stage of life. Unlike other issues contested at the UN, then, *everyone* ultimately has an intimate interest in upholding disability rights.

Second, the willingness of state delegates to cooperate with civil society representatives to the extent that they did can be attributed, at least partially, to a "diplomatic shortcoming": diplomatic delegations simply lacked the expertise, knowledge, and understanding to properly address the needs of persons with disabilities.[22] Human rights organizations shared this lack of knowledge.[23] Together, this meant that the assistance of disability-related NGOs was absolutely necessary, much more so than in other human rights developments.[24] Furthermore, having been made aware of this shortcoming, the AHC itself had continuously and formally encouraged states to include persons with disabilities within their formal delegations and many states followed suit.[25] It was enormously helpful that many official delegates wore these "dual hats." These double-duty representatives had both the expertise about the needs of persons with disabilities and a sense of collegiality with other members of the disability community, allowing them to carefully listen and endorse text proposals submitted by the IDC. And, importantly, it gave some civil society representatives a direct, unlimited, and powerful opportunity to be equal to states' delegates in influencing the negotiations. The other indirect consequence of these developments was in breaking down the "invisibility barrier": the proportion of delegates with disabilities at the AHC simply made the phenomenon impossible to ignore. While the blurred civil society/state delegate distinction and removal of the invisibility barrier were invaluable to CSO efforts to press ahead with the disability rights agenda, state actors enabled the achievement.

Third, the participation of CSOs, DPOs, and NHRIs must be seen as part of a larger movement toward expanding the modalities of participation in such international forums. In addition to the campaign led by the disability rights community, states and international agencies, too, had advocated for extensive participation. New Zealand, Mexico, Latin American and Caribbean countries, and the European Union, along with the OHCHR and the UN Secretariat, were the strongest supporters in this regard.[26] These efforts represented self-interest as well as support for the international disability rights movement. Mexico, for instance, had struggled between being the initiator of the process and lacking expertise on disability. The participation of NGOs was thus in its interest, allowing it to retain its position as a leader but also granting it access to the very much needed expertise of the disability community. In the case of GRULAC, their cooperation with the IDC and Proyecto Sur was probably motivated, at least in part, by the real concern that Southern states cannot provide for their disabled population without the assistance of the developed countries. Collaborating closely with the IDC thus enabled GRULAC to maximize its power. While pursuing its long-term goal of raising the bar of internationl cooperation beyond existing human rights instruments, it was also able to garner additional states' support by increasing the level of pressure in a way that it could not have done otherwise. Similarly, the European Union's rising policy of promoting stakeholders' participation in European forums arguably influenced its decision.[27] Finally, both the OHCHR and the Secretariat had, in light of their own missions, an inherent interest in extensive participation by CSOs. For the OHCHR, it was the effort to strengthen its own role within the UN system and to further establish its agenda of stakeholders' full participation, including the power of NHRIs in the monitoring of states' obligations with regard to human rights.[28] Conversely, the Secretariat—jointly operated by the UN Department of Economic and Social Affairs and the OHCHR—was the body authorized under the General Assembly resolution to establish the AHC. The stakes were high.

The existence of external motivations is not intended as a criticism per se. Rather, the point is to acknowledge that ultimately states retained the power to decide whether to open or close the gates for NGO involvement. Indeed, when states' interests clashed with NGO participation—as it occurred, for example, in the discussion on international cooperation—the AHC discontinued its meetings until the issue was resolved.

A fourth important external factor is the impact of the chairperson's leadership—an issue that has been raised also in the drafting of the Convention on the Rights of the Child,[29] ICBL,[30] and CICC.[31] In theory, the chairperson is responsible for the facilitation of the negotiation process and has largely procedural authority.[32] In reality, his or her power reaches further: the chairperson can summarize the opinions raised in various ways, sway the participants' attitudes and positions, and quietly pursue or dismiss specific positions. In the CRPD negotiations, the chairpersons—initially, Ambassador Luis Gallegos Chiriboga from Ecuador and, later, Ambassador Don MacKay from New Zealand—were indeed of utmost importance. While some may suggest that New Zealand's national interests prevented a substantive recognition of indigenous persons with disabilities (see Chapter 10), it is nevertheless true that New Zealand's support, including that of Ambassador MacKay, was paramount for the outcome. Utilizing all tools available to him, MacKay personally encouraged ongoing multidirectional negotiations: states-states, NGOs-states, and states-NGOs. Importantly, he was supportive of the disability rights community, including both IDC and non-IDC members. MacKay was accessible and occasionally had meetings with IDC members to hear concerns; he gave a sense of confidence not only that it would be possible to reach a consensus but also that IDC approval would be required for the Convention's adoption. Yet again, the chair's appointment was a decision that was completely in the hands of states.

A final factor to consider is international politics. States' participation in the negotiations and their support (or lack of) of specific proposals often reflected what may be seen as a onetime opportunity to change their international image and to be part of the "clique" of developed states. Arguably, states' participation in such lawmaking processes is driven by a simple desire for self-expression in, and domination over, the international community.[33]

Unsurprisingly, states' involvement in human rights treaties has often been characterized by such motives, and the CRPD negotiations were no different—perhaps even to a greater extent. As the first human rights treaty to be negotiated in the post-USSR and post-Yugoslavia era, and the first human rights treaty in the twenty-first century, it was surrounded by optimism. Both developed and developing states wanted to show human rights activism. Such involvement provided (in particular, less established) states two opportunities. First, it enabled frequently criticized states to distance themselves, at least for some time, from international denunciation. For instance, the Venezuelan and Cuban delegations scored a (relative) success when their proposal to reference indigenous persons with disabilities in the Preamble was endorsed. Similarly, IDC proposals that were endorsed by the Israeli delegation garnered support from countries such as Kenya, Chile, and Jamaica, along with Canada, New Zealand, and others—partnerships that might not otherwise be available. Second, the negotiations solidified the place of relatively "weaker" states in international politics.

A similar dynamic had been at work in the CICC, though the specifics differ. In that case, the coalition had to overcome the opposition of the countries in the Non-Aligned Movement, and the developing states' participation (particularly from North Africa and the Middle East) may have been partly mobilized by a concern of being the main targets for accusations.[34] In the disability context, states' participation in the process provided them with the opportunity to show a deep concern for a marginalized part of their population. The relatively faint U.S. involvement (rather than outright opposition, as had occurred in the CICC), the shared lack of expertise among both developed and developing nations, and, again, the desire to take a leadership position in international affairs all contributed to this effect. The fact that developing states sent delegates with disabilities (e.g., Kenya, Jordan, Ethiopia, Vanuatu, South Africa, Guatemala, Chile) and also often closely cooperated with the IDC further strengthened their position. They could show a level of expertise that they did not necessarily have, and yet come ahead as creators of the new human rights regime.

In summary it is important to recognize that state interests in creating or maintaining international reputation were a significant factor in leveraging the power of CSOs. These interests enabled the development of the best strengths of human rights networks: building relationships that are highly personalized, flexible in form but without a fixed loyalty.[35] Put differently, national interests in upholding international reputations meant that NGOs could play political partners off of one another.[36] When one country rejected a proposal, another one was given the opportunity to submit it—hence enabling it to gain power in the international forums.

The Rise of "New Diplomacy"

Although NGOs have always been active in the international arena, there is no doubt that both the extent of their contemporary existence and the scope of their participation exceeds by far any role that was originally envisioned for them.

Political scientists and international-relations scholars have proposed various theories for the increasing involvement and impact of NGOs at the UN.[37] One explanation builds on the assumption that both the UN as an intergovernmental organization and (particularly) international NGOs are at "the highest form of institutional relations in their respective category."[38] Partnership between NGOs and the UN are thus fruitful as the latter serves as a mediator for NGO activity: it opens up channels for NGOs when domestic structures are limited and reduces the resistance of states. This is known as the *transnationalist* theory. Another explanation suggests a *trans-societal* theory, whereby the internationalization of various political processes led to further international activism. The UN thus functions to uphold global civil society by providing access and allowing for greater networking among CSOs. Arguably, it is this networking that reinforces NGO participation and also allows them to have an impact. Still another explanation revives the notion of *corporatism*. It views civil society's involvement as a system-initiated phenomenon and assumes that the increased access to UN bodies aims to provide a solution to accommodate numerous actors, but also "to diffuse criticism by radical opponents by co-opting more moderate groups."[39] It therefore addresses the problem of direct democracy—having too many individual citizen participants—by limiting participation to a number of groups that presumably represent them.

The disability rights community during the negotiations seemed to exhibit aspects of all three explanations, but it fits squarely with none of them. Of particular importance are the permeability of national resistance (discussed in Chapter 3), the opportunity to network, and the vision of NGO participation as part of the international community. However, the focus on international NGOs clearly does not reflect the fabric of activists in the negotiations. Moreover, the need for accreditation, the extensive modalities of NGO involvement, and the efforts to gain input through regional meetings seem to controvert the corporatist goal of limiting the number of participants. NGO participation in the negotiations thus signals that a new explanation for civil society's participation in international processes is emerging—one that is grounded in the relationships between societal actors and governmental and international institutions. It views international lawmaking as a pluralist process in which NGO voices are an integral part simply on the basis of being the "proper" partners.

Indeed, although concerns regarding NGO participation in international negotiations have been raised,[40] NGOs are clearly increasingly visible and active actors in international forums. Again, it is in this context that the notion of "new diplomacy" was coined, in the aftermath of the ICBL and of the CICC, to express civil society's substantial and strategic involvement in international processes.[41] States' interest in having civil society's perspectives, the usefulness in having pools of ideas, the often visionary characteristic of NGOs and the (although challenged) perception of NGOs as expressing the voice of the world, have all contributed to the sense that there is no return from this development. Moreover, CSOs are viewed as an answer to the "democratic deficit" in global governance.[42] Their participation in international forums is thus perceived as "new hybrid, pluri-lateral forms of governance," that allows for "multi-stakeholder dialogues and partnership agreements institutionalizing relationships between State and nonstate actors."[43] It reinforces the first words of the UN Charter: "We, the peoples of the United Nations," acknowledging that the UN—the traditional "All States Institution"—is nonetheless a body intended to benefit the people of the world. In exchange, it also enhances the legitimacy of the global process and the status of the UN as an institution.[44] As Secretary-General Kofi Annan stated in 1999, "I see a United Nations which recognizes that the nongovernmental revolution—the new global people power, or whatever else you wish to call this explosion of citizens' concern at the global level—is the best thing that has happened to our Organization in a long time."[45]

The successes—and failures—of the disability rights movement have to be construed in this light. Following the steps of other social movements, which secured great successes at the "All States Institution," the disability rights community has thrived. It is nonetheless significant that the disability rights movement took the notion of "new diplomacy" to a new level. The

CRPD negotiations shifted the type and forms of relationships in international human rights processes. Whereas the traditional perspective was characterized by bilateral and state-centered direction, focusing on the legal outcome to be achieved, the Convention's negotiations reflected a far more relational and developmental approach.[46] The process was mobilized by both collective leadership (the IDC), as was the case with other international processes, and by many individuals.[47] Significantly, the type of activists and leaders expanded: they did not necessarily have the common prerequisite of legal expertise but they had nonetheless unmatchable life experience and disability knowledge to contribute to the UN's discussions. The method of persuasion subsequently highly relied on extralegal strategies and on the close and trustful personal relations developed with state delegates, UN officials, and other political actors. In this sense, the IDC overcame the criticism raised with regard to the CICC, whereby the presence of grassroots representatives was claimed to be mainly symbolic, and that the negotiation process overwhelmingly favored legal expertise rather than experience.[48] The blurred state delegates/civil society distinction during the CRPD negotiations further ensured greater levels of transparency—another key aspect of democratic decision making. Additionally, the creation through the Internet of a new global "imagined community" of disability rights activists—even if based on a mere sense of collegiality—was imperative. Technology enabled individuals to cut across distinctions between ability and disability, civil society representatives and formal state delegates, North-South divides, and local, national, regional, and international interests, gluing together the ingredients of the new diplomacy.

The disability rights movement succeeded, then, in achieving what social movements aspire to do: it bound itself to societal, governmental, and other political partners in such a manner that it tied many who would not be otherwise bound to the disability rights mission.[49] In this sense, it provided more than a remedy to the "democratic deficiency" in global governance; it provided a model for the way international law processes should be held. It established the understanding that just as legal instruments are "living documents," so, too, their negotiations, conclusions, and implementation have to truly encapsulate the lives and human rights of those they aim to protect. Thus, the emphasis shifted to focus on process as well as outcome; importantly, this process inherently emphasizes not only a statement in favor of human rights protection, but also a long-term strategy of building institutions and processes that may "ensure ongoing respect for human rights through social commitment, monitoring processes, and watchdog institutions."[50]

Whether the new diplomacy as obtained through the CRPD negotiations can be generalized to other social movements is harder to evaluate. The shift toward increased stakeholder participation in international processes is likely to remain and to strengthen further. Indeed, the laudatory statements about the invaluable role of CSOs, as delivered by states' delegates and the AHC chair from the negotiations to the opening ceremony for signature, reflect states' recognition that contemporary "society" now includes nonstate actors.[51] It also signals some sense of satisfaction with the type, form, and extent of interaction. There is, therefore, no reason to assume it would weaken—though the broader human rights community has a responsibility to ensure its continuation. States will continue to have their own external motivations, and the human rights community will have to find ways to navigate between states' self-interests and human rights goals. Methods of advocacy and communication strategies can be improved. And activating the characteristics of social movements—personalized relationships without long-term loyalties and the ability to unite many actors but also to play off one another—can be replicated. Other factors are, however, unique to the disability context. The significant "diplomatic shortcoming" and the universality of the phenomenon are less likely to exist in other international law processes, and yet they were certainly invaluable in the success of the disability rights movement.

There are other lessons to be learned from the experience of disability rights negotiations. Although the disability rights movement in its horizontal relations with state delegates certainly strengthened the idea of deliberative and participatory democracy, its *internal* deliberative process was arguably more limited. On the one hand, it advanced the collective democratic process in comparison to previous international processes. For instance, whereas the CICC was criticized for having "no thorough debate, still less any formal collective decision-making, among all participating NGOs,"[52] in the CRPD context, Internet communication enabled significant discussions and the IDC's decisions were often voted for by a show of hands. On the other hand, the extent of its democratic character, as discussed above, is disputed. Similarly, although the Steering Committee allowed non-IDA members to join, the extent to which their voices were truly heard is not clear, and IDA members still enjoyed a dominant position. And, while Southern NGOs seemed to have had greater access and influence than in previous processes, the participation of other traditionally excluded groups (such as persons with disabilities from island communities and indigenous persons with disabilities) was arguably either absent or mainly symbolic. Strengthening the democratic process from *within* would therefore be important in future processes.

Finally, the durability of this new diplomacy has yet to be tested. International treaties open the door to influence local policies, and they have been found to have positive effects in countries that are neither stable democracies nor stable autocracies.[53] This is an important finding considering the disproportionately high number of persons with disabilities residing in developing states. But translating the international instrument into domestic realities will not be easy. It would also require the disability rights movement to effectively shift the power it gained in the international process and channel it instead into local and national achievements (so-called "transnationalism reversed").[54]

While in some contexts (e.g., legal capacity, prohibition of torture, and others) improvements have already started taking place,[55] the mission of achieving and of fully implementing the Convention provisions is far from complete. The negative impact of institutional, attitudinal/social, physical, and information/communication barriers are yet to be internalized. Importantly, as evidenced by Chapters 5, 10, and 12, these barriers should be removed both from within and from outside the disability rights movement. Opportunities missed in the negotiations for reasons of insufficient coordination and/or willingness to listen may reopen, and no group of persons with disabilities should feel left out. Only if the disability rights network successfully integrates the many "other" voices and persists in open dialogue will it move from being a mere social agent that tackled the specific crisis of disability's exclusion from the human rights discourse and "become a part of the social and material *structure* of the international system, regionally or globally."[56] Upholding the motto "Nothing About Us Without Us"—where the "Us" truly includes *all* of us—is key to attaining this achievement.

NOTES

Introduction

1. This definition, used throughout the book, follows the UN approach. UN and Civil Society, http://www.un.org/en/civilsociety/index.shtml; UNDP and Civil Society Organizations: A Policy of Engagement (2001), 6.

2. Gerard Quinn and Theresia Degener, *Human Rights and Disability: The Current Use and Future Potential of United Nations Human Rights Instruments in the Context of Disability* (New York: UN, 2002).

3. 91 states also signed and 76 ratified the Optional Protocol, which allows individuals to submit a complaint to the relevant international bodies.

4. UN Enable, http://www.un.org/esa/socdev/enable/dissre01.htm.

5. Ibid.

6. Quinn and Degener, *Human Rights and Disability*, chap. 12.

7. World Conference on Human Rights, 14–25 June 1993, Vienna Declaration, see, e.g., Articles 18, 23, 29.

8. Report of the Secretary-General, Ad Hoc Committee, "Overview of Issues and Trends Related to Advancement of Persons with Disability," Ad Hoc Committee, New York, 16–27 June 2003, http://www.un.org/esa/socdev/enable/rights/a_ac265 _2003_2e.htm.

9. Theresia Degener, "Disability as a Subject of International Human Rights Law and Comparative Discrimination Law," in *The Human Rights of Persons with Intellectual Disabilities: Different But Equal*, ed. Stanley S. Herr, Lawrence O. Gostin, and Harold Hongju Koh (Oxford: Oxford University Press, 2003), 169, 174.

10. Ann Florini, "Lessons Learned," in *The Third Force: The Rise of Transnational Civil Society*, ed. Ann Florini (Washington, D.C.: Carnegie Endowment for International Peace, 2000), 217–28.

11. Lester Salamon, "The Rise of the Nonprofit Sector," *Foreign Affairs* 73, 4 (1994): 109–22.

12. Laurie S. Wiseberg, "The Internet: One More Tool in the Struggle for Human Rights," in *NGOs and Human Rights: Promise and Performance*, ed. Claude E. Welch, Jr. (Philadelphia: University of Pennsylvania Press, 2001), 238–47; Jessica Mathews, "Power Shift," *Foreign Affairs* 76, 1 (1997): 50–66.

13. Andreas Paulus, "Legalist Groundwork for the International Criminal Court," *European Journal of International Law* 14 (2003): 843.

14. GA Res. 56/168, para. 3, 19 December 2001, http://www.un.org/esa/socdev /enable/disA56168e1.htm.

15. Consultative status with ECOSOC through Article 71 of the UN Charter is the most formal way of NGO participation at the UN.

16. GA Res. A/RES/56/510, 26 July 2002, http://www.un.org/disabilities/default .asp?id=69.

17. Figures provided by Yao Ngoran, chief, NGO Unit, Division for Social Policy and Development of the UN Department of Economics and Social Affairs.

18. List of accredited DPOs, http://www.un.org/esa/socdev/enable/rights/ngo saccredited.htm.

19. List of NGO representatives, eighth session, http://www.un.org/esa/socdev /enable/rights/ahc8ngolistpart.htm.

20. Tara Melish, "The UN Disability Convention: Historic Process, Strong Prospects, and Why the U.S. Should Ratify," *Human Rights Brief* 14 (2007): 43.

21. Report of AHC, first sess., 2 August 2002 (A/57/357), http://www.un.org/esa /socdev/enable/rights/adhoca57357e.htm#IV.

22. Report to GA, 58th sess. (A/AC.265/2003/L.4), http://www.un.org/esa/socdev /enable/rights/a_58_118_e.htm.

23. The Chair's Draft, submitted in preparation for the WG, was the basis for subsequent negotiations.

24. For the outcome of these events see http://www.un.org/esa/socdev/enable /rights/.

25. "Timeline of Events," http://www.un.org/disabilities/default.asp?id=153.

26. Cynthia Price Cohen, "The United Nations Convention on the Rights of the Child: Involvement of NGOs," in *The Legitimacy of the United Nations: Towards an Enhanced Legal Status of Non-State Actors*, ed. Theo C. van Boven et al. (Utrecht: SIM, 1997), 169–89; Sonia Harris-Short, "Listening to 'the Other'? The Convention on the Rights of the Child," *Melbourne Journal of International Law* 2 (2001): 304–50; Sharon Detrick, ed., *The United Nations Convention on the Rights of the Child: A Guide to the "Travaux Préparatoires"* (Dordrecht: Nijhoff, 1992); Sharon Detrick, *A Commentary on the United Nations Convention on the Rights of the Child* (The Hague: Nijhoff, 1999); Lawrence J. LeBlanc, *The Convention on the Rights of the Child: United Nations Lawmaking on Human Rights* (Lincoln: University of Nebraska Press, 1995); UN Centre for Human Rights, *Legislative History of the Convention on the Rights of the Child (1978–1989)* UN Doc. HR/1996/Ser.1 (Geneva: UN, 1996); Marlies Glasius, "Expertise in the Cause of Justice: Global Civil Society Influence on the Statute for an International Criminal Court," in *Global Civil Society 2002*, ed. Marlies Glasius, Mary Kaldor, and Helmut Anheier (Oxford: Oxford University Press, 2002), 137–65.

27. E.g., Oddný Mjöll Arnardóttir and Gerard Quinn, eds., *The UN Convention on the Rights of Persons with Disabilities: European and Scandinavian Perspectives*

(Leiden: Nijhoff, 2009); Jukka Kumpuvuori and Martin Scheinin, eds., *The United Nations Convention on the Rights of Persons with Disabilities: Multidisciplinary Perspectives* (Helsinki: Center for Human Rights of Persons with Disabilities in Finland (VIKE), 2009); Lauri Philipp Rothfritz, *Die Konvention der Vereinten Nationen zum Schutz der Rechte von Menschen mit Behinderungen: Eine Analyse unter Bezugnahme auf die deutsche und europäische Rechtsebene* (Frankfurt am Main: Peter Lang, 2010); Eilionóir Flynn, *From Rhetoric to Action: Implementing the UN Convention on the Rights of Persons with Disabilities* (Cambridge: Cambridge University Press, 2011).

Chapter 1. History of the International Disability Rights Movement

1. Rannveig Traustadóttir, "Disability Studies, the Social Model and Legal Developments," in *The UN Convention on the Rights of Persons with Disabilities: European and Scandinavian Perspectives*, ed. Oddný Mjöll Arnardóttir and Gerard Quinn (Leiden: Nijhoff, 2009), 3–16, 5.

2. Tom Shakespeare, "Cultural Representation of Disabled People: Dustbins for Disavowal?" *Disability and Society* 9, 3 (1994): 292–93; Rhoda Olkin, *What Psychotherapists Should Know About Disability* (New York: Guilford, 1999), 10.

3. Traustadóttir, "Disability Studies," 6.

4. Kevin Boyle, "Stock-Taking on Human Rights: The World Conference on Human Rights, Vienna 1993," in *Politics and Human Rights*, ed. David Beetham (New York: Wiley-Blackwell, 1995), 79–95, 79.

5. Charles Norchi, "Human Rights: A Global Common Interest," in *The United Nations: Confronting the Challenges of a Global Society*, ed. Jean E. Krasno (Boulder, Colo.: Lynne Rienner, 2004), 79–114, 87–88.

6. World Conference on Human Rights, 14–25 June 1993, Vienna Declaration, para. 5.

7. General Comment No. 5, Persons with Disabilities (1994). See also Committee under ICCPR, General Comment No. 8, Liberty and Security of the Person (1982), including only a reference to persons with mental illness.

8. Harlan Hahn, "The Political Implications of Disability Definitions and Data," in *The Psychological and Social Impact of Disability*, ed. Robert P. Marinelli and Arthur E. Dell Orto (New York: Springer, 1999), 3–11, 5–6.

9. Shakespeare, "Cultural Representation of Disabled People," 287–89.

10. David L. Braddock and Susan L. Parish, "Social Policy Toward Intellectual Disabilities in the Nineteenth and Twentieth Centuries," in *The Human Rights of Persons with Intellectual Disabilities: Different But Equal*, ed. Stanley S. Herr, Lawrence O. Gostin, and Harold Hongju Koh (Oxford: Oxford University Press, 2003), 83–115, 90–91; David Pfeiffer, "Eugenics and Disability Discrimination," In *The Psychological and Social Impact of Disability*, ed. Robert P. Marinelli and Arthur E. Dell Orto (New York: Springer, 1999), 12–31.

11. Colin Barnes, *Disabled People in Britain and Discrimination: A Case for Anti-Discrimination Legislation* (London: Hurst with British Council of Organisations of Disabled People, 1991); Mike Oliver, *The Politics of Disablement* (London: Macmillan, 1990).

12. Hahn,"The Political Implications of Disability," 3, 6–7; Deborah Marks, "Models of Disability," *Disability and Rehabilitation* 19, 3 (1997): 88–89.

13. Colin Barnes and Geof Mercer, "The Politics of Disability and the Struggle for Change," in *Disability, Politics and the Struggle for Change*, ed. Len Barton (London: David Fulton, 2001), 11–23; Mike Oliver and Colin Barnes, "Discrimination, Disability and Welfare: From Needs to Rights," in Ian Bynoe, Oliver, and Barnes, *Equal Rights for Disabled People: The Case for a New Law* (London: Institute for Public Policy Research, 1991), 9–17, 13–14.

14. Tom Shakespeare, *Disability Rights and Wrongs* (London: Routledge, 2006), 10, 15.

15. Ibid., 10, 13.

16. Ibid., 10–11.

17. Ibid., 25.

18. Traustadóttir, "Disability Studies," 12–13.

19. 1967 Norwegian White Paper on disability, cited in Shakespeare, *Disability Rights and Wrongs*, 25.

20. Traustadóttir, "Disability Studies," 13.

21. Shakespeare, *Disability Rights and Wrongs*, 26.

22. Hahn, "The Political Implications of Disability," 6–7; Traustadóttir, "Disability Studies," 14.

23. Because the Deaf community is viewed as a linguistic minority group, there is a cultural distinction between "capital D" Deaf and "lower case" deaf. When describing people who have the condition of deafness, whether or not they use sign language, lower case d is used. When emphasizing deaf people as members of Deaf Community and Deaf culture, capital D is used. Similarly, sign language/s refers to sign languages in general (compare to "spoken languages"), whereas a reference to a specific sign language requires capitalization (e.g., American Sign Language or Japanese Sign Language). See also Chapter 8.

24. Katherine E. Russell, Cheryl Coffin, and Margaret Kenna, "Cochlear Implants and the Deaf Child: A Nursing Perspective," *Pediatric Nursing* 25, 4 (1999): 444.

25. Erik Parens and Adrienne Asch, "The Disability Rights Critique of Prenatal Genetic Testing," *Hastings Center Report* 29, 5 (1999): 12.

26. Anna Kirkland, "Identity and the Properly Functioning Individual: Imagining the Confluence of Fat Rights and Disability Law," University of Southern California Center for Law, History and Culture, 6 October 2004, http://lawweb.usc.edu /centers/clhc/archives/workshops/documents/kirkland_000.pdf.

27. Adrienne Asch, Lawrence O. Gostin, and Diann M. Johnson, "Respecting Persons with Disabilities and Preventing Disability: Is There a Conflict?" in Herr, Gostin, and Koh, *Human Rights of Persons with Intellectual Disabilities*, 323.

28. Alison Dundes Renteln, "Cross-Cultural Perceptions of Disability: Policy Implications of Divergent Views," in Herr, Gostin, and Koh, *Human Rights of Persons with Intellectual Disabilities*, 71.

29. Ibid., 60.

30. Mary T. Westbrook, Varoe Legge, and Mark Pennay, "Attitudes Towards Disabilities in a Multicultural Society," *Social Science and Medicine* 36, 5 (1993): 620, 622.

31. E.g., Robert Chimedza, "The Cultural Politics of Integrating Deaf Students in Regular Schools in Zimbabwe," *Disability and Society* 13, 4 (1998): 495–96.

32. Anna-Miria Muhlke, "The Right to Language and Linguistic Development: Deafness from a Human Rights Perspective," *Virginia Journal of International Law* 40 (2000): 738.

33. Richard J. Sanghas and Laila Monaghan, "Signs of Their Times: Deaf Communities and the Culture of Language," *Annual Review of Anthropology* 31 (2002): 69, 81.

34. Cheryl Wu and Nancy Grant, "Asian, American, and Deaf: A Framework for Professionals," *American Annals of the Deaf* 142, 2 (1997): 88.

35. Annie G. Steinberg et al., "'A Little Sign and a Lot of Love . . .': Attitudes, Perceptions, and Beliefs of Hispanic Families with Deaf Children," *Qualitative Health Research* 7, 2 (1997): 202–22.

36. Lindsay Moeletsi Dunn, "Education, Culture and Community: The Black Deaf Experience," *Deaf American Monograph* 45 (1995): 38–40.

37. Renteln, "Cross-Cultural Perceptions," 60, 65.

38. Theresia Degener, "Disabled Persons and Human Rights: The Legal Framework," in *Human Rights and Disabled Persons*, ed. Theresia Degener and Yolan Koster-Dreese (Dordrecht: Nijhoff, 1995), 9–39, 11–12.

39. Theresia Degener, "Disability as a Subject of International Human Rights Law and Comparative Discrimination Law," in Herr, Gostin, and Koh, *Human Rights of Persons with Intellectual Disabilities*, 158.

40. Renteln, "Cross-Cultural Perceptions," 64.

41. Ibid.

42. Theresia Degener, "Disabled Women and International Human Rights," in *Women and International Human Rights Law*, ed. Kelly D. Askin and Dorean M. Koenig (Ardsley, N.Y.: Transnational, 1999–2001), 267–93.

43. Declaration on the Right to Development, GA Res. 41/128, Annex, 41 UN GAOR, Supp. No. 53 at 186, UN Doc A/RES/41/128 (1986); Vienna Declaration, particularly provisions 10–11.

44. "'Reasonable accommodation' means necessary and appropriate modification and adjustments not imposing a disproportionate or undue burden, where needed in

a particular case, to ensure to persons with disabilities the enjoyment or exercise on an equal basis with others of all human rights and fundamental freedoms" (Article 2, CRPD).

Chapter 2. Our Lives, Our Voices

1. See, e.g., UN data, http://www.un.org/disabilities/default.asp?id=18; Susan Peters, *Education Notes: Education for All* (Washington, D.C.: World Bank, 2003); Ann Elwan, *Poverty and Disability* (Washington, D.C.: World Bank, 1999); Inclusion International, *Hear Our Voices: A Global Report; People with an Intellectual Disability and Their Families Speak Out on Poverty and Exclusion* (London: Inclusion International, 2006).

2. For Inclusion International Policy, see http://www.inclusion-international.org/about-us/policies.

3. For UN and World Bank data, see, e.g., http://www.un.org/esa/socdev/enable/diswpa04.htm; Peters, *Education Notes.*

4. E.g., Canadian Association for Community Living, *Alternatives to Guardianship* (Toronto: Canadian Association for Community Living, 1992)

5. See also Chapter 3.

6. IDC lobby sheet, "Article 15: Living and Being Included in the Community," fifth AHC session, January 2005.

7. E.g., J. Douglas Willms, *Learning Divides: Ten Policy Questions About the Performance and Equity of Schools and Schooling Systems* (Montreal: UNESCO Institute for Statistics, 2006); J. Douglas Willms, "Standards of Care: Investments to Improve Children's Educational Outcomes in Latin America," paper presented at the Conference on Early Childhood Development, Washington, D.C., 2000; Cameron Crawford, *Scoping Inclusive Education for Canadian Students with Intellectual and Other Disabilities* (Toronto: Roeher Institute, 2005); Gordon L. Porter, "Making Canadian Schools Inclusive," *Canadian Education Association* 48, 2 (2008): 62–66, http://www.inclusiveeducation.ca/documents/2MakingCanadianSchoolsInclusiveGPorter.pdf; Maryam Wagner and Vianne Timmons, "The Connection Between Inclusion and Health," 2008, http://www.ctf-fce.ca/publications/health_learning/Issue6_Article2_EN.pdf; Cameron Crawford, "Social Trajectories and the Inclusive Education of People with Disabilities," presentation to Canadian Association of Statutory Human Rights Agencies (CASHRA), 2008 National Forum, Ontario, 25–27 September 2008.

Chapter 3. Living in the Community, Access to Justice

1. http://www.bizchut.org.il/eng/.

2. HC 7081/93, *Shachar Botzer v. Maccabim-Reut*, PD 50(1) 19.

3. The Equal Rights for Persons with Disabilities Law (1998).

4. HC 1759/99, *Shtrum et al. v. Minister of Interior.*

5. HC 3989/00, *Bizchut et al. v. Minister of Transportation et al.*

6. Labor Court (Haifa) 1103/01, *Hadas Schramm et al. v. Karmiel Municipality.*

7. http://www.justice.gov.il/MOJHeb/NetzivutNEW/.

8. The Rehabilitation in the Community for Persons with Psychosocial Disabilities Law (2000).

9. E.g., HC 7443/03, *Bizchut et al. v. Ministry of Education* (decision at http://elyon1.court.gov.il/files/03/430/074/16L/03074430.16l.htm); HC 6973/03 *Martziano v. Minister of Finance et al.*, PD 58(2) 270.

10. S.H. 2038 (2005), 42.

11. In 1997 approximately 5,700 individuals resided in 49 institutions for persons with intellectual disabilities in Israel; in 2010, 6,500 individuals resided in 60 such institutions; http://www.molsa.gov.il/misradharevacha/disabilities/mentalretardation/dormitories.

12. http://www.molsa.gov.il/NR/rdonlyres/A0E972F1-8B7C-4647-87B1-9E89F36929E3/1741/nehalim1.pdf.

13. HC 4759/95, *Amir v. Minister of Labor and Welfare.*

14. HC 3304/07, *Bizchut et al. v. State of Israel*: http://www.bizchut.org.il/heb/upload/.mishpatit/diur_bakehila.html; decision: http://elyon1.court.gov.il/files/07/040/033/p19/07033040.p.19.htm; http://elyon2.court.gov.il/files/07/040/033/p32/07033040.p.32.htm.

15. A workshop conducted by Survivor Corps (then Landmine Survivors Network) in April 2004 introduced Israeli activists to the process and familiarized them with what had previously transpired at the negotiations.

16. http://www.un.org/esa/socdev/enable/rights/ahcwgreportax1.htm.

17. Chile's proposed modification to (then) Article 9, http://www.un.org/esa/socdev/enable/rights/ahc4da9.htm.

18. Summary of Costa Rica's intervention, http://www.un.org/esa/socdev/enable/rights/ahc4sumart09.htm.

19. Law on Accommodations to the Investigative and Testimonial Processes for Persons with Intellectual or Psychosocial Disabilities (2005).

20. The International Society for Augmentative and Alternative Communication defines AAC as "a set of tools and strategies that an individual uses to solve everyday communicative challenges. Communication can take many forms such as: speech, a shared glance, text, gestures, facial expressions, touch, sign language, symbols, pictures, speech generating devices, etc. Everyone uses multiple forms of communication, based upon the context and our communication partner. Effective communication occurs when the intent and meaning of one individual is understood by another person. The form is less important than the successful understanding of the message," https://www.isaac-online.org/english/what-is-aac/.

21. New Zealand proposal, sixth session: http://www.un.org/esa/socdev/enable/rights/ahc6nz.htm; summary of session discussion, http://www.un.org/esa/socdev

/enable/rights/ahc6sum1Aug.htm; IDC proposed text, http://www.un.org/esa/socdev /enable/rights/ahc5contngos.htm.

22. This policy was struck down in 2008 as a result of Bizchut's second petition to the Supreme Court on the right to live in the community, which cited CRPD Article 19: HC 3304/07, *Bizchut et al. v. State of Israel.*

23. http://www.molsa.gov.il/misradharevacha/disabilities/mentalretardation /dormitories.

24. Through this alliance, the broader issue of participation of persons with intellectual disabilities in the negotiations was taken up as well. Thus, e.g., a collaborative effort of these organizations resulted in release of several documents in plain language (available on request from the author), including a manual describing the negotiations process to newcomers and an adapted version of the draft convention, with a glossary of key terms. Additionally, guidelines were issued for assistants supporting advocates with intellectual disabilities who participated in the negotiations.

25. Israel's proposal, http://www.un.org/esa/socdev/enable/rights/ahc7israel.htm.

26. IDC proposal, http://www.un.org/esa/socdev/enable/rights/ahc7docs /ahc7idcart19.doc.

27. Israel's proposed amendment, http://www.un.org/esa/socdev/enable/rights /ahc7israel.htm. IDC proposed amendment, http://www.un.org/esa/socdev/enable /rights/ahc7docs/ahc7idcart19.doc.

28. Daily summary for 19–20 January 2006, http://www.un.org/esa/socdev/enable /rights/ahc7sum19jan.htm; 20jan.htm.

29. For further discussion about the right to live in the community see also Chapter 5.

30. Daily summary for 26 January 2005, http://www.un.org/esa/socdev/enable /rights/ahc5sum26jan.htm.

31. http://www.un.org/esa/socdev/enable/rights/ahc5docs/ahc5idcaucus.doc.

32. "Justice for All? Making the Legal Process Accessible for Persons with Disabilities," side event, 16 January 2005.

33. For the draft language see http://www.un.org/esa/socdev/enable/rights/ahc5chile .htm, presented when discussion resumed over this article on 28 January 2005.

34. Proposed new article on access to justice, http://www.un.org/esa/socdev /enable/rights/ahc5contngos.htm.

35. Israel's proposed amendment http://www.un.org/esa/socdev/enable/rights /ahc7israel.htm; IDC proposal http://www.un.org/esa/socdev/enable/rights/ahc7docs /ahc7idcchairamend1.doc.

36. Daily summary for 18 January 2006, http://www.un.org/esa/socdev/enable /rights/ahc7sum18jan.htm.

37. Full text of IDC intervention, http://www.un.org/esa/socdev/enable/rights /ahc7docs/ahc7idcart13.doc.

38. http://www.un.org/esa/socdev/enable/rights/ahc7israel.htm; http://www.un .org/esa/socdev/enable/rights/ahc7docs/ahc7idcchairamend1.doc.

39. http://www.un.org/esa/socdev/enable/rights/ahc7sum18jan.htm.

40. E.g., Frances Gibson, "Access to Justice for Persons with Disabilities: The Response of the Clinic" (La Trobe University), http://papers.ssrn.com/sol3/papers.cfm?abstract_id=1540581; "Legal Workshop Examines Access to Justice Issues in China" (March 2010), http://wikisites.cityu.edu.hk/sites/newscentre/en/Pages/201003081050.aspx.

41. See, e.g., section on Article 13 in the IDA contribution to the OHCHR ("Contribution to 2008 Thematic Study on Legal Measures for the Implementation of the CRPD," http://www.internationaldisabilityalliance.org/wp-content/uploads/2009/08/IDA-CRPD-Forum-submission-to-the-OHCHR-thematic-study-September-15.doc). See also the recommendations proposed by the National Platform for the Rights of the Disabled, India, on making the justice system accessible, at http://health.dir.groups.yahoo.com/group/namiindia/message/653. For an interesting example of a pre-CRPD program reflecting the essence of Article 13, see Beverley Dickman et al., "'How Could She Possibly Manage in Court?' An Intervention Programme Assisting Complainants with Intellectual Disability in Sexual Assault Cases in the Western Cape," in *Disability and Social Change: A South African Agenda*, ed. Brian Watermeyer et al. (Capetown: HSRC Press, 2006), 116–33.

42. Language to that effect was suggested by the IDC: http://www.un.org/esa/socdev/enable/rights/ahc7docs/ahc7idcart19.doc.

43. For a recent and powerful explication of Article 19, see Thomas Hammarberg, "The Right of People with Disabilities to Live Independently and Be Included in the Community," Comm DH/Issue Paper 3 (Strasbourg, 20 February 2012), https://wcd.coe.int/ViewDoc.jsp?id=1917847.

Chapter 4. Inclusion or Choice?

Epigraph: Vaclav Havel, *Disturbing the Peace: A Conversation with Karel Hvizdala*, trans. and intro. Paul Wilson (London: Faber and Faber, 1990), 181.

1. For further discussion and references on human rights and inclusive education, see Sharon Rustemier, *Social and Educational Justice: The Human Rights Framework for Inclusion* (Bristol: CSIE, 2002).

2. www.csie.org.uk/.

3. For significant landmarks in the development of this evidence, see Gary Thomas and Mark Vaughan, eds., *Inclusive Education, Readings and Reflections* (London: Open University Press, 2004); see also the resources and campaigns sections of the websites of UK organizations referred to in this chapter and daily summaries of AHC sessions, http://www.un.org/disabilities/default.asp?id=1423; and key CSIE written briefings, http://www.csie.org.uk/campaigns/un-lobbying.shtml.

4. www.allfie.org.uk.

5. www.crae.org.uk.

6. www.ukdpc.net/site/.

7. www.worldofinclusion.com.

8. www.eenet.org.uk.

9. Daily summary, 2–4 August 2005, www.un.org/esa/socdev/enable/rights
/ahc6summary.htm; for the original proposals for education, www.un.org/esa/socdev
/enable/rights/ahcwgreporta17.htm.

10. This summary is based on UN Convention archives, briefing papers from
CSIE and other organizations, and personal notes and papers.

Chapter 5. An Eye Toward Effective Enforcement

1. Amnesty International and Human Rights Watch, for example, undertook
early human rights campaigns in the 1970s and 1980s against forced institutionalization of political dissidents in psychiatric facilities, especially in the Soviet Union and
Eastern Europe. They did so on the understanding that such dissidents *did not have*
mental impairments, and hence could not justifiably be institutionalized. See, e.g.,
Amnesty International, *Annual Report 1980*, 17, 250; Amnesty International, *The Political Abuse of Psychiatry in Romania*, AI Index: EUR 39/20/80 (New York: Amnesty
International, 1980); Human Rights Watch, *Dangerous Minds: Political Psychiatry in
China Today and Its Origins in the Mao Era* (New York: Human Rights Watch, 2002)
(recalling Soviet practices from earlier reports and comparing to contemporary Chinese ones). Although broader abuses against persons in psychiatric institutions were
found by human rights investigators, Amnesty International concluded that forced
institutionalization of persons with real or perceived mental impairments, and even
their subjection to painful electroconvulsive shock therapy, fell outside of its mandate since such treatment was inflicted neither for political motivations nor with
deliberate intent to cause suffering. See, e.g., Amnesty International, *Psychiatry: A
Human Rights Perspective* 1–6 (New York: Amnesty International, 1995). The U.S.
Department of State took the same limited approach in its reporting on psychiatric
abuses in the Soviet Union. See, e.g., Department of State, *Country Reports on
Human Rights Practices for 1989* (Washington, D.C.: U.S. Department of State,
1990), 1274, 1276.

2. For more on DRI's work, see http://www.disabilityrightsintl.org/work/.

3. These testimonial interventions were vital to the negotiation process. They
brought vividly to life for state delegations (and other civil society members) the specific, often unrecognized, ways that day-to-day structures, attitudes and other barriers to equality inhibit the rights and dignity of persons with disabilities worldwide.
They were thus crucial for raising delegate awareness and ensuring that the Convention substantively included key concepts and particular forms of abuse widely experienced by persons with disabilities around the world. The Convention would not
have been what it is without these critical substantive contributions and the dedicated

work of countless advocates in socializing disability experiences within the negotiation process.

4. Although individuals were hired to officially record the treaty's *travaux préparatoires*, the public record includes delegate interventions in "summary" form only, often losing the nuance and specificity of what was said. It was, moreover, not available until after the conclusion of each session, limiting its utility for the negotiation process itself.

5. See, e.g., DRI intervention on Article 19, AHC seventh session ("while it is important to recognize that Article 19 derives directly from Article 12 of the ICCPR, it is equally important to recognize that the language used in Article 19 should not—indeed, *must not*—directly mirror that in ICCPR Article 12").

6. On issues where DRI had less of a direct stake it distributed copies of the precise language proposed by distinct delegations with a view to helping delegations find their own way through contentious issues (like "foreign occupation" or sexual intimacy) as expeditiously as possible.

7. See, e.g., discussion of Article 24 below, in section titled "Inclusive Education and Work Environments."

8. The WNUSP played a key role in the IDC and in the negotiation process as a whole, from start to finish.

9. See "Our Work," http://www.disabilityrightsintl.org/work/, particularly with respect to DRI's Worldwide Campaign to End the Institutionalization of Children and its global campaign to recognize abuse against persons with disabilities as "ill-treatment or torture."

10. As likewise noted in Chapter 12, this decision led to DRI's formal spurning by certain IDC members, which was very difficult and painful institutionally. This is true even as it received a great deal of privately expressed support and encouragement for the positions it took from both within and outside the IDC.

11. As a concession for the removal of inappropriate article-by-article qualifiers, the inclusion of Article 4(2) remains a major disappointment. Although containing corrective language that, if taken at its value, renders the entire provision superfluous, the provision can be expected to raise unnecessary interpretive disputes and challenges at the implementation stage with respect to many of the most important rights in the CRPD, including those of equal access by persons with disabilities to adequate and appropriate housing, work, health care, education, habilitation and rehabilitation services, and other core social rights.

12. Norm framing in this regard has been particularly problematic in enforcing the social rights enshrined in Article 26 of the American Convention on Human Rights.

13. Certain states, such as the People's Republic of China, often explicitly refused to recognize norms as rights, including the right to personal integrity. Other states seemed to propose drafting changes without much attention to the loss of the rights denomination.

14. See CRPD Articles 15 and 17. In so doing, references to the state duty to "protect [persons with disabilities] from forced interventions or forced institutionalization" were dropped from both.

15. See, e.g., *Shtukaturov v. Russia*, Application no. 44009/05, ECHR, 27 March 2008; *Salontaji-Drobnjak v. Serbia*, Application no. 36500/05, ECHR, 13 October 2009.

16. In *Glor v. Switzerland*, Application no. 13444/04, ECHR, 30 April 2009, the European Court of Human Rights identified the CRPD as a modern expression of a "European and universal consensus" on the need to protect persons with disabilities from discriminatory treatment.

17. See http://www.disabilityrightsintl.org/learn-about-the-worldwide-campaign -to-end-the-institutionalization-of-children/.

18. This exception was initially supported by all Middle Eastern, most Asian, and many African countries.

19. See, e.g., Chapter 4.

20. DRI recalled in this regard Japan's comment that where inclusive education is not available, the only "choice" is segregated or separate education—a very different kind of choice, indeed.

21. See, e.g., Convention Concerning Indigenous and Tribal Peoples in Independent Countries (ILO No. 169), 72 ILO Official Bull. 59, entered into force 5 September 1991, Article 27.

22. Council of Europe, Committee of Ministers, Recommendation (2004)10.

23. Ibid., Article 36(2)(ii),(iii).

24. Ibid., Article 37(1), Article 38.

25. Alison Hillman, "Protecting Mental Disability Rights: A Success Story in the Inter-American Human Rights System," *Human Rights Brief* 12, 3 (2005): 25–28, 25.

Chapter 6. Children with Disabilities

1. Review of recommendations by the Committee on the Rights of the Child in respect of children with disabilities, Rights for Disabled Children, Disability Awareness in Action (DAA), 2003 (paper presented to Committee, 29 September 2003).

2. The Committee has acknowledged four of the rights as also general principles that must inform implementation of all other rights: nondiscrimination, best interests of the child, right to life and development, right to be heard and taken seriously (Articles 2, 3, 6, 12, CRC).

3. See, e.g., Rachel Hodgkin and Peter Newell, *Implementation Handbook for the Convention on the Rights of the Child*, rev. 3rd ed. (New York: UNICEF, 2007).

4. UNICEF, *Promoting the Rights of Children with Disabilities* (Florence: Innocenti Research Centre, 2007).

5. See, e.g., Gerison Lansdown, *The Evolving Capacities of the Child* (Florence: Innocenti Research Centre, 2005).

6. UN Secretary-General's Study on Violence Against Children, *Summary Report of the Thematic Meeting on Violence Against Children with Disabilities* (New York: UN, 2005).

Chapter 7. Women with Disabilities

1. Gerard Quinn and Theresia Degener, *Human Rights and Disability* (New York: United Nations, 2002), 15.

2. Daniel Stubbs and Sainimilil Tawake, *Pacific Sisters with Disabilities: At the Intersection of Discrimination* (Suva, Fiji: UNDP Pacific Centre, 2009), 7.

3. Bengt Lindqvist, in *Monitoring the Implementation of the Standard Rules on Equalization of Opportunities, Report to the Commission of Social Development*, E/CN.5/2002/4, para. 56, as quoted in Tina L. Singleton, Mary Lou Breslin, and Cindy Lewis, *Gender and Disability: A Survey of InterAction Member Agencies* (Eugene, Ore.: Mobility International USA-MIUSA, 2002), 7.

4. On the 80 percent figure see Report of the UN Secretary General, *Keeping the Promise: Realizing the Millennium Development Goals for Persons with Disabilities* (A/65/173); AMDD (Averting Maternal Death and Disability Program), http://www.amddprogram.org/d/; see also UNFPA, *Maternal Mortality Update 2006, Expectation and Delivery: Investing in Midwives and Others with Midwifery Skills*, http://www.unfpa.org/public/home/publications/pid/390.

5. CESCR, General Comment No. 5, Persons with Disabilities (1994), para. 19.

6. Marieke Boersma, *Violence Against Ethiopian Children with Disabilities: The Stories and Perspectives of Children* (The Hague: DCDD, 2009).

7. Note, though, the mention in the World Programme of Action Concerning Disabled Persons, Special groups: "In families, the responsibility for caring for a disabled parent often lies with women, which considerably limits their freedom and their possibilities of taking part in other activities," A/RES/37/52. For discussion on role of family, see Chapter 2.

8. Quinn and Degener, *Human Rights and Disability*, particularly Chapter 1.3., The "core" problem: The invisibility of people with disabilities in the system of freedom.

9. Clearly, a stand-alone provision on women with disabilities would not provide an automatic panacea to the rights of women with disabilities. In fact, as Quinn and Degener's seminal study has clearly shown, inclusion of such a provision on the rights of children with disabilities has had only limited impact (*Human Rights and Disability*, chap. 8). It is nonetheless an initial and essential step for recognition, as, at the very least, it requires states to report and acknowledge the existence of children with disabilities under their jurisdiction and provides a platform for further discussion and inclusion.

10. Nairobi Forward-Looking Strategies for the Advancement of Women, UN Doc. A/CONF.116/28/Rev. (1985), http://www.un-documents.net/nflsaw.htm.

11. *Report of the World Conference to Review and Appraise the Achievement of the United Nations Decade for Women: Equality, Development and Peace*, UN Doc. A/CONF.116/28/Rev.1 (1985), para. 296, http://www.un.org/womenwatch/daw/beijing/otherconferences/Nairobi/Nairobi%20Full%20Optimized.pdf.

12. Ibid.

13. CEDAW Committee, General Recommendation No. 18 (1991), Disabled Women.

14. CESCR, General Comment No. 5, para. 19.

15. Standard Rules on the Equalization of Opportunities for Persons with Disabilities, A/RES/48/96 (1993), para. 15.

16. Declaration on the Elimination of Violence Against Women, UN A/RES/48/104 (1993).

17. The proposed article was originally numbered Article 15 bis in line with the then draft.

18. Quoted by International Service for Human Rights, Ad Hoc Committee on a Comprehensive and Integral International Convention on the Protection and Promotion of the Rights and Dignity of Persons with Disabilities, sixth session, New York, 1–12 August 2005

19. See Chapter 6.

20. Definition by ECOSOC, *Report of the Economic and Social Council for 1997*, UN Doc. A/52/3 (1997).

21. *Report of the Fourth World Conference on Women*, UN Doc. A/CONF.177/20/Rev.1, Platform for Action, p. 79.

22. The EU proposal (UK on behalf, sixth session) read: "States Parties undertake to take all necessary measures to ensure the full and equal enjoyment of all human rights and freedoms by women with disabilities on an equal basis with others, bearing in mind the general obligation to ensure equality between women and men." http://www.un.org/esa/socdev/enable/rights/ahc6eu.htm

23. Cf. Chapter 6.

24. Cf. Republic of Korea proposal, http://www.un.org/esa/socdev/enable/rights/ahc3sum28may.htm.

25. For Holy See proposal, August 2005, http://www.un.org/esa/socdev/enable/rights/ahc6.htm.

26. IDC, "The Convention and Women with Disabilities: We Need the Twin Track Approach!!" 14 August 2006, http://www.un.org/esa/socdev/enable/rights/ahc8docs/ahc8idcwomgen.doc.

27. Women's IDC Update, "Proposals on Inclusion of Gender Aspects in a Specific Article and Other Relevant Articles of the UN Convention," http://www.un.org/esa/socdev/enable/rights/ahc7docs/ahc7widc1.doc.

28. Sigrid Arnade and Sabine Haefner, "Gendering the Draft Comprehensive and Integral International Convention on the Protection and Promotion of the Rights and

Dignity of Persons with Disabilities: Legal Background Paper," Disabled People's International (Berlin, January 2006), http://v1.dpi.org/lang-en/resources/topics_detail ?page=446.

29. AHC Report, sixth session, Para. 23.

30. Ibid., 24.

31. *Report of the Fourth World Conference on Women,* Beijing Declaration, para. 32.

32. Ibid., 1995 Beijing Declaration, Para 14.

33. Compare the reference to families in the Preamble of the CRC and to the reference in Rule 9 of the Standard Rules.

34. General Recommendation 24, Article 12, CEDAW.

Chapter 8. Including Deaf Culture and Linguistic Rights

1. For information on the WFD see http://www.wfdeaf.org/.

2. Deaf People and Human Rights, 2009, http://www.wfdeaf.org/pdf/Deaf%20Peo ple%20and%20Human%20Rights%20Report%20-%2023%20Feb%2009%20Version .pdf.

3. For information on the International Disability Alliance, including its composition during the negotiations and today, see http://www.internationaldisabilityalliance.org/.

4. Daily summaries, third AHC session, http://www.un.org/esa/socdev/enable /rights/ahc3.htm.

5. Faith McLellan, "Controversy over Deliberate Conception of Deaf Child," *Lancet* 359, 9341 (2002): 1315; Bonnie Poitras Tucker, "Deaf Culture, Cochlear Implants, and Elective Disability," *Hastings Center Report* 28, 4 (1998): 7.

6. Oliver Sacks, *Seeing Voices: A Journey into the World of the Deaf* (London: Picador, 1990), 113; Elissa L. Newport and Ted Supalla, "Sign Languages," in *MIT Encyclopedia of Cognitive Sciences,* ed. Robert A. Wilson and Frank C. Keil (Cambridge, Mass.: MIT Press, 1999), 758–60; see also Nora Ellen Groce, *Everyone Here Spoke Sign Language:Hereditary Deafness on Martha's Vineyard* (Cambridge, Mass.: Harvard University Press, 1988).

7. Article 3(d), CRPD; see also Marianne Schulze and Kirsten Young, "Respect for Difference: A Value or a Value-Add to Discrimination and Equality Norms?" *Juridikum* 1 (2008): 45–48.

8. Johannes Borgstein, "A Sense of Language," *Lancet* 357, 9261 (2001): 1036–37.

9. Anna-Miria Muhlke, "The Right to Language and Linguistic Development: Deafness from a Human Rights Perspective," *Virginia Journal of International Law* 40 (2000): 710.

10. Compare Article 24 (1)(c) CRPD.

11. WFD Comments Concerning Draft CRPD, third AHC session, http://www.un
.org/esa/socdev/enable/rights/ahc3wfd.pdf.

12. On file with authors, http://www.un.org/esa/socdev/enable/rights/ahc5summary
.htm.

13. Muhlke, "Right to Language and Linguistic Development," 713, 719.

14. WFD Comments Concerning Draft CRPD.

Chapter 9. Imagine: To Be a Part of This

1. The European Disability Forum convened the meeting held in Madrid, 13–15
December 2003.

2. IDC proposal on the right to life, AHC fourth session (August 2004), http://un
.org/esa/socdev/enable/rights/ahcstata10fscomments.htm#idc.

3. Document on file with the author's estate.

4. See also Chapter 4.

Chapter 10. Indigenous People with Disabilities

1. Statement by Special Rapporteur on Indigenous People, Geneva, 9 September
2010.

2. Report by Special Rapporteur to Human Rights Council, 9th sess., UN Doc.
A/HRC/9/9 (2008).

3. Russel L. Barsh, "Indigenous Peoples in the 1990s: From Object to Subject of
International Law?" *Harvard Human Rights Journal* 7 (1994): 33, 81–82.

4. José Martínez Cobo, *Study of the Problem of Discrimination Against Indigenous
Populations*, vol. 5, UN Doc. E/CN.4/Sub.2/1986/87.

5. Convention Concerning Indigenous and Tribal Peoples in Independent Countries (ILO No. 169), ILO Official Bull. 59, entered into force 5 September 1991.

6. Martínez Cobo, *Study of the Problem*; Subcommission on the Promotion and
Protection of Human Rights, *Indigenous Peoples and Their Relationship to Land: Final
Working Paper by the Special Rapporteur, Mrs. Erica-Irene A. Daes* (11 June 2001), UN
Doc. E/CN.4/Sub.2/2001/21; Article 13 of ILO Convention No. 169 also recognizes
this relationship to the land; see also Jean-Bernard Marie, "Relations Between Peoples'
Rights and Human Rights: Semantic and Methodological Distinctions," *Human
Rights Law Journal* 7 (1986): 195.

7. Christine Cheyne, Mike O'Brien, and Michael Belgrave, *Social Policy in
Aotearoa New Zealand: A Critical Introduction* (Oxford: Oxford University Press,
1997).

8. Mason Durie, "The Treaty of Waitangi: Equality of Citizenship and Indigene-

ity," address to HRC Workshop on the Relationship between the Treaty of Waitangi and Human Rights, Wellington, 8 July 2003, www.hrc.co.nz/hrc/worddocs/Mason %20Durie%20presentation.doc, 9.

9. Jeff Corntassel and Tomas Hopkins Primeau, "Indigenous 'Sovereignty' and International Law: Revised Strategies for Pursuing 'Self-Determination,'" *Human Rights Quarterly* 17, 2 (1995): 343–65; Ian Brownlie, *Principles of Public International Law* (Oxford: Clarendon, 1990); Russel L. Barsh, "Indigenous Peoples and the UN Commission on Human Rights: A Case of the Immovable Object and the Irresistible Force," *Human Rights Quarterly* 18, 4 (1996): 782–813.

10. Commission for Human Rights Resolution 1999/52, 27 April 1999, Geneva; subsequently, the Permanent Forum on Indigenous Issues was established by ECOSOC Resolution 2000/22, 28 July 2000.

11. UN GA Res. A/RES/57/191 (2002).

12. Cindy L. Holder and Jeff Corntassel, "Indigenous Peoples and Multicultural Citizenship: Bridging Collective and Individual Rights," *Human Rights Quarterly* 24, 1 (2002): 126–51; Helen Quane, "The Rights of Indigenous Peoples and the Development Process," *Human Rights Quarterly* 27, 2 (2005): 652–82.

13. Ulrich Beck, "The Truth of Others: A Cosmopolitan Approach," *Common Knowledge* 10, 3 (2004): 430.

Chapter 11. At the United Nations . . . "The South Also Exists"

1. For more information in Spanish about CRESOR, see http://www.cresor.cl/.

2. Handicap International and Christian Blind Mission, *Making Poverty Reduction Strategies Inclusive*, 2006, http://siteresources.worldbank.org/DISABILITY/Resources/280658-1172608138489/MakingPRSPInclusive.pdf.

3. See Seamus Hegarty, *Education of Children and Young People with Disabilities: Principles and Practices* (Paris: UNESCO, 1990), http://www.unesco.org/education/pdf/281_65_s.pdf; International Disability Rights Monitor, *Regional Report on the Americas, 2004* (Chicago: International Disability Network, 2004), http://www.ideanet.org/cir/uploads/File/IDRM_Americas_2004.pdf; World Bank and WHO, *World Report on Disability* (New York: United Nations, 2011), http://siteresources.worldbank.org/DISABILITY/Resources/WRD_Summary_Spanish_EMBARGO.pdf

4. Rosemary Thorp, *Progress, Poverty and Exclusion: An Economic History of Latin America in the Twentieth Century* (Washington, D.C.: Inter-American Development Bank, 1998).

5. Rosángela Berman-Bieler, "Desarrollo inclusivo: Un aporte universal desde la Discapacidad," working document, World Bank, 2011.

6. IDRM, *Regional Report of the Americas.*

7. Organization of American States, Inter-American Convention on the Elimination of All Forms of Discrimination Against Persons with Disabilities, 7 June 1999, AG/RES. 1608 (XXIX-O/99) (Guatemala Convention), Article 1.

8. For a different view, see Chapter 10.

9. For a different view, see Chapter 3.

10. For a discussion on the Optional Protocol, see Chapter 13.

11. For a different perspective, see Chapter 4.

Chapter 12. Voices Down Under: An Australian Perspective

1. Res 58/168, "Strengthening United Nations action in the field of human rights through the promotion of international cooperation and the importance of non-selectivity, impartiality and objectivity"

2. Second AHC session, 16–27 June 2003; Australian delegation statement at agenda item 5, http://www.un.org/esa/socdev/enable/rights/contrib-australia.htm.

3. Comprehensive and Integral International Convention to Promote and Protect the Rights and Dignity of Persons with Disabilities, UN A/RES/57/229 (2002).

4. This is the term used in the Australian Disability Discrimination Act 1992, sec. 11.

Chapter 13. Monitoring the Convention's Implementation

1. The term "treaty bodies" refers to forums established to monitor core UN human rights treaties at the international level.

2. Compare, generally, Chapter 14.

3. See Chapter 1.

4. Compare Article 28, International Covenant on Civil and Political Rights; Article 8, Convention on the Elimination of All Forms of Racial Discrimination, GA Res. 2106 (XX), annex, 20 UN GAOR Supp. (No. 14) at 47, UN Doc. A/6014 (1966), 660 U.N.T.S. 195, entered into force 4 January 1969; Article 17, Convention on the Elimination of All Forms of Discrimination against Women; Article 17, Convention Against Torture, GA Res. 39/46, annex, 39 UN GAOR Supp. (No. 51) at 197, UN Doc. A/39/51 (1984), entered into force 26 June 1987; Article 72, International Convention on the Protection of the Rights of All Migrant Workers and Members of Their Families, GA Res. 45/158, annex, 45 UN GAOR Supp. (No. 49A) at 262, UN Doc. A/45/49 (1990), entered into force 1 July 2003.

5. UN Doc. A/RES/56/168 (2001).

6. Report of the Secretary-General, *Strengthening the United Nations: An Agenda for Further Change*, UN Doc. A/57/387 (2002); the GA endorsed the report in its resolution A/RES/57/300 (2002).

7. Compare, inter alia, Report by the Secretary-General, *In Larger Freedom: Towards Development, Security and Human Rights for All*, UN Doc. A/59/2005 (2005).

8. Side event "UN Human Rights Treaty Monitoring Bodies and Mechanisms: Achievements and Challenges," held 25 January 2005. All statements based on notes by the author, document on file with author.

9. Report of the AHC, sixth session, to the GA, UN Doc. A/60/266, para. 155.

10. OHCHR Expert paper on existing monitoring mechanisms, possible relevant improvements and possible innovations in monitoring mechanisms for a comprehensive and integral international convention on the protection and promotion of the rights and dignity of persons with disabilities, sec. 2.4–9, UN Doc. A/AC.265/2006/CRP.4 (18 January 2006).

11. Declaration of Quito, annex to letter dated 23 May 2003 from Permanent Representative of Ecuador to the UN addressed to the Secretary of the AHC, http://www.un.org/esa/socdev/enable/rights/a_ac265_2003_crp8.htm; see also Marianne Schulze, "Die Verpflichtung zur Einrichtung eines nationalen 'Mechanismus' im Rahmen des Übereinkommens über die Rechte von Menschen mit Behinderungen," in *Völkerrecht im innerstaatlichen Bereich*, ed. Christina Binder, Claudia Fuchs, Matthias Goldmann, Thomas Kleinlein, and Konrad Lachmayer (Baden-Baden: Nomos, 2010), 111.

12. Bangkok Draft: Proposed Elements of a Comprehensive and Integral Convention to Promote and Protect the Rights of Persons with Disabilities (Bangkok Draft), Article 34(1), http://www.worldenable.net/bangkok2003a/bangkokdraftrev.htm.

13. UN Doc. A/RES/48/134 (1993), annex.

14. Cf. Chapter 1.

15. See, e.g., daily summary of WG discussions, vol. 3, nos. 9, 10, http://www.un.org/esa/socdev/enable/rights/wgsuma25.htm.

16. Report of WG to AHC, A/AC.265/2004/WG/1, Annex I, http://www.un.org/esa/socdev/enable/rights/ahcwgreporta25.htm.

17. "Draft Text on Monitoring Presented by the National Human Rights Institutions," 10 August 2005, http://www.un.org/esa/socdev/enable/rights/documents/ahc6nhrida25.doc.

18. Ibid., Article 27 ("Establishment of a National Monitoring Body").

19. Proposals by Israel at the sixth AHC session, http://www.un.org/esa/socdev/enable/rights/ahc6israel.htm;see also proposal by the ILO at the same session.

20. Amnesty International, "Strengthening Implementation at the National Level," Enable Negotiations Archive, http://www.un.org/esa/socdev/enable/rights/ahc6contngos.htm.

21. Ibid., sec. 2 ("The Government Focal Point and Intra-Governmental Coordination").

22. Cf. OHCHR, Expert Meeting on Possible Monitoring Mechanisms for the New Disability Convention, 24/25 November 2005, http://www2.ohchr.org/english/issues/disability/egm.htm.

23. OHCHR, Expert Paper on Existing Monitoring Mechanisms, para. 77.

24. The debate about the role of the Special Rapporteur on Disability of the Commission for Social Development in accordance with the UN Standard Rules vis-à-vis the CRPD can only be flagged here.

25. Thematic study by OHCHR on the structure and role of national mechanisms for the implementation and monitoring of the CRPD, UN Doc. A/HRC/13/29.

26. Human Rights Council, Resolution 10/7 (2009), "Human Rights of Persons with Disabilities: National Frameworks for the Promotion and Protection of the Human Rights of Persons with Disabilities."

27. Ibid., para. 76.

28. UN Doc. A/RES/46/119 (1991), annex.

29. Ibid., principle 22.

30. "States Parties shall ensure that all facilities and programmes, both public and private, where persons with disabilities are placed together, separate from others, are effectively monitored to prevent the occurrence of violence, injury or abuse, neglect or negligent treatment, maltreatment or exploitation, including sexual exploitation and abuse" (WG draft text, Background Documents, Article 16, Enable Negotiations Archive, http://www.un.org/esa/socdev/enable/rights/ahcstata16bk grnd.htm).

31. Compare the comments made by NGOs (Children's Rights Alliance for England, International Disability Caucus, Landmines Survivors Network, People with Disability Australia, Working Meeting of NGOs for people with disabilities from Ukraine, Russia, Belarus and Moldova) at the fourth AHC, as well as comments by IDC at the fifth AHC, Enable Negotiations Archive, http://www.un.org/esa/socdev /enable/rights/ahcstata16bkgrnd.htm.

32. See University of Bristol/Arts & Humanities Research Council, "The Optional Protocol to the UN Torture Convention and the UN Convention on the Rights of People with Disabilities: Some Common Issues," which, notably, does not discuss the role of Article 16(3) CRPD vis-à-vis Optional Protocol to the Convention Against Torture implementation.

33. See note 4, above.

34. See note 7, above

35. See, for those in particular, the recommendations made by OHCHR, "Expert Paper."

36. Compare, e.g., national monitoring, discussed above, access to justice, Chapter 3.

37. Report of AHC, sixth session.

38. See proposals by IDC and NHRIs during the sixth session in particular.

39. In line with the Standard Rules a special rapporteur has been appointed since 1994.

40. Anna Bruce, "Negotiating the Monitoring Mechanism for the Convention on the Rights of Persons with Disabilities: Two Steps Forward, One Step Back," in *Inter-*

national Monitoring Mechanisms: Essays in Honor of Jakob Th. Möller, ed. Gudmundur Alfredsson et al., 2nd ed. (Leiden: Nijhoff, 2009), 135.

41. Compare Articles 4(3), 32(1), 33(3), CRPD.

42. Compare, e.g., the committee requirements under the Covenant on Economic, Social and Cultural Rights: "The Committee shall have eighteen members who shall be experts with recognized competence in the field of human rights, serving in their personal capacity, due consideration being given to equitable geographical distribution and to the representation of different forms of social and legal systems; to this end, fifteen seats will be equally distributed among the regional groups, while the additional three seats will be allocated in accordance with the increase in the total number of States parties per regional group" (ECOSOC Res. 1985/17).

43. Bruce, "Negotiating the Monitoring Mechanism," 137.

44. Ibid.

45. Exceptions are Optional Protocol to the Convention Against Torture, Optional Protocol on Sale of Children, and Optional Protocol on Children in Armed Conflict.

46. Compare CEDAW, adopted in 1979; for which the Optional Protocol was adopted twenty years later.

47. UN GA Res. A/RES/2200 (XXI) (1966).

Chapter 14. The Role of National Human Rights Institutions

I am grateful to Laura Ferraro for her research assistance. This chapter also draws on research conducted as part of an Australian Research Council Linkage project between the Australian Human Rights Centre and the Asia Pacific Forum of National Human Rights Institutions (LP0776639).

1. Optional Protocol to the CRPD, UN GA Res. A/RES/61/106, Annex II (2006), entered into force 3 May 2008.

2. The Optional Protocol to the Convention against Torture (GA res. A/RES/57/199, adopted 18 December 2002, entered into force 22 June 2006) also provides for designation of "national preventive mechanisms," some envisaged to be NHRIs (many countries have so designated their NHRIs).

3. Report of the AHC, UN Doc. A/57/357 (2002), para. 11.

4. International Workshop on National Institutions for the Promotion and Protection of Human Rights, Paris, 7–9 October 1991.

5. UN Commission on Human Rights, Resolution 1992/54.

6. UN Doc. A/RES/48/134 (1993).

7. See the position as of late 2011: OHCHR, "Information for National Human Rights Institutions," http://www2.ohchr.org/english/bodies/hrcouncil/nhri.htm.

8. Brian Burdekin (with Jason Naum), *National Human Rights Institutions in the Asia Pacific Region* (Leiden: Nijhoff, 2006), 7.

9. This paragraph is taken from Catherine Renshaw, Andrew Byrnes, and Andrea Durbach, "Testing the Mettle of National Human Rights Institutions: A Case Study of the Human Rights Commission of Malaysia," *Asian Journal of International Law* 1 (2011): 165.

10. Originally known as the International Coordination Committee of NHRIs.

11. These are the Asia Pacific Forum of NHRIs (APF); European Group of NHRIs; Network of National Institutions in the Americas (http://www.rindhca.org.ve/); and Network of African NHRIs (NANHRI) (http://www.nanhri.org/), the 2007 evolution of the earlier Coordinating Committee of African NHRIs. On the European and African groupings, see Gauthier de Beco, "National Human Rights Institutions in Europe," *Human Rights Law Review* 7 (2007): 331–70; Rachel Murray, *The Role of National Human Rights Institutions at the International and Regional Levels: The Experience of Africa* (Oxford: Hart, 2007).

12. Europe, the Americas, Africa, and Asia Pacific.

13. All "A" status NHRIs are members of the entity; the board comprises sixteen members selected according to regional groupings; see ICC-NHRI Statute—Explanatory Note, http://www.nhri.net/2008/226004.doc. (Classification as an "A" status NHRI indicates that the ICC-NHRI considers the institution in full compliance with the Paris Principles.)

14. Morten Kjærum, *National Human Rights Institutions Implementing Human Rights* (Copenhagen: Danish Institute for Human Rights, 2003), 16.

15. See Andrew Byrnes, Andrea Durbach, and Catherine Renshaw, "Joining the Club: The Asia Pacific Forum of National Human Rights Institutions, the Paris Principles, and the Advancement of Human Rights Protection in the Region," *Australian Journal of Human Rights* 14, 1 (2008): 63, 70–73; Andrea Durbach, Catherine Renshaw, and Andrew Byrnes, "'A Tongue But No Teeth?' The Emergence of a New Human Rights Mechanism in the Asia Pacific Region," *Sydney Law Review* 31 (2009): 211, 229–34.

16. Richard Carver, "A New Answer to an Old Question: National Human Rights Institutions and the Domestication of International Law," *Human Rights Law Review* 10, 1 (2010): 1, 32.

17. "Report on the International Workshop for NHRIs for the Commonwealth and Asia Pacific Region on 'Promoting the Rights of Persons with Disabilities,'" 26–30 May 2003, New Delhi, 3, http://www.asiapacificforum.net/services/training/regional-workshops/disability/.

18. Statement of Brian Burdekin, OHC Special Advisor on National Institutions to the OHCHR to the AHC, New York, 30 July 2002, http://www.nhri.net/pdf/Burdekin%20statement%20to%20Ad%20Hoc%20Cttee.pdf.

19. Report of the AHC, para. 11.

20. Ibid., para.16.

21. GA resolution 57/226, UN Doc. A/RES/57/229 (2002), item 7.

22. More than 15 NHRIs attended the second AHC session: Joint Statement of National Human Rights Institutions, presented by Charlotte Vuyiswa McClain-Nhlapo, 18 June 2003, http://www.un.org/esa/socdev/enable/rights/contrib-jnhri.htm.

23. Second Joint Statement of Australian Human Rights and Equal Opportunity Commission, Danish Institute for Human Rights, Irish Human Rights Commission, Mexican National Human Rights Commission, Northern Ireland Human Rights Commission, New Zealand Human Rights Commission, and South African Human Rights Commission, 19 June 2003, delivered by Charlotte Vuyiswa McClain-Nhlapo (South African Human Rights Commission and ICC-NHRI representative), http://www.nhri.net/pdf/Second-joint-statement-Ad-Hoc-disability.pdf; and (Third) Joint Statement of the Australian Human Rights and Equal Opportunity Commission, Danish Institute for Human Rights, Irish Human Rights Commission, National Human Rights Commission of the Republic of Korea, Mexican National Human Rights Commission, Northern Ireland Human Rights Commission, New Zealand Human Rights Commission, South African Human Rights Commission, and the Swedish Office of Disability Ombudsman, delivered by William Binchy (Irish Human Rights Commission), 25 June 2003, http://www.un.org/esa/socdev/enable/rights/contrib-inhri.htm.

24. See (Third) Joint Statement, above.

25. Report of the AHC, New York, 16–27 June 2003, 15, A/58/118 & Corr.1 (2003).

26. APF, Proposed UN Convention on the Rights of Persons with Disabilities, background paper prepared for the Seventh Annual Meeting of the Asia Pacific Forum of National Human Rights Institutions, 11–13 November 2002, New Delhi, India, 8 n 22, http://www.asiapacificforum.net/about/annual-meetings/7th-india-2002/downloads/thematic-issues/disability.pdf.

27. Ibid., 8–9.

28. Ibid., 9.

29. APF, "Concluding Statement," Seventh Annual Meeting of the APF, 11–13 November 2002, New Delhi, India, para. 13, http://www.asiapacificforum.net/about/annual-meetings/7th-india-2002/downloads/concluding.pdf.

30. APF, Proposed UN Convention, 10, recommendations 6 and 7.

31. The WG comprised the NHRIs of Australia, India, New Zealand, and the Philippines; they were assisted by Rosemary Kayess, an NGO expert on disability, and the author; see APF, "Concluding Statement," Eighth Annual Meeting of the APF, 16–18 February 2004, Kathmandu, Nepal, para. 20, http://www.asiapacificforum.net/about/annual-meetings/8th-nepal-2004/downloads/concluding.pdf.

32. Other submissions were made by individual NHRIs; see, e.g., Danish Institute for Human Rights, "Discussion Paper on Founding Principles of Convention on Rights of Persons with Disabilities," UN Doc. A/AC.265/2003/CRP/9, http://www.un.org/esa/socdev/enable/rights/a_ac265_2003_crp9.htm.

33. Conclusions of the Workshop on the Human Rights of Persons with Disabilities of the Network of National Institutions for the Promotion and Protection of

Human Rights of the Americas, San José, Costa Rica, 28 March 2003, 2, http://www
.un.org/esa/socdev/enable//rights/contrib-americas-e.htm.

34. Represented at the meeting were NHRIs from Afghanistan, Australia, Fiji, Ghana, Iran, Korea, Malawi, Malaysia, Mauritius, Mongolia, Nepal, New Zealand, Nigeria, Northern Ireland, Philippines, South Africa, Sri Lanka, Thailand, and Uganda.

35. Conclusions and Recommendations, International Workshop for NHRIs from the Commonwealth and Asia Pacific Region, New Delhi, 26–29 May 2003, "Promoting the Rights of People with Disabilities: Towards a New UN Convention," http://www.nhri.net/pdf/Conclusions-Recommendations-290503-NewDelhi.pdf.

36. The NHRIs represented were from Kenya, Niger, Malawi, Mauritius, Rwanda, South Africa, Tanzania, Uganda and Zambia. Final Declaration, Regional Workshop on Promoting the Rights of Persons with Disabilities: Towards a New UN Convention, Munyonyo-Kampala, Uganda, 5–6 June 2003, para. 1, http://www.un.org/esa/socdev/enable/rights/contrib-uganda.htm.

37. Position paper of the European NHRIs attending the second AHC session, 16 June 2003, http://www.nhri.net/old/pdf/Position-Paper-EU-NHRI's-Disability.pdf.

38. Representatives of the NHRIs of Afghanistan, Fiji, India, New Zealand, and Thailand attended; see the report of the expert group meeting and seminar on an international convention to protect and promote the rights and dignity of persons with disabilities, Bangkok, 2–4 June 2003, E/ESCAP/EGM-PWD/Rep 4, Annex I.

39. Bangkok Recommendations on the Elaboration of a Comprehensive and Integral International Convention to Promote and Protect the Rights and Dignity of Persons with Disabilities, outcome of the expert group meeting and seminar held in Bangkok at the headquarters of the Economic and Social Commission for Asia and the Pacific, 2–4 June 2003, A/AC.265/2003/CRP/10.

40. This workshop was attended by representatives of the NHRIs of Australia, India, Malaysia, Thailand and Sri Lanka; *Report of Regional Workshop Towards a Comprehensive and Integral International Convention on Protection and Promotion of the Rights and Dignity of Persons with Disabilities*, Bangkok, 14–17 October 2003, Annex I, http://www.worldenable.net/bangkok2003a/finalreport.htm.

41. Bangkok Draft: Proposed Elements of a Comprehensive and Integral International Convention to Promote and Protect the Rights of Persons with Disabilities (Bangkok Draft), in ibid., http://www.un.org/esa/socdev/enable//rights/bangkokdraft.htm.

42. For the documents before the WG, see http://www.un.org/esa/socdev/enable//rights/comp-element0.htm.

43. Regular attendees at the sessions and participants in the meetings of NHRIs were representatives of NHRIs from South Africa, India, Ireland, Canada, New Zealand, and the Swedish Office of the Disability Ombudsman. NHRIs from the Republic of Korea, Uganda, Guatemala, and Honduras attended some of the sessions.

44. APF submissions to AHC, third session, May 2004, http://www.un.org/esa/socdev/enable/rights/ahc3apf.doc; and fourth session, August–September 2004, http://www.un.org/esa/socdev/enable/rights/ahc4asiapacific.doc.

45. See, e.g., Frédéric Mégret, "The Disabilities Convention: Human Rights of Persons with Disabilities or Disability Rights?" *Human Rights Quarterly* 30 (2008): 494.

46. Andrew Byrnes, "Second-Class Rights Yet Again? Economic, Social and Cultural Rights in the Report of the National Human Rights Consultation," *University of New South Wales Law Journal* 33 (2010): 193.

47. Report of the WG to the AHC, UN Doc. A/AC.265/2004/WG.1, Annex I (2004), http://www.un.org/esa/socdev/enable/rights/ahcwgreporta25.htm [hereafter WG Report].

48. APF submission to AHC third session (May 2004), paras. 202–8.

49. Ibid., para. 207.

50. See NHRI intervention on draft Article 4, AHC third session, http://www.un .org/esa/socdev/enable/rights/ahc3nhricomments.htm.

51. "Letter dated 7 October 2005 from Chairman to all members of the Committee," UN Doc. A/AC.265/2006/1 (hereafter, Chair's letter), Annex I (11 October 2005).

52. Chair's letter, para. 23.

53. NHRI intervention on draft Article 4, seventh AHC session, 31 January 2006, http://www.un.org/esa/socdev/enable/rights/ahc7nhri.htm.

54. See "Article 4—General Obligations, Seventh Session, Comments, Proposals and Amendments Submitted Electronically," http://www.un.org/esa/socdev/enable /rights/ahcstata4sevscomments.htm; the IDC proposal was to replace the chair's text with a text based closely on the Bangkok Draft.

55. Ibid.

56. The Chair's Draft (December 2003), closely following the Bangkok Draft, included a draft article on remedies. A number of NGOs also proposed including a remedies provision; see NGO contributions to the elements of a convention (2003), http://www.un.org/esa/socdev/enable/rights/a_ac265_2003_crp13_add1.htm

57. Comments on Chair's Draft Article 4, General Obligations (2003), http://www .un.org/esa/socdev/enable/rights/wgdca4.htm.

58. Daily summary related to draft Article 4—General Obligations, vol. 3, no. 1 (5 January 2004), http://www.un.org/esa/socdev/enable/rights/wgsuma4.htm.

59. WG Report, 10 n 18.

60. APF submission to AHC third session, May 2004, paras. 202–8.

61. Ibid., paras. 209–17.

62. See NHRI intervention on draft Article 4.

63. Daily summary of discussions related to Article 4, AHC fourth session, vol. 5, 2–7 (24–31 August 2004), http://www.un.org/esa/socdev/enable/rights/ahc4sumart04 .htm. Costa Rica's proposed inclusion in Article 9(g) of the compilation document for the fourth session, read: "Take all necessary measures to ensure evomperyone whose rights and freedoms as recognised in this convention are violated should have an effective remedy before a national authority, notwithstanding that the violation has been committed in an official capacity."

64. Daily summary of discussions related to Article 4, AHC fourth session, Vol. 5, 2–7 (Costa Rica, Israel, Kenya, Lebanon, IDC, LSN (Landmine Survivors Network), and NHRIs, all supported inclusion of a provision on remedies). See also APF submission to AHC fourth session, August–September 2004, paras. 129–37.

65. Chair's letter, paras. 23–31.

66. NHRI intervention, AHC seventh session, 31 January 2006.

67. Costa Rica (with the support of Chile, Argentina, Mexico, Guatemala, Colombia, Uruguay, Brazil, Trinidad and Tobago, Panama, Honduras, Dominican Republic, El Salvador, and Venezuela) proposed the addition to draft Article 4 of a new paragraph requiring states parties "To ensure legal protection of the rights of persons with disabilities on an equal basis with others and ensure an effective remedy by the competent national tribunals for acts violating their fundamental rights," http://www.un.org/esa/socdev/enable/rights/ahc8gpcart4.htm. The inclusion of a remedial provision continued to be supported by influential NGOS, including the IDC (News Page, 21 August 2006, 2, http://www.un.org/esa/socdev/enable/rights/ahc8docs/ahc8idcreactcomp1.doc), and the Japan Disability Forum (JDF comment on the working text, eighth session, 14–25 August 2006, 6–7, http://www.un.org/esa/socdev/enable/rights/ahc8docs/ahc8jdf1.doc).

68. A number of states pointed out during the negotiations that states parties to the ICCPR would be obliged to provide remedies for at least some instances of discrimination against persons with disabilities under ICCPR Articles 2 and 26, and that this would cover discrimination on the basis of disability with regard to both civil and political and economic, social, and cultural rights.

69. See the submissions at http://www.un.org/esa/socdev/enable/rights/comp-ele ment0.htm; see also the Chair's Draft Elements on Implementation, December 2003, http://www.un.org/esa/socdev/enable/rights/wgcontrib-chair2.htm, which itself drew on and added to the proposals in the Bangkok Draft.

70. E.g., Working paper by Mexico, UN Doc. A/AC.265/WP.1 (2003), Articles 17, 19–24, http://www.un.org/esa/socdev/enable/rights/adhocmeetaac265w1e.htm.

71. Compilation of Proposals for a Comprehensive and Integral International Convention to Promote and Protect the Rights and Dignity of Persons with Disabilities (2003), AHC second session, http://www.un.org/esa/socdev/enable/rights/a _ac265_2003_crp13.htm; see also draft submitted by the Government of the Bolivarian Republic of Venezuela, annex to the letter dated 18 June 2003 from Deputy Permanent Representative of Venezuela to UN, addressed to Secretary of the AHC, UN Doc. A/AC.265/2003/WP.1 (2003).

72. Articles 34–50, Bangkok Draft. http://www.un.org/esa/socdev/enable/rights /bangkokdraft.htm

73. Compilation of Proposals for Elements of a Convention, Part VII—Monitoring Mechanisms, 5 January 2004, http://www.un.org/esa/socdev/enable/rights/comp-ele ment7.htm.

74. Chair's Draft Elements on Implementation.

75. Working paper by Mexico, Article 17.

76. Chair's Draft Elements on Implementation, Article 29bis.

77. Ibid., Article 30.

78. WG Report, 30, 31, nn. 112, 113.

79. Daily summary related to draft Article 25—Monitoring, vol. 3, no. 9, 15 January 2004, http://www.un.org/esa/socdev/enable/rights/wgsuma25.htm.

80. WG Report, nn. 112–14.

81. Draft Article 25, WG Report, 31.

82. APF submission to AH fourth session, August–September 2004, 207–8.

83. Report, AHC, sixth session, A/60/266, paras. 155–60 (2005).

84. NHRI Draft Text on Monitoring, 10 August 2005, http://www.un.org/esa/socdev/enable/rights/ahc7docs/ahc7nhrimonitoraug05.doc; see also Towards an Innovative Monitoring Mechanism for the Convention—Taking Domestic Sovereignty Seriously, submission by Irish Human Rights Commission and Swedish Disability Ombudsman on behalf of European Grouping of National Institutions, www.un.org/esa/socdev/enable/rights/documents/ihrcse.doc.

85. NHRI Draft Text on Monitoring, 18.

86. See also NHRI intervention on Article 25, 10 August 2005.

87. Chair's letter, para. 111.

88. Monitoring (Article 25): Monitoring and Implementation Mechanism at the International and National Levels," NHRI intervention, 23 January 2006, http://www.un.org/esa/socdev/enable/rights/ahc7docs/ahc7nhrimonit.doc; and NHRI response to the questions proposed by the Chair on Monitoring, http://www.un.org/esa/socdev/enable/rights/ahc7nhri.htm.

89. See draft Article 33(2), International CRPD Working Text, in Report of the AHC seventh session, UN Doc. A/AC.265/2006/2, Annex II (2006).

90. Ibid., draft Article 33(3).

91. Thematic study by OHCHR on enhancing awareness and understanding of the Convention, UN Doc. A/HRC/10/48 (2009), http://www2.ohchr.org/english/bodies/hrcouncil/docs/10session/A.HRC.10.48.pdf.

Chapter 15. The New Diplomacy

1. Marlies Glasius, "Expertise in the Cause of Justice: Global Civil Society Influence on the Statute for an International Criminal Court," in *Global Civil Society 2002*, ed. Marlies Glasius, Mary Kaldor, and Helmut Anheier (London: Oxford University Press, 2002), 164; Andreas Paulus, "Legalist Groundwork for the International Criminal Court," *European Journal of International Law* 14 (2003): 849.

2. List of NGO representatives, eighth AHC session, http://www.un.org/esa/socdev/enable/rights/ahc8ngolistpart.htm.

3. Frédéric Mégret, "The Disabilities Convention: Towards a Holistic Conception of Rights," *International Journal of Human Rights* 12, 2 (2008): 266–69.

4. Nicholas Pedriana, "Help Wanted NOW: Legal Resources, the Women's Movement, and the Battle over Sex-Segregated Job Advertisements," *Social Problems* 51 (2004): 194–95; Beth A. Simmons, *Mobilizing for Human Rights* (New York: Cambridge University Press, 2009), 168.

5. Glasius, "Expertise," 141. On the different expertise in the ICBL, see Motoko Mekata, "Building Partnerships Toward a Common Goal: Experiences of the International Campaign to Ban Landmines," in *The Third Force: The Rise of Transnational Civil Society*, ed. Ann Florini (Washington, D.C.: Carnegie Endowment for International Peace, 2000), 146, 155.

6. Summary of experts' panels, http://www.un.org/esa/socdev/enable/rights/a_58 _118_e.htm.

7. Mekata, "Building Partnerships," 143–45.

8. Glasius, "Expertise," 142, 156.

9. *Brown v. Board of Education of Topeka*, 347 U.S. 483 (1954).

10. List of side events for each session, http://www.un.org/esa/socdev/enable /rights/adhoccom.htm.

11. *39 Pounds of Love*, http://www.39poundsoflove.com/main.html (clip on UN event on file with the author).

12. Thomas Keenan, "Mobilizing Shame," *South Atlantic Quarterly* 103, 2/3 (2004): 435–49; Ronit Avni, "Mobilizing Hope: Beyond the Shame-Based Model in the Israeli-Palestinian Conflict," *American Anthropologist* 108, 1 (2006): 205–14.

13. Glasius, "Expertise," 146; Margaret E. Keck and Kathryn Sikkink, *Activists Beyond Borders* (Ithaca, N.Y.: Cornell University Press, 1998), 1–38; William E. DeMars, *NGOs and Transnational Networks* (London: Pluto Press, 2005), 54.

14. DeMars, *NGOS and Transnational Networks*, 56.

15. Simmons, *Mobilizing for Human Rights*, 140. For a different view, see Edward L. Rubin, "Passing Through the Door: Social Movement Literature and Legal Scholarship," *University of Pennsylvania Law Review* 150, 1 (2001–2): 12–17, 42.

16. DeMars, *NGOs and Transnational Networks*, 45–48.

17. Peter J. Spiro, "New Global Potentates: Nongovernmental Organizations and the 'Unregulated' Marketplace," *Cardozo Law Review* 18 (1996–97): 965; Glasius, "Expertise," 162.

18. GA Res. A/RES/57/229.

19. Barbara K. Woodward, *Global Civil Society in International Lawmaking and Global Governance: Theory and Practice* (Leiden: Nijhoff, 2010), 208.

20. Report of the second AHC session, para. 19, http://www.un.org/esa/socdev /enable/rights/a_58_118_e.htm.

21. Handicap International, Disability—Key Figures 2005.

22. Gráinne de Búrca, "The EU in the Negotiation of the UN Disability Convention," *European Law Review* 35 (2010): 189.

23. See, however, Chapter 14.

24. De Búrca, "EU in the Negotiation," 189. See in contrast, the ICBL and CICC processes (Mekata, "Building Partnerships"; Glasius, "Expertise".

25. Among the states that had a disability expert/DPO representative as a delegate were Australia, Canada, Germany, Thailand, Korea, Kenya, Jordan, Vanuatu, and Venezuela.

26. De Búrca, "EU in the Negotiation," 189.

27. Ibid., 177–78, 195–96.

28. UN OHCHR and Civil Society, http://www.ohchr.org/EN/AboutUs/Pages/CivilSociety.aspx.

29. Maya Sabatello, *Children's Bioethics* (Leiden: Nijhoff, 2009), 41, 47, 50.

30. Mekata, "Building Partnerships," 165.

31. Glasius, "Expertise," 147; William R. Pace and Jennifer Schense, "The Role of Non-Governmental Organizations," in *The Rome Statute of the International Criminal Court: A Commentary*, ed. Antonio Cassese, Paola Gaeta, and John R. W. D. Jones (London: Oxford University Press: 2002), 1:113.

32. UN GA, Rules of Procedure, http://www.un.org/en/ga/about/ropga/cttees.shtml.

33. Matti Koskenniemi, "Carl Schmitt, Hans Morgenthau, and the Image of Law in International Relations," in *The Role of Law in International Politics*, ed. Michael Byers (London: Oxford University Press, 2000), 20.

34. Glasius, "Expertise," 140, 144–45; yet see Simmons, *Mobilizing for Human Rights*, 12–13.

35. DeMars, *NGOs and Transnational Networks*, 51.

36. Ibid., 49.

37. Woodward, *Global Civil Society*, 78–103; Kerstin Martens, "NGOs in the United Nations System: Evaluating Theoretical Approaches," *Journal of International Development* 18 (2006): 691–700.

38. Martens, "NGOs in the United Nations System," 693.

39. Woodward, *Global Civil Society*, 79.

40. Of particular concern are issues of representation, accountability, the tag of elitism, and the historical domination of Western NGOs.

41. Glasius, "Expertise," 164; Paulus, "Legalist Groundwork," 849.

42. Woodward, *Global Civil Society*, 213.

43. Ibid.

44. Marcia E. Greenberg, "NGO Participation in International Law and Its Processes: An Eastern European Perspective," *ASIL Proceedings* 95 (2001): 303.

45. UN Information Services press release, 8 December 1999, http://www.unis.unvienna.org/unis/pressrels/1999/sg2465.html.

46. Janet E. Lord, "On the Possibilities and Limitations of NGO Participation in International Law and Its Processes," *ASIL Proceedings* 95 (2001): 295; Greenberg, "NGO Participation," 301.

47. Individual leaders certainly existed in previous international processes; their qualifications, however, were mostly legally oriented; see also Woodward, *Global Civil Society*, chap. 5.

48. Glasius, "Expertise," 163.

49. DeMars, *NGOs and Transnational Networks*, 45.

50. Greenberg, "NGO Participation," 301.

51. Elisabeth J. Friedman, Kathryn Hochstetler, and Ann Marie Clark, *Sovereignty, Democracy, and Global Civil Society* (Albany: State University of New York Press, 2005), 33.

52. Glasius, "Expertise," 162.

53. Simmons, *Mobilizing for Human Rights*, 17.

54. Friedman, Hochstetler, and Clark, *Sovereignty*, 171.

55. *Alajos Kiss v. Hungary*, European Court of Human Rights, May 2010, Application no. 38832/06; OHCHR report, *Expert Seminar on Freedom from Torture and Ill Treatment and Persons with Disabilities* (Geneva: UN, 2007).

56. DeMars, *NGOs and Transnational Networks*, 58.

CONTRIBUTORS

Andrew Byrnes is Professor of Law at the University of New South Wales, and Chair of the Australian Human Rights Centre, having previously been on the Faculties of Law of the Australian National University, University of Hong Kong and University of Sydney. He is also a Member of the Management Committee of the UNSW Disability Studies and Research Centre. From 2003 to 2006, he was involved in the development of the Convention on the Rights of Persons with Disabilities, participating in the UNESCAP meetings, which adopted the Bangkok Draft convention, and as an adviser to the delegation of the Asia-Pacific Forum of National Human Rights Institutions.

Heidi Forrest is an Australian woman with disability (that she acquired in high school) and the mother of a child with a developmental disability. She has been actively involved in disability rights for most of her life and participated in Ad Hoc Committee sessions in her capacity as president of People with Disability Australia Inc. Among the institutions in which she involved with are Women with Disability Australia, Pacific Disability Forum and Disability and Research Institute, Australian Disability and Development Rights Consortium, and Disability Discrimination Legal Centre. She is currently a law student at Newcastle University.

Phillip French is a lawyer who specializes in the law and disability. He has been responsible for establishing a number of Australian disability rights and advocacy organizations. As Executive Director of People with Disability Australia, a national disability rights and advocacy organization, he was involved in the CRPD negotiations; he is now a Life Member of the organization. His work focuses on CRPD implementation in Australia.

Lex Grandia was born premature, leading to deaf-blindness. He obtained a Ph.D. in Theology from the University of Amsterdam. Active in many organizations in the Netherlands, he became chair of European Deafblind Network (EDbN) in 1994 and secretary in 1995. He was also a board member of the European Disability Forum. He supported the founding of the European Deafblind Union in 2003 and the African Federation of the Deaf-Blind in 2009, serving as Secretary General and President of the World Federation of the DeafBlind and subsequently Chair of the International Disability Alliance (IDA) in 2007–8. He wrote two books on using Bibliodrama. Lex passed away in April 2012.

Huhana Hickey is a scholar of disability with a PhD in Law and Tikanga Maori from the University of Waikato. Both a disability activist and Human Rights Lawyer Huhana has undertaken professional roles in the government and nongovernment sectors of New Zealand, including involvement in developing the UN Convention on the Rights of Persons with Disabilities. Dr Hickey is of Ngati Tahinga descent, identifies as *whanau haua*, is in a wheelchair and the parent of an adult child with disabilities. Dr. Hickey works at the Auckland Disability Law, the first Community Law Centre in New Zealand dedicated to free services for persons with disabilities.

Markku Jokinen, As executive director of the Finnish Association of the Deaf and president of the World Federation of the Deaf (2003–2011), Dr. Jokinen was closely involved in the CRPD negotiations in 2004–2006. He continues to be one of the key figures in the Finnish disability movement with special focus on the language policy work elevating the status of Finnish Sign Language. He continues his cooperation with the WFD as a human rights and education expert and he is part of the working group preparing Finland's ratification of the CRPD.

Liisa Kauppinen, former WFD President and Secretary General, was the World Federation of the Deaf' main representative at the CRPD Ad Hoc meetings for the duration of the negotiations leading to the adoption of the CRPD in August 2006. She continues to be a prominent figure in both the Finnish and international disability movement and has received numerous awards for her work in human rights of deaf people and persons with disabilities. She continues to work with the WFD as a special advisor on human rights and is particularly interested in deaf women's rights and inclusion of persons with disabilities in developing countries.

Mi Yeon Kim is a South Korean civil society expert who worked closely with her country's delegation. In addition to her vast national, regional and international experience she brought significant UN knowledge to the table: she was already a participant in the Beijing World Conference on Women in 1998. As a regular advisor to South Korean Ministries, she was one of the participants whose access to the State's delegation proved crucial.

Gerison Lansdown is an international children's rights consultant, and has published and lectured widely over many years in the field of the human rights of children. She was involved throughout the negotiations of the CRPD, on behalf of Save the Children, to ensure the visibility of children with disabilities in the text. She was the rapporteur for the General Day of Discussion on children with disabilities held by the Committee on the Rights of the Child in 1997 and actively involved in the development of the Committee's General Comment on the Rights of Children with Disabilities, published in 2006

Connie Laurin-Bowie, Executive Director, Inclusion International, headed Inclusion International's representation at the Ad-Hoc Committee. She directed Inclusion International's global project on poverty and disability and produced the document "Hear Our Voices; A Global report on the situation of people with intellectual disabilities and their families" in relation to the UN Millennium Development Goals; recently she co-authored the Global Report on Education. She has 18 years experience in public policy, government relations and international development.

Tirza Leibowitz is legal adviser for the Open Society Foundations' Disability Rights Initiative. She previously was a legal advisor for Bizchut – The Israel Human Rights Center for People with Disabilities and directed the international advocacy team at Survivor Corps. Leibowitz holds an LLB from the Hebrew University of Jerusalem. She participated in the negotiations on the CRPD on behalf of Bizchut, and contributed to the discussion and draft language on the articles on Access to Justice and Living Independently and Being Included in the Community.

Don MacKay, former New Zealand Ambassador to the United Nations in New York and Geneva. He was initially facilitator, and then Chair (2005–06), of the Ad-Hoc Committee. He has also chaired and facilitated a wide range of other international processes, including at the United Nations. A graduate in law, he has served as the International Legal Adviser to the New Zealand Ministry of Foreign Affairs and has represented New Zealand before the International Court of Justice. He is currently working as a consultant on human rights and international legal issues.

Anna MacQuarrie works for Inclusion International, she was previously the director of policy and programs for the Canadian Association for Community Living. She has a Masters degree in Human Rights from the University of Essex. She has worked with the Canadian Association for Community Living for the past seven years with a domestic and international focus on the rights of persons with intellectual disabilities and their families. She worked actively on the development of the CRPD. She continues to work on making the CRPD real and meaningful for people with intellectual disabilities and their families.

Ron C. McCallum AO was the foundation Blake Dawson Waldron Professor in Industrial Law in the Faculty of Law of the University of Sydney, and also served as Dean of Faculty of Law of the University of Sydney. He is the first totally blind person to have been appointed to a full professorship in any field at any university in Australia or New Zealand, as well as to be appointed to the Deanship of a Law School in Australia or New Zealand. Professor McCallum is also the inaugural president of the Australian Labour Law Association. He is a member of the Committee on the Rights of Persons with Disabilities and has served as its President since October 2009.

Tara J. Melish is an Associate Professor and Director of the Human Rights Center at SUNY Buffalo Law School, The State University of New York. She taught as a Visiting Assistant Professor of Law at the University of Notre Dame, the University of Virginia, George Washington University, the University of Georgia, Oxford University, and Abo Akademi University. She received her J.D. from Yale Law School and her B.A. from Brown University. She served as Disability Rights International's United Nations representative in the drafting negotiations of the CRPD. Prior to that, she served as Associate Social Affairs Officer in the U.N. Department of Economic and Social Affairs.

Pamela Molina Toledo, holds a B.A. in Latin American Literature from the University of Chile; a MS in Disability Studies and Human Development, University of Illinois, at Chicago (UIC), and is a PhD Candidate in Disability Studies. She was Chair of the Ethics Committee of the Latin American Network of organizations of People with Disabilities and their Families, RIADIS, and is a board Member of the Inter-American Institute on Disability and Inclusive Development and President of DECIDE Foundation (Civil Rights and Equal Development for People with Disabilities in Latin America). She was a Deaf advocate representative of the South in the Ad-Hoc Committee. Currently, she is Program Manager on HH.RR, Democracy and Governance Initiative for the Trust for the Americas, an NGO affiliated to the Organization of American States, OAS, in Washington, D.C.

Maya Sabatello teaches at NYU's Center for Global Affairs and is appointed as Visiting Research Fellow at Columbia University Law School and as Research Fellow in Medical Ethics at Harvard Medical School. A lawyer with a Ph.D. in Political Science from the University of Southern California, she specializes in international and comparative human rights law, disability, public health, and bioethics and has published extensively on these issues, including authoring *Children's Bioethics* (Martinus Nijhoff, 2009). For over a decade, she has also promoted human rights and disability issues in national and international forums.

Marianne Schulze studied law at the University of Sydney, Australia, and the University of Vienna, Austria, from which she graduated. She holds an LL.M. in international human rights from the Center for Civil and Human Rights at the University of Notre Dame du Lac. She was a monitor, analyst and reporter in the Ad Hoc Committee and developed a handbook, Understanding the Convention on the Rights of Persons with Disabilities, published by Handicap International. A free-lance human rights consultant, she serves as the inaugural chair of the Austrian CRPD Monitoring Committee.

Belinda Shaw joined the Centre for Studies on Inclusive Education, Bristol, as co-director in 1988 after working as a journalist and broadcaster in this country and overseas. She retired in 2007 and is currently a trustee with the Alliance for Inclusive Education, London. Belinda has an MA with distinction in Inclusive Education, from the Institute of Education, University of London (2004) and BA from the Open University (1999).

INDEX

Individual CRPD are listed following the other index entries.

ACKNOWLEDGMENTS

When we concluded our initial conversation about co-editing a book on the Convention process, we had no idea what a thoroughly inspiring, fun and particularly rewarding journey we were about to embark upon. The (hi) story of the Convention on the Rights of Persons with Disabilities is unique in so many ways and trying to capture some of that magic in a book has been a real privilege.

Getting to this point has meant support from a variety of institutions and persons. Whilst the list of people who assisted on the path to this book extends throughout the community involved with the process, and well beyond, we would like to specifically acknowledge a few individuals who helped pave the way for this publication. First of all the authors of this book: a heartfelt "thank you" to Anna MacQuarrie, Connie Laurin-Bowie, Tirza Leibowitz, Belinda Shaw, Tara J. Melish, Gerison Lansdown, Mi Yeon Kim, Huhana Hickey, Liisa Kauppinen, Markku Jokinen, Pamela Molina Toledo, Lex Grandia, Heidi Forrest, Phillip French, and Andrew Byrnes. Many had to squeeze the writing of their chapters into their weekends, vacation, or other well-deserved rest time, and for that we are deeply grateful. Knowing that personal assistants, family members and others were supportive in many ways, we wish to acknowledge them, too. We are particularly grateful to Ambassador Don MacKay of New Zealand, who so ably led the negotiations, for generously offering to write a foreword. With the Convention in force and its Committee established, we are grateful to its Chair, Professor Ron McCallum, for writing a preface.

The process of bringing this book together was immensely supported by our immediate support group a.k.a. family and significant others: thanks for the sustenance, understanding, encouragement, and patience.

We would not have been able to carry this to the finishing line without the editorial ability of Edith Friedlander who lent her formidable skills and boundless enthusiasm for all things language and human to this project.

Additionally, a special thank you for the invaluable editorial assistance of Audra Wolfe. Kathrin Meyer came to our rescue in transcribing edits and putting it all into form with a good balance of patience and speed as well as an amazing attention to detail. Agnieszka Gasparska generously shared her design passion by capturing "Human Rights and Disability Advocacy" graphically.

Finally, we want to express our deep gratitude to the staff at University of Pennsylvania Press—including Bert Lockwood (Series Editor), Peter Agree (Editor-in-Chief), and Rachel Taube (Acquisitions Assistant), the invaluable and constructive comments by the reviewer, and the formidable editors Alison A. Anderson (Managing Editor) and Jennifer Shenk—for believing in this project and supporting us so thoughtfully and professionally through the various stages of production.